MAN'S RESPONSIBILITY FOR NATURE

MAN'S RESPONSIBILITY FOR NATURE

Ecological Problems and Western Traditions

John Passmore

Duckworth

First published in 1974
by Gerald Duckworth & Co. Ltd.,
The Old Piano Factory,
43 Gloucester Crescent,
London N.W.1

© John Passmore 1974

Cloth ISBN 0 7156 0756 1
Paper ISBN 0 7156 0819 3

Printed in Great Britain by
Unwin Brothers Limited
The Gresham Press, Old Woking, Surrey, England
A member of the Staples Printing Group

CONTENTS

The blessing is not in living but in living well   Seneca

Rest and quiet? Leave them to the dead, where they belong   Heraclitus

PREFACE

This book arose by accident and I have many times resolved to abort it. My friends—or I hope they are my friends—dissuaded me. So I have carried it for its full term, for all that I am more than ordinarily conscious of its imperfections. If it contributes only slightly to clearer thinking about the problems which confront us, I shall be more than satisfied.

My indebtedness is wide ranging—to economists, biologists, political theorists, historians, philosophers, in conversation, in seminars, as well as through their writings. As usual, I owe much to the late Professor John Anderson, especially to his lectures on Heraclitus. One book—C. J. Glacken's *Traces on the Rhodian Shore*—served to stimulate more of my thinking than my meagre references to it make clear; it is a vast storehouse of learning, giving me many clues which I later followed up. The help of my Research Assistant, Miss Janette Paris, has been particularly valuable in keeping me in touch with a literature now so vast as to encourage despair; Miss Isabel Sheaffe has had typing duties more arduous than usual in coping with a constantly reshaped manuscript. My wife, as ever, has supplemented their efforts in innumerable ways. At the final stages of the book Mr Harris Dienstfrey made a number of useful suggestions and my daughter Diana cast a final eye over my references. It was seen through the press in the hospitable surroundings of Clare Hall, Cambridge.

John Passmore   Canberra 1973

A NOTE TO THE READER

The structure of this book is perhaps a little unusual. It begins with two chapters which are essentially historical, in which I set out to describe those Western traditions which tend to encourage and those which might serve to curb man's ecological destructiveness. Then I examine in turn, now in a manner which is analytical rather than historical, what are by general consent the four major ecological problems: pollution, the depletion of natural resources, the destruction of species, over-population. In the final chapter I set in confrontation Western traditions and ecological problems. I ask what the West has to jettison, and what to retain, if it is to have any prospect of solving the problems which confront it. This chapter can also be read as a note of warning to those countries which have not yet fully absorbed Western traditions.

The peculiarities of my method of procedure, partly historical, partly analytical, partly critical, are to be explained by the fact that I write out of a sense of alarm, but an alarm which is double-edged. The scientific literature fully convinces me, so far as personal observation does not suffice, that men cannot go on living as they have been living, as predators on the biosphere. But I find no less alarming the suggestion in so much of that literature that the West can solve its problems only by forgetting what it has so gradually learnt, only by reverting to attitudes and modes of thought which it painfully shook off.

This conclusion is often associated with a particular thesis about the origin of Western attitudes. The West has learnt from Genesis, so the argument then runs, to be wholly despotic, totally irresponsible, in its attitudes to nature. If my argument begins from history, this is partly in order to dispute so simple an account of Western traditions; if my historical chapters are relatively detailed, this is because the actual situation is far more complex than has commonly been supposed.

The present intellectual mood is anti-historical. I do not share it. Not merely in order to understand why men behave as they do but also in order to estimate what the prospects are that they can be persuaded to act differently, we have to take account, I firmly believe, of the traditions they have inherited. So it is not *merely* for controversial reasons that I have begun with history. But such of my readers as are convinced that the past is now of no importance will find that they can, without too great a sense of confusion, turn at once to the four central chapters—although what they there read may, I hope, eventually persuade them that the opening historical chapters cannot be dismissed as an antiquarian flourish.

So far as the content of those central chapters is concerned, I should at once make it clear that I have not in any way sought to compete with the many distinguished scientists who have drawn attention to the physical and biological consequences of the West's technological rashness. I assume, indeed, a general acquaintance with their work—of the sort, at least, which no intelligent reader of the daily newspaper can wholly avoid. What I have tried to do, rather, is to bring out the fundamental moral, metaphysical and political assumptions which so often underlie their arguments. I have asked in what the solution to an ecological problem consists; I have tried to show why the solution of such problems cannot be safely left to scientists. I have asked whether, and how far, we should think of ourselves as having a duty to conserve resources for posterity and why it matters when wildernesses and wild species are destroyed. I have asked how we can determine whether our population growth is too rapid and what moral objections there are to attempts to control it. And all the while I have had in mind my over-arching intention: to consider whether the solution of ecological problems demands a moral or metaphysical revolution.

These preliminary explanations may, I hope, help to guide the reader through the twists and turnings of my argument. But in the long run that argument must speak for itself or not at all.

Part One
THE TRADITIONS

CHAPTER ONE MAN AS DESPOT

As a direct consequence of our agricultural and industrial technology, we are rapidly causing to degenerate our sole habitation, that narrow strip of soil, air and water—the biosphere—in which we live and move and have our being. So much must be granted: the evidence in its favour is daily made more apparent to our nose, our ears, our palate, our eyes, and is reinforced by scientific investigation. That action must be taken, that if Western civilisation is to survive, it must, in important respects, change its ways, is also sufficiently obvious.

The only point at issue is just how fundamental these changes will need to be. It is one thing to suggest that Western societies must learn to be more prudent in their attitude to technical innovations, less wasteful of natural resources, more conscious of their dependence on the biosphere. It is quite another thing to suggest that they can solve their ecological problems only if they abandon the analytical, critical approach which has been their peculiar glory and go in search of a new ethics, a new metaphysics, a new religion. That is the conclusion I wish to dispute—not wholly, indeed, but at least in those extremer forms in which it finds expression as mysticism, primitivism, authoritarianism. The traditions of the West, I shall be trying to show, are far richer, more diversified, more flexible than its critics allow.

The ecologist Aldo Leopold, writing in the nineteen-forties, was one of the first* to suggest that the West now stands in need of a 'new ethic'—an 'ethic of conservation'. Like so many schematic historians before him, from Joachim of Flora to Hegel and Comte, Leopold divided the history of moral judgment into three stages. In the first stage, as represented by the Ten Commandments, the emphasis, he says, was on the individual's relationship to other individuals, whom he was commanded not, for example, to kill or to bear false witness against. (There is no mention in Leopold of the duties to God so prominent in the decalogue; to mention them

---

* Not the first, however. The early proponents of kindness to animals, as we shall see, were propounding a 'new ethic', in Leopold's sense of the phrase. Victor Hugo was convinced that a 'new ethic', of the sort Leopold had in mind, would inevitably come to birth. 'In the relations of man with the animals, with the flowers, with the objects of creation, there is a great ethic, scarcely perceived as yet, which will at length break forth into the light and which will be the corollary and complement to human ethics.' Note that for Hugo this 'new ethic' is already nascent; there is no question of our having to create it *de novo* by a deliberate act of choice.

would have impaired the triune simplicity of his analysis.) In the second stage, moralists began to emphasise men's duties to society, as distinct from their duties to particular individuals. But what the West still lacks, Leopold tells us, is an 'ethic dealing with man's relation to land and to the animals and plants which grow upon it'.[1]

Leopold looked forward, then, to an extension of the area of moral judgment, so as to subject to moral criticism types of conduct which have traditionally been set aside as morally neutral. As matters stand, he says, men do not feel morally guilty if they maltreat the land, extract from it whatever it will produce, and then move on to fresh fields and pastures new. Nor do their actions arouse the moral indignation of their fellows. 'A farmer who clears the woods off a 75 per cent slope, turns his cows into the clearing, and dumps its rainfall, rocks, and soil into the community creek, is still (if otherwise decent) a respected member of society.'[2] An 'ethic of conservation', in contrast, would judge man's dealings with the land in moral terms, just as the decalogue, silent on this point, judges his dealings with his fellow-men.

Leopold's *Sand County Almanac* was first published in 1949; by 1970 a leader-writer in England's *New Scientist* was convinced that Leopold's project for an 'extension of ethics' could not be carried into effect, that Western ethics would have to be not extended but abandoned. He agrees with Leopold that the West stands in need of 'a more ecological approach in which man regards the soil as a partner to be cherished rather than as a captive to be raped'. But in search of such an ecological approach, he tells us, men will turn in vain to a Western-type ethic, however extended. They will need to look, rather, to 'Hindu and Buddhist faiths . . . or the peasant cultures of Asia'.[3]

One leading article does not make a social movement. But it is easy to match the spirit, if not the details, of the *New Scientist* leader elsewhere. According to the historian of science and technology Lynn White, our ecological problems derive from 'Christian attitudes towards man's relation to nature which are almost universally held not only by Christians and neo-Christians but also by those who fondly regard themselves as post-Christians'— attitudes which lead us to think of ourselves as 'superior to nature, contemptuous of it, willing to use it for our slightest whim'.[4] Since the roots of the West's troubles are so largely religious, 'the remedy', he goes on to argue, 'must also be essentially religious, whether we call it that or not'. He writes with some approval of the 'beatniks'— who are, he says, 'the basic revolutionaries of our time'—and of the Zen Buddhism to which they turn in search of a new man-nature relationship.* Unlike the *New Scientist* editorialist, he doubts whether the West can simply take over a form of thought 'as deeply conditioned by Asian history as Christianity is by the experience of the West'. But he is equally convinced, first, that 'orthodox Christian arrogance towards Nature' must somehow be dispelled and, secondly, that science and technology are so imbued with Christian or post-Christian 'arrogance' that 'no solution for our ecological crisis can be expected from them alone'. White's article has become something of a classic, much reprinted in anthologies. How widely his attitudes are shared, it is difficult to say, but widely enough, I fear, and in sufficiently respectable quarters to demand our close attention.

When the critics of contemporary Western civilisation demand a 'new ethic', they do not mean, of course, what this phrase would mean in the mouths of most contemporary British moral philosophers—a new way of analysing and inter-relating such ethical concepts as 'good' and 'right' or a new method of characterising moral judgments. As the virologist Frank Fenner puts it, 'the primary need is a change in human values and our ideas of morality'[5]—where 'ideas of morality' means 'our ideas about what kinds of action are moral and which are criminal'. He goes on to give an example: men will have to recognise that it is morally wrong to produce more than a limited number of children. In the language now current among philosophers, Fenner and his fellow-ecologists are demanding changes not in meta-ethics but in 'normative' or 'substantive' ethics.[6]

Only gradually can we explore this view that the West now needs a 'new ethic'; only gradually, as our argument proceeds, will it emerge to what a degree such a 'new ethic' is already inherent, if only as a minor theme, in Western thought. We shall begin, rather, with the principal accusation—that Western attitudes to nature are infected with 'arrogance', an arrogance which has continued into the post-Christian world and makes men think of nature as a 'captive to be raped' rather than as a 'partner to be cherished'. Genesis will be our starting-point, a Genesis so often assailed as the fount and origin of the West's ecological troubles. That it is justly so condemned we shall find reason for questioning.

* I wish I could wholly avoid the word 'nature'. But if it is one of the most ambiguous it is also one of the most indispensable words in the English language. For the most part I shall, of necessity, be using it in that sense in which it includes everything except man and what obviously bears the mark of man's handiwork. For what is in question is man's moral relationships to a nature thus defined. In another fundamental sense of the word—'whatever is subject to natural law'—both man and man's artifacts belong to nature; nature can then be contrasted, if at all, only with the supernatural. And sometimes it will be necessary to use the word in that broader sense. The word 'environment' is often substituted for the collective 'nature'. But other people, their actions, their customs, their beliefs are the most important ingredient in our environment.

The Lord God created man, so Genesis certainly tells us, to have 'dominion over the fish of the sea, and over the fowl of the air, and over the cattle, and over all the earth and over every creeping thing that creepeth upon the earth' (1: 26). This has been read not only by Jew but by Christian and Muslim as man's charter, granting him the right to subdue the earth and all its inhabitants. And God, according to Genesis, also issued a mandate to mankind: 'Be fruitful and multiply and replenish the earth and subdue it' (1: 28). So Genesis tells men not only what they can do, but what they should do—multiply and replenish and subdue the earth.

God is represented, no doubt, as issuing these instructions before the Fall. But the Fall did not, according to the Genesis story, substantially affect man's duties. What it did, rather, was to make the performance of those duties more onerous. After the Flood—man's position in the intervening period is more than a little obscure—God still exhorted Noah thus: 'Be fruitful, and multiply, and replenish the earth.' But then he added two significant riders. The first rider made it clear that men should not expect to subdue the earth either by love or by the exercise of natural authority, as distinct from force: 'And the fear of you and the dread of you shall be upon every beast of the earth, and upon every fowl of the air, upon all that moveth upon the earth and upon all the fishes of the sea: into your hand are they delivered.' The second rider—'every moving thing that liveth shall be meat for you'—permitted men to eat the flesh of animals. In the Garden of Eden, Adam, along with the beasts,* had been a vegetarian, whose diet was limited to 'every herb bearing seed . . . and every tree, in the which is the fruit of a tree yielding seed'. Now, in contrast, not only the 'green herb' but all living things were handed over to Adam and his descendants as their food.[7]

As late as the eighteenth century the poet James Thomson could still sum up man's prelapsarian condition thus: quite 'unfleshed in blood' man was 'the lord and not the tyrant of the earth',

> A stranger to the savage arts of life,
> Death, rapine, carnage, surfeit and disease.[8]

The soil, the plants and the animals all recognised his natural dominion over them. After the Fall, in contrast, he had no choice but to play the tyrant, not only over animals but over plants and soil. 'Cursed,' God told Adam, 'is the ground for thy sake.' A

---

* Aquinas denies this (*Summa Theologiae*, 1a, 96, 1) and quotes Bede as his authority. But Bede in fact takes the view outlined above—the only one the Biblical text appears to allow. Aquinas did not like the idea that man's sin had changed the nature of the beasts. One can see why.

paradisiacal garden no more, 'thorns also and thistles shall it bring forth to thee'.[9] The gentlemanly gardening which, according to Aquinas, was man's sole occupation in Paradise, the Fall converted into unremitting toil.[10]

The Hebrews, this much is clear from the Genesis story, were puzzled and disturbed about their relationship with nature. On the one side they were struck by their capacity to domesticate animals, so that one man could govern a herd of oxen. No other living thing had this power; it suggested that man possessed an inherent authority over the beasts of the field. On the other side, they found their own violence and carnivorousness disconcertingly barbarous, standing in need of explanation and justification.* Were it not for Adam's sin, the Hebrews could tell themselves by way of explanation—and after the Hebrews those other religions, Christian or Muslim, which accepted Genesis as a sacred book—they would have been vegetarians, they would not have had to live by violence.

There is nothing peculiarly Judaic, of course, in such a picture of an idyllic past conjoined with discomfiture about man's present aggressiveness and destructiveness. Another familiar instance is the Greek Golden Age, which Hesiod poetically describes as a time when men were 'free of toil and grief' and 'the earth spontaneously bore them abundant fruit without stint'.[11] A little later Empedocles tells that once 'all things were tame and kindly to man' and the trees bore fruit the year around.[12] Like Genesis but unlike Hesiod, he went on to ascribe to man's sin the destruction of that beneficent world. The primal sin, the cause of man's fallen state, was on Empedocles' view man's slaughter of animals, even although at first only for sacrificial purposes. In the Age of Love, the Golden Age, as Empedocles describes it, 'no altar was wet with the shameful slaughter of bulls' (DK fr. 128).

Nor was it only in the West that men looked back nostalgically to a Golden Age, an Age of Love, when tyranny, whether over man or beast, was unknown. The Taoist Chuang Tsu, writing in the fourth century BC, deplored the passing of 'the age of perfect virtue' when 'men lived in common with birds and beasts'.[13] The belief that the world is 'out of joint' and that its disharmony is reflected in man's relationship with the animals around him is indeed a widespread one. Uniquely Judaic, only, is the suggestion that even before the Fall man *ruled over* his fellow-creatures. Neither Empedocles nor Chuang Tsu suggests that in the age of perfect virtue man had dominion over the beasts; man and beast then

* Notice the way I have put this point. It has a wider import. By the time the Genesis stories were composed—in Mesopotamia—man had already embarked on the task of transforming nature. In the Genesis stories man *justifies* his actions. He did not set about mastering the world—any more than he set about multiplying—because Genesis told him to. Rather, Genesis salved his conscience.

lived together, according to Chuang Tsu, on terms of equality 'as forming one family'. This is characteristic of a great many other such stories. A myth of the Cherokee Indians, for example, relates that man once lived on terms of perfect amity not only with beasts but even with plants, all of which then had the gift of speech.[14] In the apocryphal Book of Jubilees, the beasts are said to have lost the power of speech with Adam's Fall, a power of speech often identified, as we shall see, with the possession of reason and, through reason, rights.[15]

Genesis, in contrast, is quite clear that from the very beginning man ruled, however benevolently, over the beasts. The first creation story tells us explicitly that man was given dominion over the animals. The second story does not go so far as this: it says that they were created as man's auxiliaries, as 'help meet for him'. But Adam is also represented in that story as giving *names* to the animals. And in primitive thought to have possession of a thing's name is to have power over it.

Nevertheless, although the Old Testament insists on man's dominion, it is far from suggesting that God has left the fate of animals entirely in man's hands, whether before or after the Fall. In the Garden of Eden, God gave 'every green herb' as food to 'every beast of the earth, and to every fowl of the air and to everything that creepeth upon the earth'; the green herb, that is, was not created solely for man's use. When, so the Genesis story runs, God flooded the earth, he took pains to ensure the preservation of beasts as much as men—even if he used a man, Noah, as his instrument in so doing. After the Flood, he instructed every type of living creature, not man alone, to 'breed abundantly in the earth, and be fruitful, and multiply upon the earth'. The so-called 'covenant of the rainbow' was a promise not only to Noah and his descendants but to 'every beast of the earth'.[16] God, according to the Book of Job, causes 'it to rain on the earth, where no man is; on the wilderness, wherein there is no man; to satisfy the desolate and waste ground; and to cause the bud of the tender herb to spring forth'.[17] He is depicted as telling Job that he has made the wilderness and the desert as a home for the wild ass.[18] And according to the psalmist: 'He sendeth the springs into the valleys which run amongst the hills. They give drink to every beast of the field; the wild asses quench their thirst.'[19]

Men, it is also made clear, ought to care for their sheep and their cattle. 'A righteous man,' according to Proverbs 12: 10, 'regardeth the life of his beast.' The image of the good shepherd, whose flocks 'will not want', comes as naturally to the lips of the psalmist as it does to Ezekiel. Early Christian art depicts Jesus as a shepherd—or sometimes, even more strikingly, as Orpheus charming the animals with his lute—rather than as a crucified God or, in the Byzantine manner, a divine Emperor.

To the analogy of the shepherd, however, a crucial ambiguity attaches. In Plato's *Republic*, the sophist Thrasymachus, criticising Socrates' suggestion that a good ruler always devotes himself to the interests of his subjects, invokes by way of analogy the care of a shepherd for his flock. 'You surely don't imagine,' says Thrasymachus sardonically, 'that shepherds or herdsmen look after the good of their sheep or cattle, fattening and tending them, with any other view than the good of their masters and themselves.' In reply, Socrates argues that the shepherd's art consists, purely and simply, in looking after the interests of his sheep; it is not *qua* shepherd that he tries to profit by them. And something similar is true, he goes on to say, of the art of the ruler. The art of the ruler *qua* ruler 'considers only what is best for that which it governs or tends'.[20] It is in this spirit that the Lord God, according to Ezekiel, rebuked 'the shepherds of Israel'—the kings of Judah—who fed themselves rather than their sheep. 'Ye eat the fat, and ye clothe you with the wool, ye kill them that are fed: but ye feed not the flock. The diseased have ye not strengthened, neither have ye healed that which was sick . . . but with force and with cruelty have ye ruled them.'[21]

There are two possible interpretations, then, of the Old Testament view about man's dominion: the first, that he is an absolute, or Thrasymachean, ruler who cares for the world God made subject to him only in so far as he profits from doing so; the second, that like the Platonic shepherd he takes care of the living things over which he rules for their own sake, governing them not 'with force and with cruelty' but in the manner of a good shepherd, anxious to preserve them in the best possible condition for his master, in whose hands alone their final fate will rest. Of these two ways of interpreting the Biblical view, the second has recently come into favour. But the first interpretation, that man is entitled to rule like an absolute despot, was for long predominant; that is what critics have in mind when they condemn 'Christian arrogance' and find in it the source of Western man's maltreatment of nature. For the present we shall be restricting ourselves to it.

It rests on assumptions which Hebraic prophets and Greek cosmologists share and which converge in Christianity. Although the Old Testament, I have said, by no means suggests that whatever exists was created for man's sake, there is one point on which it is absolutely clear: nature is not sacred. And while the rejection of the view that nature is sacred does not justify an irresponsible attitude towards it, it at least leaves the way open to that attitude, does not at once condemn it as sacrilegious.

9

The view that man in any sense rules over nature inevitably presumes that nature is not itself divine. And the striking peculiarity of the religion of the Hebrews, when we compare it with the middle Eastern religions which surrounded it, is its sharp distinction between God and nature. The Hebrew God, to put the difference technically, is transcendent, not immanent; he creates and rules nature but is not to be identified with it. 'The keeping of Jahweh's covenant,' Frankfort therefore writes, 'meant . . . sacrificing the greatest good ancient Near East religion could bestow—the harmonious integration of man's life with the life of nature.' Man's dealings with nature were sharply separated from his dealings with God. And it was his relationship with God which really mattered. 'Man,' Frankfort sums up, 'remained outside nature, exploiting it for a livelihood, offering its first fruits as a sacrifice to Jahweh, using its imagery for the expression of his moods, but never sharing its mysterious life.'[22]

We may well cavil at Frankfort's suggestion—so typical of Romanticism—that in nature there is a 'mysterious life' from which the Hebrews somehow cut themselves off. But the Hebrew desacralisation of nature certainly left man free to exploit it with none of the qualms which, in many other societies, he would have felt when he cut down a tree or killed an animal. There are societies in which the axeman or the slaughterer, before taking up his axe or his knife, would first have begged the tree's or the animal's pardon, explaining the necessity which forced him to destroy it. Indeed, such an attitude to nature lingered on among German foresters as late as the nineteenth century.[23] But this feeling is not compatible with orthodox Hebraic or Christian teaching.*

It is certainly a mistake to suggest, as the biologist L. C. Birch has recently suggested, that 'the doctrine of creation'—the Hebrew doctrine, that is—'stands for the sacredness of all things'.[24] Nothing is sacred, on this tradition, except God and what, like Sinai, is specifically dedicated to God. 'The Lord is in his holy temple; the Lord's throne is in heaven.'[25] No doubt God owns the earth and all it contains, 'every beast of the forest and the cattle upon a thousand hills'.[26] But man is at liberty, under a special charter from God, to exploit it as he wills—subject only to restrictions specifically imposed by God. He is not, when he kills 'the cattle upon a thousand hills', killing something sacred.

Greek science, similarly, began by rejecting the view that nature

---

* In many parts of Europe, Christianity was a late arrival. And nowhere did it quite succeed in destroying, especially amongst peasant peoples, that older feeling that there were mysterious divine powers in rivers, trees and mountains. Compare Old Ekdal's conviction in Ibsen's *The Wild Duck*, first performed in 1884, that the forest will 'take its revenge' for being thinned. Popular attitudes to animals and to the life around them were by no means necessarily the same as those embraced by philosophers and theologians.

was sacred; the fifth-century B.C. philosopher-scientist Anaxagoras, so the story runs, was condemned for impiety and exiled from Athens for calling the sun a fiery stone, i.e. for denying its divinity. And in this denial he was typical of his fellow-cosmologists. Modern science has been no less emphatic that nature is not sacred. At the beginning of the modern period, Robert Boyle, devout Christian and scientific pioneer, conjoins the Hebraic and the Greek tradition when he insists that men must think of nature not as a sacred force but simply as a collection of plants, animals, rocks, seas, forests, plains. 'The veneration wherewith men are imbued for what they call nature,' he writes, 'has been a discouraging impediment to the empire of man over the inferior creatures of God: for many have not only looked upon it, as an impossible thing to compass, but as something of impious to attempt . . . and whilst they look upon her as such a venerable thing, some make a kind of scruple of conscience to endeavour so to emulate any of her works, as to excel them.'[27] (Consider, as an example of what Boyle had in mind, the way in which the view that the body is 'sacred' held up medical research.) Science and technology, Boyle is suggesting, could not progress so long as nature was still thought of as 'venerable', as something which it was impious to attempt to control, to modify, or even to understand. That he had to make this point suggests that the older view was by no means dead. But in making it he was certainly not breaking with the Hebraic-Christian tradition. Indeed, science and technology, as the Roman Catholic theologian Charles Davis has more recently argued, are far more in conformity with Christianity than any view which 'sees nature as the embodiment of the divine . . . as inaccessible to man's understanding and outside his intelligent control'. Nature itself, so he sums up, 'is not sacred for the Christian'.[28] In the early decades of the present century, Christian apologists were particularly anxious to establish that science and technology were of Christianity's making. For science and technology were widely esteemed as the secular saviours of mankind. Now, ironically enough, Christianity finds itself condemned as the progenitor of a diabolic technology. If both views exaggerate Christianity's historical role in this regard, it is still not an accident that technology flourished in a West for which nature was not sacred.*

On this much, Jew and Christian were in complete agreement; there was nothing sacrilegious in eating the flesh of animals or in cultivating crops. Nature was one thing, God quite another. And

---

* We might in general define 'the West' as those civilisations whose major ideas and attitudes derive from Greek and Hebrew sources. Taken thus, it includes, of course, the Muslim regions. But the most 'Western' parts of the West felt Greek and Hebrew influence twice, the second time during the Revival of Learning and the Reformation. In that sense, Russia, for example, has never been thoroughly Westernised.

this agreement, I have been suggesting, was of fundamental importance in determining the attitudes of the West. It is still necessary to insist on the points on which Jew and Christian differed, for they are highly relevant to our theme. These differences derive from two connected facts. First, the Old Testament, unlike so many Christian theologians, does not set up an unbridgeable gap between man and his fellow-creatures. Secondly, it is uncompromisingly theocentric: nature, on its view, exists not for man's sake but for the greater glory of God. And it will at once be obvious that, in the Christian separation of man from the animals and the Christian view that nature was made for man, there lie the seeds of an attitude to nature far more properly describable as 'arrogant' than the purely Old Testament conception of man's dominion.

There are, of course, problems in talking about 'the Old Testament' as if it were a single book with, in all respects, a single point of view. Running through it there is a conflict between the new man-centred agriculture and the old nature-oriented nomadic pastoral life to which so many of the Jews looked back with nostalgia. (Cain's offer to Yahweh of the fruits of the earth was, it will be remembered, spurned; God accepted Abel's oxen, only.) The nomadic pastoralist is more conscious than is the agriculturalist that he shares the earth with other living things, which go their own way largely indifferent to his presence; the agriculturalist deliberately transforms nature in a sense in which the nomadic pastoralist does not. The conflict of attitudes persists in later Jewish thought, influenced as it also was by Greek humanism. The Egyptian-Jewish Saadia, writing in the tenth century A.D., committed himself very firmly to the view that 'the entire universe was created on account of man'.[29] The greatest Jewish orthodox philosopher, Maimonides, at first took the same view in his early commentary on the Mishnah. 'All things in the sublunary world', he there writes, 'exist only for the sake of man.'[30] But he later rejected that view as in essence profoundly non-Jewish. Genesis makes it perfectly clear, he then argues, that the world was good *before* man was created: 'It should not be believed', he concludes, 'that all beings exist for the sake of the existence of man. On the contrary, all the other beings, too, have been intended for their own sakes and not for the sake of something else.'[31] And this is the more typically Jewish attitude.

Christianity, on the other hand, with its God who took human shape, is, or tends to be, anthropocentric, at least so far as the things of this world are concerned. For the Jews, as for the Muslims, it is blasphemous to suppose that God could become a man; for many other religions, God was as likely to become a bull, or a monkey, as a man. The peculiarities of Christian attitudes to nature derive in large part from its man-centredness. So Calvin, for example, is quite confident that God 'created all things for man's sake'.[32] God, Calvin's argument runs, could have created the universe, had he so chosen, in one day. He chose, however, to take six days in order to demonstrate to man that everything had been made ready for him, that he entered the earth like a royal guest whose importance is indicated by the fact that he enters last. 'But he willed to commend his providence and fatherly solicitude towards us, in that before he fashioned man, he prepared everything he foresaw would be useful and salutory for him.'*

Calvin's description of a creation prepared for man was echoed, in an ecological form, by G. P. Marsh in his *Man and Nature*, published in 1864, and the first work to describe in detail man's destructiveness. Nature, according to Marsh, 'has left it within the power of man irreparably to derange the combinations of inorganic matter and of organic life, which through the night of aeons she had been proportioning and balancing, to prepare the earth for his habitation, when, in the fulness of time, his Creator should call him forth to enter into its possession'.[33] Although with very different intentions, Calvin and Marsh both emphasise man's ingratitude when, whether by Adam's sin (Calvin) or by man's destructive acts (Marsh), they vandalise the home which God (Calvin) or nature (Marsh) had in six days (Calvin) or over aeons (Marsh) prepared for their residence. The difference between Marsh and Calvin is nevertheless crucial: for Christianity men entered nature as its rightful master, for the ecologist as a potentially dangerous intruder. To that extent the critics of Christianity are right. Christianity has encouraged man to think of himself as nature's absolute master, for whom everything that exists was designed. They are wrong only in supposing that this is also the Hebrew teaching; it originates with the Greeks.

Traditional Greek religion, admittedly, did nothing to encourage the view that man either was, or should seek to become, master of the world. To seek that mastery would be *hubris*, an attempt on man's part to set himself up as a god; such presumption would undoubtedly bring calamities about his head, as the fate of Prometheus served to illustrate. The situation was very different, however, after the Greek Enlightenment, with its rejection of the concept of *hubris*. One then finds it explicitly maintained that animal life exists purely and simply for man's sake. Aristotle argues

* This is true only of the first Creation story, yet only in the second story were the animals specifically created to help man. In that story, Eve was created *after* Adam when God discovered that he had *not* created all that man needed. Genesis has been very discriminately employed by theologians.

in his *Politics* that 'plants are created for the sake of animals, and the animals for the sake of men; the tame for our use and provision; the wild, at least for the greater part, for our provision also, or for some other advantageous purpose, as furnishing us with clothes, and the like'.[34] He takes this conclusion to follow necessarily from the premise that 'nature makes nothing either imperfect or in vain' —as indeed it does follow if the test of a thing's 'perfection' and 'usefulness' is first presumed to be its suitability for man's purposes.

Not all Greek philosophers, no doubt, agreed with Aristotle. Man's place in nature was a major point of dispute between Epicureans and Stoics. 'That filthy dog Lucretius'—to quote Calvin's amiable description of the Epicurean poet[35]—developed in a primitive form a theory of natural selection. It is quite absurd, according to Lucretius, to suppose that the world—'so foolish the design, contrived so ill'—was created by a god for human use.[36] He foreshadowed the Darwinian doctrine that if we can speak of man as being born into a world made ready for his reception, this is only in a very limited sense: it was the kind of world in which men could survive, if with difficulty, and multiply, if at first very slowly. As much can be said of any other species which has succeeded in establishing itself.

It by no means follows that, as Calvin puts it, the world was 'prepared for man's coming'—except in the same sense that it was prepared for the coming of those parasitic vines which can survive only by killing the trees on which they climb or those bacteria and viruses which must pass through human beings to complete their life-cycle. They could not have survived had they appeared on the scene before the hosts on which they depend for their existence. Not until after Darwin, however, did the Epicurean way of looking at man's relation to nature prevail: it entails thinking of men, in a quite un-Stoic and un-Christian manner, as not only using but being used by the living things which surround them.

In Cicero's *Concerning the Nature of the Gods* the spokesman for Stoicism, Balbus, replies to the Epicureans with a detailed defence of the view that the world was made for men. 'The produce of the earth,' he says, 'was designed for those only who make use of it; and *though some beasts may rob us of a small part*, it does not follow that the earth produced it also for them . . . Beasts are so far from being partakers of this design, that we see that even they themselves were made for man . . . Why need I mention oxen? We perceive that . . . their necks were naturally made for the yoke, and their strong broad shoulders to draw the plough.'[37] (Notice that it is the beasts, not men, who figure in the Stoic world drama as 'robbers'. So in Australia the kangaroos 'rob' the pastures which were once entirely at their disposal.)

The Stoics knew no Revelation, no 'sacred books'. So they had to seek philosophical premises for their conclusion that whatever exists was made for men. Sometimes, like Cicero's Balbus, they fell back on a crude version of the 'argument from design', deducing from the premise that man is able to make advantageous use of certain living things the conclusion that they were created precisely in order to procure that advantage for him. Indeed, the Stoics, and after them patristic and mediaeval apologists, carried to extraordinary lengths the view that all creatures are designed to serve man. The Stoic Chrysippus is said to have argued that the flea is useful to man because he wakes the sluggard from his sleep and the mouse because he discourages untidiness.[38] In a somewhat more subtle fashion, Christian apologists like to describe nature as a book, a book designed for man's reading, as in that familiar passage in *As You Like It* where the Duke

> Finds tongues in trees, books in the running brooks,
> Sermons in stones, and good in everything.[39]

Bishop Berkeley, as late as the eighteenth century, treats the whole of nature as a vast system of signs through which God teaches man how to behave—'informing, admonishing and directing incessantly, in a most evident and sensible manner'.[40] On such a way of looking at the world, Providence, in guiding it, cares only for men. Nature appears in it only a means to man's survival and instruction.

This—if we add the gods to men—was the explicit Stoic teaching. The universe, as they saw it, is a vast body, providentially governed to serve the interests of its only rational members—men and gods. Like the argument from design, still flourishing in the nineteenth century, this Stoic view that man's dominion over nature, his god-like superiority, is based on his rationality, was destined to have a long life. It is constantly assumed that whatever else exists does so only for the sake of the rational. One finds this assumption not only in Augustine and Aquinas but in Kant. 'As the single being upon earth that possesses understanding,' Kant was to write, 'he is certainly titular lord of nature and, supposing we regard nature as a teleological system, he is born to be its ultimate end.'[41] And from this it was deduced, as we shall see later, that his relationships with nature are not subject to moral censure.

The Old Testament, pre-Stoic, sense of a particular providence ruling over the beasts, as over men, is still, no doubt, to be found in Luke, where Jesus is reported as saying: 'Are not five sparrows sold for two farthings, and not one of them is forgotten before

God?' God's providential watch over sparrows is there introduced, however, only in order to contrast it, at least in degree, with his care for men. 'But even the very hairs of your head are all numbered'—as not, presumably, the very feathers of the sparrow. 'Fear not therefore; ye are of more value than many sparrows.'[42] Paul is more forthright: citing Deuteronomy's 'Thou shalt not muzzle the mouth of the ox that treadeth out the corn', he asks: 'Doth God take care for oxen?' And the answer, he thinks, is clear. God does not care for oxen, but only for men. 'For our sakes, no doubt, this is written: that he that ploweth should plow in hope; and that he that thresheth in hope should be partaker of his hope.'[43] Thus what at first sight appears to be an example of God's concern for the welfare of animals turns out, according to Paul, to be a lesson for man, in allegorical form. As so often, Paul stands closer to Stoicism than he does to the Old Testament, whether or not he actually came under Stoic influence.[44]

In opposition to the intellectual lineage we have suggested, Origen, writing in the third century AD, attempts to derive from Old Testament sources the Christian doctrine that everything is made for man's use. Arguing against the Epicurean-influenced pagan Celsus, who typically asserts that 'everything was made just as much for the irrational animals as for men',[45] Origen quotes Psalm 104: 'He causes the grass to grow for the cattle and herb for the service of man.'[46] In that very same psalm, however, the psalmist makes it perfectly clear that God is no less interested in the birds, the wild asses and the young lions, the wild goats and the beavers, than he is in man and his cattle. 'As for the stork, the fir trees are her house. The high hills are a refuge for the wild goats; and the rocks for the conies . . . Thou makest darkness and it is night; wherein all the beasts of the forest do creep forth. The young lions roar after their prey, and seek their meat from God.'[47] Notice that phrase 'and seek their meat from God'. It could scarcely be more strongly asserted that God is directly concerned with the welfare of the beasts as much as with the welfare of men.

Indeed, Origen has to turn to Stoicism, not to the Old Testament, to find any support for his view that 'even the wildest of animals . . . were made for the exercise of our rational being'. He concludes thus, very like Balbus: 'Just as in cities those who are in charge of the stalls and the market-place are concerned only with men, although dogs and other irrational animals share the surplus; so providence cares for the rational beings, while the fact that irrational animals also share in what is made for men has been a subsidiary result.'[48] Animals seek their meat, that is, not from God but from man's leavings. Stoic, certainly, but not Old Testament teaching.

If, then, one can speak of 'Christian arrogance' in supposing that all things are made for men, it must be with the proviso that it is not Hebraic-Christian but Graeco-Christian 'arrogance'; its roots do not lie, as Origen and many others after him have supposed, in teachings which derive from Judaism and are taken over from that source by Christianity. It is one thing to say, following Genesis, that man has dominion over nature in the sense that he has the right to make use of it: quite another to say, following the Stoics, that nature exists only in order to serve his interests.

Furthermore, and this is a very important fact, even the Graeco-Christian doctrine can be taken as a guide to practice in one of two quite distinct ways: the first conservative, the second radical. The conservative interpretation is that since God has designed everything for man's use, it is impious for man to seek to change it; this would suggest that he can do better than God.* Such popular sayings as 'If God had meant us to fly, he would have given us wings' reflect that interpretation. Christianity, at least in its Hellenistic and mediaeval forms, certainly did not encourage man to undertake the transformation of nature. With one important exception: Christianity did encourage, as we shall see later, the transformation of wildernesses, those dreaded haunts of demons, the ancient nature-gods, into farm and pasture. But in general terms, what men had to transform was not nature, but themselves, and even that was possible only with the aid of God's grace. Men were free to use nature as they chose—provided they did not worship it as sacred—but otherwise it was best left alone, created as it was in the form most suitable for their needs. Preservationism in its extremer forms, with its horror of 'disturbing the balance of nature', has its emotional roots in this conservative, theological attitude—especially pronounced in the Eastern Church.

A second interpretation, however, was radical. And this, for our purposes, is the crucial interpretation. Since everything on earth is for man's use, he is at liberty to modify it as he will. So Cicero's Balbus tells us that 'we alone have the power of controlling the most violent of nature's offspring, the sea and the winds, thanks to the service of navigation . . . Likewise the entire command of the commodities produced on land is vested in mankind . . . the

* From the twelfth century onwards—as a result of its encounters with other civilisations during the Crusades—mediaeval Europe began to develop the 'mechanical arts' as exemplified in the water-wheel, windmills, the compass, clocks. But those inventions were in many quarters feared as the work of the devil. In a wonderful example of Heideggerian etymology, the word 'mechanical' was derived from 'moecha', an adulteress. As late as the sixteenth century a Spanish commission rejected proposals for making two rivers navigable on the ground that it would be an infringement of the rights of Providence. Man should not try to finish, so the commission argued, what God has deliberately left unfinished. (Compare Edward Shillebeeckx: *God and the Future of Man*, trans. N. D. Smith, London, 1969, pp. 54–5.) That the mechanical arts were diabolic was still a favourite theme of nineteenth-century itinerant evangelists.

rivers and the lakes are ours . . . we give fertility to the soil by irrigating it, we confine the rivers and strengthen or divert their courses . . . by means of our hands we try to create as it were a second Nature within the world of Nature.'[49]

Balbus, then, for all the technological limitations of Greece and Rome, already saw man as a demi-god, constructing with his hands a new nature. It is not so far from Balbus to that modern attitude which Robert Jungk ascribes particularly to America, but which is widespread far beyond that country: 'America is striving to win power over the sum total of things, complete and absolute mastery of nature in all its aspects . . . To occupy God's place, to repeat his deeds, to recreate and organize a man-made cosmos according to man-made laws of reason, foresight and efficiency: that is America's ultimate objective . . . It destroys whatever is primitive, whatever grows in disordered profusion or evolves through patient mutation.'[50]

Balbus and Jungk are not so far apart, at least, if we think only in terms of parallel attitudes, parallel ambitions. Historically, of course, the gap is immense. They are separated not only by the West's experience of Christianity, with its emphasis on man's sinfulness and unworthiness, but by a long history of technical innovation, at first dependent upon the inventiveness of craftsmen and engineers, later, after about 1870, on scientific discovery. Although Cicero had already recommended 'applying the hand of the artificer to the discoveries of thought',[51] man's 'hand' was immensely strengthened by the discovery of new tools and his 'thought' by the growth of science. The sort of control over nature which Cicero had in mind was by no means without its dangers; irrigation, the diversion of rivers, could create grave enough ecological problems. But he could not foresee the creation of a science-based technology, of a 'second nature' which would consist of compounds and structures which had never previously found a place in the biosphere.

In the seventeenth century, however, Bacon and Descartes could already prophesy what was to come—as to its potential benefits, if not its potential dangers. As early as 1597, indeed, Bacon had proclaimed that 'knowledge itself is power'.[52] Eight years later, he was to argue once more that 'learning should be referred to use and action'. He now added that this is true not only in the case of such obviously 'practical knowledge' as navigation, but also in the case of what Bacon called 'philosophy and universality' and we should call scientific theory.[53] 'The empire of man over things', as he elsewhere puts it, 'depends wholly on the arts and sciences'.[54] Man does not, on this view, 'rape nature'. Rather, to continue the metaphor, he seeks to gain intellectual knowledge of her, overcoming her resistance not by force but by his intimate knowledge of her secrets, by seduction.

Bacon still wrote, in one sense, within the Judeo-Christian tradition. He thought of his projects for the advancement of science as restoring man to his prelapsarian dominion over the animals, that dominion which was ceremonially symbolised when God called upon Adam to give them names. 'It is,' he says, 'a restitution and reinvesting (in great part) of man to the sovereignty and power (for whensoever he shall be able to call the creatures by their true names [i.e. understand them scientifically] he shall again command them) which he had in his first state of creation.'[55] But his attitude is Pelagian, not Augustinian, heretical in a manner that was essential if Christianity was to be reconciled with technological optimism. With Pelagius, that is, Bacon emphasised what man could achieve by his own efforts; against Augustine, he reduces to a minimum the corrupting effects of Adam's sin. Only in so far as they rejected the view that man is essentially depraved could Bacon and his successors find ground for optimism in their conviction that through science man could greatly extend his power over the world. God's curse on Adam, Bacon certainly grants, cannot be wholly lifted: morally, man's efforts will always be blemished by some degree of self-love; practically, man's power 'cannot otherwise be exercised and administered but with labour, as well in inventing as in executing'. The fact remains that man will eventually live by 'the sweat of the brow, more than of the body'.[56] What sin had shattered, science could in large part repair: man could become not only the titular but the actual lord of nature. This was by no means the orthodox Christian teaching; it amounted to saying that *man*, as distinct from God, could bring the world into the ideal state which Isaiah had prophesied.

The ambition of restoring to man his original dominion over nature and restoring it through science—not through the magical arts which already promised men control over the world—informs Bacon's philosophy. 'Let the human race recover,' he exhorts mankind, 'that right over Nature which belongs to it by divine bequest.'[57] But the idea of 'restoration' can be quietly dropped so as to leave behind it an ambition the most secular-minded of scientists could happily share. 'The end of our foundation is the knowledge of causes, and secret motions of things; and the enlarging of the bounds of human empire, *to the effecting of all things possible*.'[58] That is Bacon on the scientific society—Salomon's house—of his *New Atlantis*; there need be no surprise that the Royal Society, on its foundation, invoked his name. Not until the nineteenth century did Bacon's dream of a science-based technology, with the applied scientist replacing the craftsman, come near to realisation. But Bacon had dreamt the dream, the dream that now, we are told, has turned out to be a nightmare.

Across the Channel, Descartes agreed with Bacon's objectives, even if he did not adopt Bacon's Biblical manner of formulating them. And if he could not write, as Bacon did, with the authority of a Lord Chancellor, he had the advantage over Bacon that he had contributed in fundamental ways to the science they both extolled. Descartes aspired, he tells us, to 'a practical philosophy by means of which, knowing the force and the action of fire, water, the stars, heavens, and all the other bodies that environ us, as distinctly as we know the different crafts of our artisans, we can in the same way employ them in all those uses to which they are adapted, *and thus render ourselves the masters and possessors of nature*'.[59] Like Bacon, that is, he looked forward to new techniques, as successful as the old crafts, but based on science. But it is important to observe that he wholly rejected what he calls the 'pious thought that God has created all things for us', on the sufficiently obvious ground that 'an infinitude of things exist, or did exist . . . which have never been beheld or comprehended by man and which have never been of any use to him'. (Later metaphysicians were to dispute that view by arguing that things exist only as objects of perception—the ultimate in anthropocentrism.) He commits himself only to the much weaker position that 'there is nothing created from which we cannot derive some use'.[60] The emphasis now is on the scientist-technologist, who freely makes use of a nature which was not created only to serve him but which is so constituted as to be potentially useful to him.

To sum up, it is just not true that, as is commonly supposed, there was an immediate transition from the Stoic-Christian doctrine that 'everything is made for man's sake' to the attempt to transform the world by science. As it stands, this doctrine would rather encourage quietism. It is only when it is coupled with a Pelagian, humanistic, attitude to man, which sees him not as essentially corrupt but as having the duty to create, by his own efforts, a second nature—identified, in the Christian West, with a second Garden of Eden—that it can either provoke or be used to justify a scientific-technological revolution. What can properly be argued, however, is that Christianity encouraged certain special attitudes to nature: that it exists primarily as a resource rather than as something to be contemplated with enjoyment, that man has the *right* to use it as he will, that it is not sacred, that man's relationships with it are not governed by moral principles.

These attitudes, certainly, are all to be found in Descartes who carries them, indeed, to an extreme point. On his view every finite existence except the human mind—identified by Descartes with consciousness—is a mere machine, which men, in virtue of that fact, can manipulate without scruples. Animals not only cannot reason but cannot even feel. Descartes' philosophy, rather than Bacon's, is the charter of the Industrial Revolution. When in 1848 the radical American economist, H. C. Carey, told his readers that 'the earth is a great machine, given to man to be fashioned to his purpose' it is Descartes he is unwittingly echoing, under the impression that it is Genesis.[61]

Cartesianism, it should be observed, does not rest on Revelation, any more than does Stoicism. No doubt, as we suggested, Descartes has taken over from the Graeco-Christian tradition that attitude to man which thinks of him as nature's governor. He does not feel it necessary to demonstrate—and this is equally true of his successors —that men should 'render themselves the masters and possessors of nature'; in a different tradition he would have been obliged specifically to argue that such an ambition does not amount to *hubris*. But to him, and to his many successors, it is *self-evident* that men should attempt to make the world a better place to live in— Descartes was himself hypochondriacally obsessed by the need to develop a science of medicine. He ignores, that is, that side of the Christian tradition which insists on man's limitations, on his sinfulness, on his need to humble himself, on the grace he can derive from suffering. In short, he inherits the Stoic ingredients in Christianity rather than its more distinctive teachings; man is lord of nature in virtue of his rationality, and that rationality has not been irremediably perverted by the Fall. The ideal of mastery could thus persist in Europe even when the Bible had lost much of its old authority; it could be transferred to countries like China where the Bible had no weight.

From the beginning, of course, there were objectors. The Cambridge Platonist Henry More, at first an admirer but subsequently a critic of Descartes, was led to protest against the anthropocentric tradition we have been examining. 'Creatures,' he writes, 'are made to enjoy themselves, as well as to serve us.' 'In some senses,' he is ready to admit, 'all things are made for man'—much of the argument in his *Antidote against Atheism* is, indeed, directed towards establishing that point. We do wrong to conclude, he nevertheless argues, that 'they are not in the least made for themselves'. God 'takes pleasure that all his creatures enjoy themselves, that have life and sense and are capable of enjoyment'. To think otherwise, More tells us, is 'provinciality and ignorance'.[62] In arguing thus, he is seeking in some measure to restore the Old Testament position.

The biologist John Ray was More's pupil and younger contemporary and quotes him with approval. He firmly opposes the view—which, as I have just done, he traces back to Cicero—that nature exists only to 'serve man', at least in that most obvious sense of 'service' in which it is equated with the provision of resources which man can employ in his practical tasks. This, he says, is a view which comes naturally to those—the reference, obviously, is to Descartes and his followers—who believe that man alone, among finite beings, is capable of sensation and perception, that 'all other animals are mere machines or puppets'.[63] To Ray, fascinated by the diversity and intricacy of nature, what he took to be not only the Stoic but the Cartesian doctrine was monstrously wrong. The only sense in which everything in nature is made for man, he argues, is that everything in it is worthy of his study. 'There is a greater depth of art, and skill, in the structure of the meanest insect, than thou [man] art able for to fathom or comprehend.'[64] When the psalmist (Psalm 148) calls upon insects to praise the Lord, he cannot mean this literally: what he must rather mean, Ray says, is that even the most 'vile and contemptible' of God's creatures can fruitfully be studied as illustrations of his glory.

A little later Ray's fellow-biologist Linnaeus adopted a rather different approach. The soil, it had conventionally been argued, exists to produce grass, grass to be eaten by the herbivora, the herbivora to be eaten by the carnivora, the carnivora to be used by man. One could as well say, Linnaeus replies, that the herbivora exist only to keep down what would otherwise be a choking excess of grass, the carnivora to set limits to the voracity of the herbivora, man to ensure, by reducing the numbers of the carnivora, that there is some equilibrium in their numbers relative to the herbivora.[65] Linnaeus had discovered the interplay characteristic of an ecological system, for which the language of means and ends is totally inappropriate. Men, of course, have ends and they can use nature to serve those ends. They plant a tree, let us say, to shade their house. But from an ecological point of view, the intention is unimportant: what matters are the ecological consequences of the fact that the tree is now growing in that place, whether by accident or design.*

Ray and Linnaeus were not for a time to prevail: the Baconian-Cartesian approach to nature dominated the West, at first merely as an aspiration, eventually as an achievement. Its emphasis was not on the diversity of forms but on the uniformity of laws. The qualities which make nature so attractive, notably colour, it denied

---

* Kant's reaction to Linnaeus is illuminating. He agrees that there is no sign that nature is designed to favour man, that if one looks at the world empirically man is as much used as user. But he still argues that in a wider transcendental sense man is the 'final end of creation'—as a 'noumenal' although not as a 'phenomenal' being. Thus it is that metaphysicians protect old doctrines against modern criticisms.

nature to possess; it looked, for control over nature, to the structure of particles rather than to roles in a wider system. It saw in man's operations on nature not destruction—for what man transformed had, in its eyes, no intrinsic value—but simply the reshaping of matter and energy to a form more suitable for human use. So the only obstacles, in its eyes, to man's dominion over nature were set by the limits of his knowledge and skill, and these limits were never more than temporary. Goethe might protest, and after Goethe the German Romanticists and the 'philosophers of Nature', but in the long run even biology succumbed to the scientific enthusiasm for particulate analysis, in the form of cellular and, later, of molecular biology. Only quite recently have biologists begun again to decry, with Ray, man's ignorance of the intricate interplay characteristic of nature and to insist on the importance of even its most 'vile and contemptible' constituents.

For a time in the nineteenth century, indeed, biology was interpreted as fortifying man's belief in his right to deal with nature however he chose. Darwin's theory of natural selection was transformed by Spencer into the doctrine of the 'survival of the fittest'. Man, it was alleged, not only had to struggle against nature in order to survive, but demonstrated his moral superiority by his success in doing so. One finds an echo of this view as late as Freud's *Civilisation and its Discontents*; he sets up as the human ideal 'combining with the rest of the human community and taking up the attack on nature, thus forcing it to obey human will, under the guidance of science'.[66]

Against this Cartesian picture of the relationship between man and nature, modern ecologists have particularly protested. It has led men to suppose that they can do what they will, subject only to resistance from God—a proviso which came to be of less and less significance when men either ceased to believe in God or took it for granted that his sole interest was in the welfare of human beings. G. P. Marsh's *Man and Nature*, as we have already seen, was the first work to describe in detail man's destructiveness, a destructiveness arising, he says, out of his 'ignorant disregard of the laws of nature' and often enough accentuated—a point of some importance—by such political acts as excessive taxation. Marsh drew attention to the crucial fact that in its original state, as man inherited it, nature was not adapted to supporting a civilisation. In order to civilise the world, that is, man was forced to transform the relationships holding within it, e.g. by clearing ground for crops. Where he went wrong was in supposing that he could act thus with impunity. 'The ravages committed by man subvert the relations and destroy the balance which nature had established between her organised and her inorganic creations; and she avenges

C

herself upon the intruder, by letting loose upon her defaced provinces destructive energies hitherto kept in check by organic forces destined to be his best auxiliaries, but which he has unwisely dispersed and driven from the field of action.'[67]

Marsh's rhetoric is unfortunately typical of much else that was later to be written on this theme; man, we are told, 'commits ravages'—although in fact he has in large part acted out of ignorance; nature is represented as a semi-divine being which 'establishes balances' and, quite in the manner of a military power, seeks to 'avenge' the loss of her 'defaced provinces'. Man, too, is depicted as if he were somehow favoured by nature, which 'was destined' to provide him with auxiliaries had he only chosen to recognise that fact. But the importance of Marsh's general line of argument shines through these highly misleading metaphors.

What Marsh saw, and later ecologists have emphasised, is that when men act so as to transform their environment, they never do only what they want to do. And this is a consequence of the fact that nature never is, and never can become, anything in the least like a soft piece of wax. (We cannot, so far as that goes, do what we like with a piece of wax; its nature binds us, for all its flexibility.) As men have recently been reminded, in a variety of unpleasant ways, nature is not a passive recipient of human action. When they operate upon it, they are affecting existing modes of interaction as distinct from merely modifying a particular characteristic. Nature, in other words, does not simply 'give way' to their efforts; adjustments occur in its modes of operation, and as a result their actions have consequences which may be as harmful as they are unexpected. That is the force of the dictum, now so popular amongst ecologists, 'it is impossible to do one thing only'.

Marsh's revelations about human destructiveness were at first, however, by no means sufficient to disturb the technological optimism of the Bacon-Descartes tradition, whose power was such, as I have already suggested, as to survive transmission into cultures and ideological systems very different from those which had originally spawned it. Marxism, in particular, has served as a medium of transmission. The classical Western view is nowhere more forcibly expressed than in the *Grundrisse* Marx wrote early in his life. The 'great civilising influence of capital', as he saw the situation, lay in its rejection of the 'deification of nature'. Thus it was that 'nature becomes for the first time simply an object for mankind, purely a matter of utility'.[68] And this has been the typical Marxist position. Admittedly, Engels, in a now much-quoted essay he wrote in 1876 but which remained unpublished for some twenty years, showed himself aware of the facts to which

Marsh had drawn attention. 'Let us not however, flatter ourselves overmuch,' he writes, 'on account of our victories over nature. For each such victory it takes its revenge on us. Each of them, it is true, has in the first place the consequences on which we counted, but in the second and third places it has quite different, unforeseen effects which only too often cancel the first . . . Thus at every step we are reminded that we by no means rule over nature like a conqueror over a foreign people, like someone standing outside nature—but that we, with flesh, blood and brain, belong to nature, and exist in its midst, and that all our mastery of it consists in the fact that we have the advantage over all other creatures of being able to know and correctly apply its laws.' As our knowledge grows, Engels is nevertheless confident, we will more and more be in a position to 'learn and hence control even the more remote natural consequences of at least our most ordinary productive activities'.[69] So ignorance, not some inevitable consequence of the very process of civilisation, is, according to Engels, at the heart of man's ecological problems.

Ignorance and greed—for it is a characteristic of capitalism, Engels maintains, that it does not concern itself with the remote consequences of its actions. 'What cared the Spanish planters in Cuba,' Engels rhetorically asks, 'who burned down forests on the slopes of the mountains and obtained from the ashes sufficient fertiliser for *one* generation of highly profitable coffee trees—what cared they that the heavy tropical rainfall afterwards washed away the now unprotected upper stratum of the soil, leaving behind only bare rock!'[70] So far from its being the case, Engels therefore argues, that communism, in respect to man's treatment of nature, shares the ideology of capitalism and Christianity, the true situation is that communism alone can *save* nature, through its destruction both of capitalism and of Christianity—from the greater profits demanded by the former, the 'senseless and unnatural' contrast between man and nature typical of the latter.[71]

The Soviet Union, however, certainly *has* shared, in this respect, the ideology of capitalism. The Soviet historian Pokrovskiy—later to be condemned, ironically enough, for allowing too much importance to the environment—makes this attitude explicit: 'It is easy to foresee that in the future, when science and technique have attained to a perfection which we are as yet unable to visualise, nature will become soft wax in his [man's] hands which he will be able to cast into whatever form he chooses.'[72] Now that the consequences of agriculture and industry have made it only too obvious, whether on the virgin plains of Siberia or on Lake Baikal, that ecological problems are not peculiar to capitalism, Engels' warning has come into greater prominence in Soviet geographical thought.[73] But the old ambition remains—the childish illusion of omnipotence, an illusion the more precious just because the lands of the Soviet Union are so difficult to master, agriculturally so unreliable.

What of the East? In Japan, as in pre-Christian Europe, nature was accounted sacred: indeed, Shinto shrines might be dedicated to a mountain or a hot-spring, not even represented, in the Greek manner, by a human-like dryad but worshipped directly. Anyone who cares to wander through the hills around Kyoto may still meet with rocks or trees draped with sacred aprons and altars dedicated to them, or he may at Nikko observe some elderly member of an air-conditioned bus tour break away from his fellow-passengers to pray to a mighty tree. Yet this reverence for nature and, what went with it, a fondness for contemplating it in the most delicate ways— can one imagine a moon-watching ceremony in the West?—has not prevented Japan from developing an industrial civilisation second to none in its offensiveness to ear, eye and nose. The power of the Western outlook, with no Genesis to lend it support, is nowhere more manifest than in Osaka or Nagoya.

The position of China is somewhat different. Unlike classical India or Japan, China was technologically inventive, although it never developed pure science or even logic—with the possible exception of the short-lived and uninfluential 'School of Names' in the fourth century BC.[74] It was the scene, too, of great engineering achievements, especially in the field of water-control, and it counted as its culture-heroes the emperors who are said to have introduced into China fire, agriculture, animal husbandry and flood control.[75] Yet undoubtedly the ideal of 'conforming to nature', of working with, rather than against, its grain, has been tremendously powerful in Chinese thought,[76] affecting even such everyday actions as the way to remove a leg from a chicken.

There have been, of course, exceptions, like that radical thinker from the third century BC, Hsün Tzu:[77]

> You glorify Nature and meditate on her:
> Why not domesticate her and regulate her?
> You depend on things and marvel at them:
> Why not unfold your own ability and transform them?

Hsün Tzu's radicalism consisted in his denial of the Confucian view, most clearly affirmed by Mencius, that everything—including man—is by nature good. It is not enough, Hsün Tzu argues, to let nature develop, conforming to it as it does so; it will go astray unless man corrects it by acting upon it, just as human beings will go astray unless they are educated. But in any history of Chinese thought Hsün Tzu stands out as a startling exception, whereas in the West his teachings would be the norm.

China's new masters have, of course, sought to introduce into China Western modes of thought. The familiar rhetoric—nature must be 'defied' or 'conquered'—is now characteristic of Chinese newspapers, along with such headlines as 'The Desert Surrenders' or 'Chairman Mao's Thoughts Are Our Guide to Scoring Victories in the Struggle Against Nature'.[78] But the vehemence of the rhetoric, now old-fashioned and suspect in the West, is a reflection of the resistance which has to be overcome, the foreignness of attitudes of mind with which the West has been for centuries familiar.

To sum up, so far as we can yet do so, the critics of Western civilisation are to this extent justified in their historical diagnosis: there is a strong Western tradition that man is free to deal with nature as he pleases, since it exists only for his sake. But they are incorrect in tracing this attitude back to Genesis. Genesis, and after it the Old Testament generally, certainly tells man that he is, or has the right to be, master of the earth and all it contains. But at the same time it insists that the world was good before man was created, and that it exists to glorify God rather than to serve man. It is only as a result of Greek influence that Christian theology was led to think of nature as nothing but a system of resources, man's relationships with which are in no respect subject to moral censure.

This attitude to nature sometimes gave rise to conservative conclusions: nature had been made by God for man's use and it would be presumptuous of man to think he can improve on God's handiwork. But it could also be interpreted in a radical way: nature was there for man to modify and transform as he pleases. Bacon and Descartes interpret it in the second way, and their interpretation—although there were objectors—was absorbed into the ideology of modern Western societies, communist as well as capitalist, and has been exported to the East. It found expression in a metaphysics, for which man is the sole finite agent and nature a vast system of machines for man to use and modify as he pleases. That is the metaphysics the ecologists are particularly, and rightly, rejecting. But this metaphysics by no means constitutes the entire Western tradition. Nor, as we shall see, does its rejection entail the rejection of the science with which it has so often been associated.

CHAPTER TWO

STEWARDSHIP AND CO-OPERATION WITH NATURE

Western civilisation—the same is true, of course, of Asian civilisation—is anything but monolithic. I shall have a little to say later about the Western mystical tradition. For although nature-mysticism, with its veneration of nature as sacred or divine, is incompatible with the central, Christian or scientific, Western tradition, it has nevertheless had a continuing importance, with such influential representatives as, in their different ways, Wordsworth and Emerson—to say nothing of the more quirky Thoreau. It has helped to establish the value of the contemplative enjoyment of nature; it has insisted on the unifying links between human life, on the one hand, and the life of nature on the other. On that last point, if on scarcely any other, the Darwinians and the nature-mystics could find themselves at one. They both rejected that view of man, Platonic in origin, which saw him, in respect to his soul at least, as an alien in a world of change and decay.

Two other traditions are also of considerable importance, in so far as they both deny that man, in relation to nature, is essentially a despot: the tradition that sees him as a 'steward', a farm-manager, actively responsible as God's deputy for the care of the world, and the tradition that sees him as co-operating with nature in an attempt to perfect it. The tradition of 'stewardship'—never strong but persistent—dates back to the post-Platonic philosophers of the Roman Empire and especially to the teachings of Iamblichus, in the third century AD. The Platonists believed that every soul existed before the birth of the man whose body it now inhabits, but in that earlier state in ideal intercourse with ideal forms. And they had to face the difficult question: why did the soul ever 'immerse itself in matter', entering this world of sin and misfortune and decay? They tried to answer this question in a number of rather different, if related, ways. But some of them, including Iamblichus, took as their point of departure an observation in Plato's *Phaedrus*: 'It is everywhere the responsibility of the animate to look after the inanimate.' Man, they said, is sent to earth by God, 'to administer earthly things', to care for them in God's name.[1]

At this point in our discussion, it is time to revert to the *Republic*, with its debate between Socrates and the sophist Thrasymachus which, as we have already seen, turns around the responsibility of governors. Thrasymachus thought it self-evident that the ruler acts entirely in his own interests; Socrates denied this. As ruler, his responsibility, according to Socrates, is the welfare of those he governs. That is the sort of government over nature Iamblichus had in mind when he said that man is sent to administer earthly things. It is now sometimes argued that this, too, is what Yahweh intended when he told the Hebrews to subdue the world. Or at the very least—for the Hebrew word translated as 'subdue' is a very strong one, with military connotations—that this is how Christianity interprets man's governorship. 'Men hold their dominion over all nature,' so the Anglican Bishop Hugh Montefiore tells us, 'as stewards and trustees for God.' And he goes on to deduce a crucially important consequence. 'They are confronted,' he writes, 'by an inalienable duty towards and concern for their total environment, present and future; and this duty towards environment does not merely include their fellow-men, but all nature and all life.'[2]

Genesis, the environmentalist John Black maintains in the same spirit, makes this duty clear when it tells us that God put Adam into the Garden of Eden 'to dress it and to keep it', i.e. to manage and protect it.[3] Man, Black goes on to argue, is made in God's image; this implies that he should act 'in a responsible way in relation to the lower order of creation, in the same way as God acts upon man'.[4] Man is to nature, that is, as God is to man. On this interpretation, then, it is a gross error to suppose that Christianity passes no moral judgment on man's relationship to nature, to suppose that it not only permits but actually enjoins him to deal with it as he pleases, in the manner of an absolute despot. His responsibilities rather are those of the shepherd ruler, as Socrates described them.

What evidence is there in support of such an interpretation of Christian teaching? Very little, I should say. Admittedly, there is a recurrent New Testament image, as Black points out, in which man figures as a steward and as, in his stewardship, representing God. Man's stewardship, however, relates to the Church, not to nature; the vineyard functions, in Christian teaching, only as a down-to-earth analogue of man's relationship to God. In Paul's words, Christian ministers are 'stewards of the mysteries of God' or, as Peter puts it, 'good stewards of the manifold grace of God'.[5] Calvin, no doubt, made great play with the concept of stewardship. But for him 'stewardship' meant the rule of the elect over the reprobate. In America the concept of 'stewardship' was used to justify strict control over the moral behaviour of the community. 'You will hereafter be called to an account,' a nineteenth-century preacher told his congregation, 'for all the violations of the Sabbath, all the profanity, all the intemperance, all the vice of every kind of which you have made yourselves partakers by neglecting to employ those means for their prevention, which God and the laws of your country have put into your hands.'[6] No mention, and characteristically, of his congregation's being 'called to account' for their treatment of nature. The stewardship they are called upon to exercise is over the lives of their profane brethren, not over 'the beasts of the field'.

For an explicit presentation of the idea of stewardship over nature Black refers us only to a passage from the seventeenth-century Chief Justice, Sir Matthew Hale—a passage so often quoted in this connexion that one has good reason for suspecting that it would be embarrassing to ask for another example. 'The end of man's creation,' Hale tells us in his characteristically legal terminology, 'was, that he should be the viceroy of the great God of heaven and earth in this inferior world; his steward, *villicus* [farm-manager], bailiff or farmer of this goodly farm of the lower world.' Only for this reason was man 'invested with power, authority, right, dominion, trust and care, to correct and abridge the excesses and cruelties of the fiercer animals, to give protection and defence to the mansuete [tame] and useful, to preserve the species of divers vegetables [growing things], to improve them and others, to correct the redundance of unprofitable vegetables, to preserve the face of the earth in beauty, usefulness and fruitfulness'.[7]

Man is still to think of himself, on Hale's view, as master over the world, not as simply contemplating it or simply preserving it in its original condition. But his high estate does not entitle him to use nature as he wills, to exploit its resources without regard to the effects of his actions. The fiercer animals he is at liberty to restrain, but the tame and useful he must protect. He can weed his farms 'to correct the redundance of unprofitable vegetables' and cut down trees to make new farms only if, in so doing, he does not destroy the beauty, the usefulness and the fecundity of the earth. Like a farm-manager, he can be called to account if he wilfully or carelessly degrades the earth's resources.

With Hale's eloquent description of man's responsibilities, modern conservationists—although not preservationists—would be in complete sympathy, whether or not they suppose these responsibilities to derive from man's being God's deputy. But this interpretation of man's relationship to nature stems from seventeenth-century humanism, with its Pelagian emphasis on what can be accomplished by the human will and its playing-down of original sin, rather than from the standard Augustinian tradition. Hale still grants, no doubt, that in some measure Adam's sin deformed the face of nature. But, like Black after him, he admonishes us to take as our guiding principle the prelapsarian injunction to 'dress and keep the garden', quite as if Adam had never been driven out of the garden to till a soil cursed for his sake.[8]

Indeed, should we go in search of images in the New Testament which relate man to God and nature we shall find many more references to man as the *servant* of God than to man as his steward. If, as Black suggests, man is to nature as God is to man, this would suggest that nature is man's servant just as, according to the Augustinian tradition, man is God's servant, at his absolute disposal, preserved or destroyed according as God chooses, or refuses, to grant his grace. That is the explicit teaching of the seventeenth-century 'laureate of the Church of England', George Herbert. After making it clear that nothing happens except for man's sake—a view Hale rejected:

> For us the winds do blow;
>   The earth doth rest, heaven move, and fountains flow.
>   Nothing we see, but means our good,

he goes on to pray

>   Since then, my God, thou hast
>   So brave a Palace built; O dwell in it,
>   That it may dwell with thee at last!
>   Till then, afford us so much wit,
>   That, as the world serves us, we may serve thee,
>   And both thy servants be.[9]

(The 'palace', of course, is man, and 'wit' has its normal seventeenth-century meaning—'intelligence'.) Man, that is, serves God; nature serves man and God. But there is no suggestion that man, in any respect, serves nature. Yet the last lines of this poem are sometimes quoted in support of the view that man, for Christianity, is nature's steward!

It is certainly a mistake, indeed, to describe as 'typically Christian' the view that man's duty is to preserve the face of the earth in 'beauty, usefulness and fruitfulness'. One should not be in the least surprised that ecological concern is sometimes condemned as heresy—'a kind of subtle undermining, in its theoretical origins, of the destiny and dignity of man himself'.[10] Just as God will not judge men, so Aquinas tells us, by their treatment of animals, so more generally, on the typically Christian view, he will not judge them by their treatment of nature. No one can hope to save himself from damnation by telling God: 'I have left the world a more beautiful, a more useful, a more fruitful place.' The sole question, as Augustine particularly emphasised, is whether he has acted entirely out of the love of God. And this implies that he has treated the world as something to be used—not as something to be enjoyed, worthy of being loved for its own sake. It is a not unimportant fact, all the same, that the tradition of stewardship has had its exponents in the past, both in classical and modern times. The view that man has a responsibility for handing over to his descendants a nature made more fruitful by his efforts is not, that is, entirely a contemporary innovation, or an attempt to appeal to moral feelings which simply do not exist: it has deeper roots in Western civilisation, if only, or so I have suggested, as a minority tradition.

Perhaps it has such roots in the Muslim world, too; latterly at least, Mahomet's teaching that man is God's vicegerent on earth has often been interpreted in this way—although concern for nature is anything but conspicuous in the Koran. But certainly it would be fruitless to look further East for a tradition of stewardship. The ideal of an active care for nature, as it is presented by Hale, forms no part of Eastern religion, whether Hindu or Buddhist. Such religions not infrequently teach, as Hale does not, that men should take all possible steps not to destroy any living thing. But the Western stewardship tradition goes further than that. It demands from man an active concern for the earth's fertility, quite incompatible with an all-absorbing quest, in the Buddhist manner, for a salvation to be achieved only by freeing oneself from every kind of earthly bondage.

To a certain degree, the tradition of stewardship coalesces with the second of the two traditions I distinguished at the beginning of this chapter—the tradition that man's responsibility is to perfect nature by co-operating with it. The word 'nature' derives, it should be remembered, from the Latin *nascere*, with such meanings as 'to be born', 'to come into being'. Its etymology suggests, that is, the embryonic, the potential rather than the actual. We speak, in this spirit, of an area still in something like its original condition as 'not yet developed'. To 'develop' land, on this way of looking at man's relationship to nature, is to actualise its potentialities, to bring to light what it has in itself to become, and by this means to perfect it. (Scarcely, of course, the attitude current amongst modern 'developers', for whom the potentialities of an area of land consist solely in the profits they can make out of it, at whatever cost to its original character.) Just as for Aquinas God's grace perfects human nature so, on this view, man's grace—commonly thought of, no doubt, as derived from God—perfects nature.* The perfecting of nature, it is admitted, requires skill and, in this sense, mastery. But a mastery which perfects, not a mastery which destroys or enslaves. Man's duty in respect to nature, then, is to seek to perfect it by working with its potentialities.

How is perfection to be judged? The presumption is still, in Aristotle's manner, that nature is at its best when it fulfils men's needs—that this, indeed, is its reason for existing, what its potentialities are for. So to perfect nature is to humanise it, to make it more useful for men's purposes, more intelligible to their reason, more beautiful to their eyes. But like good artists, men should, it is urged, respect their material; they should not try to shape it in ways which cut across its own tendencies, any more than a good sculptor treats bronze as if it were marble or marble as if it were bronze.

This attitude to nature is sometimes formalised as a metaphysics. As such, it may originate with the Stoic Posidonius, writing in the first century BC, if this is how we are to interpret his teaching that man's task is 'to live contemplating the truth and order of all things and *doing one's part in helping* to establish that order'.[11] It at least dates back to the *Hermetica Asclepius*, written somewhere about the second century AD: 'God willed that the Universe should not be complete until man had done his part.'[12] Man does not complete the universe simply by being in it, as both the Hebrew creation myth and Plato's *Timaeus* would seem to suggest: he helps to create it.

On the face of it, Genesis rules out any such supposition for the Jew or the Christian. The world, for Genesis, was created complete, by a series of divine acts; it was perfect until Adam sinned. Bacon might suggest that men had the task of recreating by their own efforts the Garden from which Adam had been driven, but Augustinian Christianity neither laid that task on man's shoulders nor promised him God's help if he should undertake it. It was left to Fichte, and the German metaphysicians who followed him, to reinstate the idea of a universe-in-the-making which man helps to form, in co-operation with a Spirit intent on civilising it. No doubt in Fichte the element originally supplied by nature, as distinct from Spirit, is reduced to a minimum—little more than an undiffer-

* This view, however, is not traditional Christianity. The minority report of the Papal Commission on birth control is orthodox in condemning the doctrine that it is man's duty to 'promote earthly culture by humanising nature' as an 'exceedingly humanistic altruism' which allows 'insufficient place in human life for the action of the Holy Spirit and for his mission of healing sin'. Sinful, unregenerate man is far from having a duty to remake nature in his own image; only 'the Holy Spirit', not the human spirit, can perfect. The minority report can conveniently be read in Leo Pyle (ed.): *Pope and Pill* (London, 1968); the passages quoted are on pp. 285, 290.

entiated chaos or, as in Hegel, 'negativity'. 'Nature, taken abstractly, for itself, and fixedly isolated from man, is *nothing* for man,' so wrote, in this same tradition, the young Marx.[13] But if we consider nature as it now presents itself, he goes on to argue, the position is very different.

The German metaphysicians emphasise the fact that what we commonly call 'nature' has already been largely modified by man— this, of course, is most obviously true in Europe with its tamed landscapes. So co-operation with Spirit means co-operation with a spiritualised nature, co-operation, indeed, with one's human predecessors. And men, at first forced to dominate, are now able to deal with nature in a gentle way; it no longer resists but welcomes their attentions—somewhat like a horse that has been broken-in. They can rule over it as its natural lord, not as tyrants. 'Cultivation,' Fichte writes, 'shall quicken and ameliorate the sluggish and baleful atmosphere of primaeval forests, deserts and marshes; more regular and varied cultivation shall diffuse throughout the air new impulses to life and fertility; and the sun shall pour his most animating rays into an atmosphere breathed by healthful, industrious and civilised nations. . . . Nature [shall] ever become more and more intelligible and transparent even in her most secret depths; human power, enlightened and armed by human invention, shall rule over her without difficulty.'[14] There could scarcely be a better expression of the optimistic spirit of civilisation—a civilisation restoring in a higher form the Garden of Eden, converting man the tyrant into man the lord—which prevailed during the nineteenth century and well into our own century; we read Fichte now with a sigh or an ironic smile.

In our own time, Teilhard de Chardin set out to formulate an evolutionary metaphysics in which the idea of co-operating with nature—or, as Teilhard mostly prefers to say, 'the world'—is central. Traditional Christianity, according to Teilhard, has made two fundamental mistakes. In the first place it has supposed nature to be static, created once and for all by God at the creation. 'Nature,' writes Teilhard in contrast, 'is the equivalent of "becoming", self-creation: this is the view to which experience irresistibly leads us.'[15] The etymological meaning of 'nature', that is, takes over in Teilhard as it does in the German Idealists. The second Christian mistake was to suppose that in order to save themselves men must free themselves from, must rise above, the world. Rather, according to Teilhard, they must work *with* the world. They are the first beings sufficiently rational to see what nature, through gradual evolution, is doing, and sufficiently powerful to help it on its path towards that final consummation for which 'the whole creation groaneth and travaileth until now'.[16]

The importance of such metaphysical systems, from our present point of view, is that they testify to the operation in Western civilisation of an attitude to nature not reducible either to despotism or to stewardship. As opposed to both of these it rejects the conception of a nature which is complete in itself, simply *there*, to be struggled against or conserved. Nature, for it, is still in the making. Teilhard sees it as capable, to a considerable degree, of developing itself through evolution. For the German metaphysicians, in contrast, it can only be elevated above primaeval chaos by the operation of Spirit, whether 'Spirit' is thought of as a supra-personal entity or as the human spirit. But for both Teilhard and the Germans, nature is already partly perfected by man's operations upon it, and that is why he can now co-operate with it.

Herbert Marcuse, an inheritor of the German Idealist tradition, distinguishes, like Fichte, 'two kinds of mastery: a repressive and a liberating one'.[17] Man's relationship to nature, Marcuse is prepared to admit, must at first be repressive, but as he civilises nature, he at the same time liberates it, frees it, as Hegel also suggests, from its 'negativity', its hostility to spirit. Civilisation, Marcuse argues, has most noticeably achieved that liberating transformation of nature in parks and gardens and reservations. 'But outside these small, protected areas', he adds, 'it has treated Nature as it has treated man—as an instrument of destructive productivity.'[18] So what is wrong with our treatment of nature is not that we have failed sufficiently to contemplate it but that we have used it destructively, as distinct from seeking to humanise it, spiritualise it.

The boundaries between the metaphysical and the metaphorical interpretation of such phrases as 'perfecting nature' are anything but sharp; passages which their author, one presumes, intends to be read solely as metaphor may disconcertingly employ the language of the metaphysicians. Consider this example from a book which is primarily anthropogeographical. 'Man has implanted so much of his own design that he appears less a subject of Nature's decrees than a partner who enables her to reveal new amplitudes of power, to render new services to material well-being, and not without grace and beauty to share with Man the great experiment of life.'[19] Nature, it would appear, can not only 'reveal new amplitudes of power' and 'render new services to material well-being'— which we might take to be a metaphorical way of saying that men can still discover fresh resources of power and food—but it is also 'not without grace and beauty to share with man the great experiment of life'. Not too easy to translate this into an intelligible literal form!

The temptation to think of nature, in the Stoic manner, as a semi-divine or divinely activated being with whom men can choose to co-operate or not to co-operate is indeed a powerful one. But it would be wrong to suggest that the metaphysicians and the looser rhetoricians are nothing more than victims of hypostatisation. They have something to say about man's relationship with nature, even when they wrongly suppose that it is a relationship between two entities—'Man' and 'Nature'. To find out what that 'something' is, I shall take a hint from Marcuse's remark that parks and gardens and reservations represent a liberating as opposed to a tyrannical mastery over nature. It is the more enlightening to do so in that Western thought has been obsessed with the ideal of a garden, that Paradisiacal garden from which Adam and Eve were driven.

In the seventeenth-century formal garden the idea of mastering or conquering nature is pre-eminent. 'Perfecting nature' is understood as imposing form on it. Man shows his unique rationality—identified with *l'esprit géométrique*—by constructing gardens on a geometrical plan. The severe simplicity of the design contrasts with the waywardness of nature. Shrubs are pruned into triangles, spheres or cones, or into the likeness of men or animals—into shapes, in either case, which could not possibly occur without human intervention. Nothing could be more autocratic, better calculated to display man's power over nature. 'Our British gardeners,' wrote Addison in 1712, ' . . . instead of humouring Nature, love to deviate from it as much as possible. Our trees rise in cones, globes and pyramids. We see the marks of the scissors upon every plant and bush.'[20] Interestingly enough, the seventeenth century sometimes thought of the Garden of Eden in exactly these same terms, with 'clipt hedges, square parterres, strait walls, trees uniformly lopt, regular knots and carpets of flowers, groves nodding at groves, marble foundations, and water works'.[21]

In contrast, the late eighteenth-century gardener sought to construct gardens which would have the same sort of relation to wild nature as does a landscape painting to the landscape it portrays. The gardener was to take his materials from nature, to treat them reverently, but to arrange them in a better composition. To 'perfect' was not to *impose* form, but to *improve* form. We are told of the most famous of landscape gardeners, Lancelot Brown, that it was his object 'to bring to life an improvement on rough Nature, . . . a raw goddess who was always struggling for improvement but never achieved it without the Aristotelian dressing of man's divinely natural faculties'.[22] His nickname 'Capability' arose out of his habit of describing a site as 'having capabilities'; his task, he thought, was to convert those capabilities into actualities.

Nature supplied the matter but only suggested the form. As a poetic contemporary put it, Brown was 'born to grace Nature and her works complete'. There could scarcely be a nicer example of the ideal of co-operative perfection—to grace nature, to complete her works, by realising their capabilities.

The civilising of nature, as its eighteenth- and nineteenth-century advocates saw the situation, has two advantages over leaving it as it is. It converts nature into something at once more agreeable and more intelligible than a wilderness; man understands domesticated nature, because he has helped to make it. He arranges nature in such a way that he 'can enter her world and enjoy our origins'.[23] From the wilderness he is always in some measure alienated; it stands in a relationship to him of pure externality. Yet at the same time the civilised garden does not involve the mutilation of nature, at least in the topiarist's manner. Its trees are still recognisably elms and limes and oaks, but by skilful placing and pruning they have been brought to a perfection of shape they rarely achieve in the forest.

The geometrical gardeners were, in a general sense, Platonists, convinced that to perfect nature it had first to be reshaped. The Cartesian-Platonist Malebranche once wrote: 'The visible world would be more perfect if the seas and lands made more regular figures'[24]—in contrast to the followers of Rousseau, for whom everything is good as it comes from the hands of the Creator and man's task is to remove hindrances to its free development. In removing dead limbs, in cutting off branches the tree is not strong enough to bear or which would prevent the free growth of other branches, the pruner, on the Rousseau view, helps the tree to assume its perfect form. To the Platonic topiarist, in contrast, no natural shape, but only a humanly-imposed and geometrical form, can be perfect.* The first view encourages man in his relationship with nature to think of himself as a ruthless despot, imposing order on what would otherwise be a meaningless chaos; on the second view he shows his skill, rather, by bringing to light the potentialities of the nature on which he operates.

Town planning will serve as a second example of this conflict of ideals. Nothing could better display the despotic concept of perfection than the American-style grid town, with its echoes of Rome and, more remotely, of Pythagoras. Whatever the character of the landscape, the roads run straight. The blocks are evenly square, whether on a hillside or on a flat plain, just as Roman

---

* The more practically minded, of course, lop trees into any shape which will ensure that they 'keep their place', so that they will not interfere with such civilised projects as overhead transmission wires. One sometimes feels, indeed, that trees are planted only in order to be thus lopped; their mutilated branches are the modern equivalent of the mutilated men with which some tyrants have liked to decorate their cities—a reminder of power.

centuriation was superimposed as much on the valley of the Po as on the near-deserts of Tunisia.[25]

In contrast, the town planner now often seeks to 'design *with* Nature', to take over the title of a book written by a leading exponent of this type of town planning, Ian McHarg. It is interesting to observe the assumptions on which McHarg works: 'Canvas and pigments lie in wait, stone, wood and metal are ready for sculpture, random noise is latent for symphonies, sites are gravid for cities.'[26] Notice the language: it is not just that stone, metal, wood, noise, sites are 'at hand', as Heidegger would say, ready for man to use; they 'lie in wait', they are 'ready', 'gravid', for man the deliverer. Lewis Mumford sums up McHarg's purpose in a way which still more closely links it with the German tradition I have already described: 'He seeks, not arbitrarily to impose design, but to use to the fullest the potentialities—and with them, necessarily, the restrictive conditions—that nature offers. So, too, in embracing nature, he knows that man's own mind, which is part of nature, has something precious to add that is not to be found at such a high point of development in raw nature, untouched by man.'[27]

The designers with nature, it will be observed, are by no means primitivists; they do not think of man as being wholly a despoiler. Nor do they imagine that they can 'perfect' nature without effort, as if what they try to do will always be aided by an invisible, guiding hand. But they seek to break down the attitude enshrined in Mill's essay on 'Nature': 'All praise of civilisation, or art, or contrivance is so much dispraise of Nature.'[28] If we praise the architects of the *tholos* at Delphi, this is not a way of depreciating the beauty of the site the architects chose for it. Men can—and this is what the 'designers with nature' are talking about—use their ingenuity to enhance rather than to destroy the qualities of a site. The road or city builder too often adopts as his principle of action Isaiah's (and Luke's): 'Every valley shall be filled, and every mountain and hill shall be brought low; and the crooked shall be made straight, and the rough ways shall be made smooth.'[29] But alternatively, he can try so to construct his city or his road that mountains and valley are, as with some Alpine roads or the Tuscan hill cities, more strikingly related than before. He will not always choose to make a road smooth or straight, if this involves too extensive a destruction.

The great virtue of the doctrine that it is man's task to perfect nature by designing *with* it is that it is a half-way house between the despotic view that he should seek, merely, to dominate over it and the primitivist view that he should do nothing to modify nature, since it is perfect as it is. No doubt, this way of looking at the relationship between man and nature can, at the hands of some of its exponents, reduce the potentialities of nature to so low a point that they constitute nothing more than the rawest of raw material. It cannot then readily be discriminated from the tyrannical interpretation of man's task. At the hands of other exponents, it can so emphasise preservation as to be scarcely distinguishable from primitivism. But in principle it offers an alternative to despotism and primitivism alike.

There are, then, two important minority traditions in Western civilisation both of which think of men as having responsibilities towards nature. The first is, in feeling, conservationist. It emphasises the need to conserve the earth's fertility, by culling and pruning and good management. The second is rather bolder: it looks to the perfection of nature by man, but a perfection which always takes account of nature's own resources and of what man has already achieved in his civilising of the world. It has often been formulated, and still is often formulated, in a metaphorical way, as if nature were a friendly power or, in the Hegelian version, a prisoner to be liberated from her fetters. We ought not to think of it as for this reason useless in our present situation. It suggests an attitude to nature which would warn us against setting up sea-walls as a substitute for yielding dunes, building freeways as gashes on the hillside, designing towns and buildings out of relationship to their sites.

How far it will carry us is quite another matter. Mill warns us against loose and sentimental talk about 'harmony with nature'. 'There still exists a vague notion', he writes, 'that . . . the general scheme of nature is a model for us to imitate: that with more or less liberty in details, we should on the whole be guided by the spirit and general conception of Nature's own ways: . . . and that, if not the whole, yet some particular parts of the spontaneous order of nature, selected according to the speaker's predilections, are in a peculiar sense, manifestations of the Creator's will; a sort of fingerposts pointing out the direction which things in general, and therefore our voluntary actions, are intended to take.'[30] The geometrical garden has a beauty of its own—remember *Last Year at Marienbad*—and so has the city of great boulevards, however 'unnatural' the square and the straight line. A road cannot imitate a riverbed, and it may be dangerous for it to follow closely at all points the contours of the countryside. But without sentimentality, without recourse to metaphysics, we can still recognise that it is better to look first at the way things happen in nature and help them to work more effectively than to try to ride rough-shod over them merely in order to demonstrate the superiority of a rationality defined in wholly mathematical, or wholly economic, terms.

Does it matter whether, as I have suggested in these two chapters, the traditions of the West are more complex, more diversified, than some of its critics have supposed? If we think of human society as something that men can reshape as they desire, whether by force or by admonition, then it does not matter in the least. On that view all the reformer has to do is to think up a better moral or metaphysical outlook and then propagate it. But that, I shall again and again be suggesting in what follows, is not the actual situation. Important changes in moral outlook can occur, have occurred; in producing some of these changes, individual reformers, whether statesmen or prophets, have played an important part. But the degree to which their reforms have been in the long run successful depends on the degree to which they have been able to appeal to and further develop already existing traditions. The fact that the West has never been wholly committed to the view that man has no responsibility whatsoever for the maintenance and preservation of the world around him is important just because it means that there are 'seeds' in the Western tradition which the reformer can hope to bring into full flower.[31] Were something like this not the case, the momentary agitation to which his strictures give rise is unlikely to issue in firm and consistent action over a long period of time; the familiar traditions are almost certain to reassert themselves. The history of the Russian Revolution is only one witness to this fact.

Part Two

ECOLOGICAL PROBLEMS

CHAPTER THREE   POLLUTION

I have set out to consider whether Western civilisation can, in principle, solve its ecological problems within the framework of its central traditions. A logically prior question, however, has first to be asked: what constitutes 'the solution of an ecological problem'? In this context, 'ecological' is used in a loose way, now current; a problem is 'ecological' if it arises as a practical consequence of man's dealings with nature. So pollution, the depletion of natural resources, the extinction of species and the destruction of wildernesses, the increase in human numbers—which I shall consider each in turn in the chapters which follow—all count as 'ecological problems'. But in what sense do they present 'problems' and what would it be like to 'solve' them?

An ecological problem is not, in the first place, the same thing as a problem in ecology. A problem in ecology is a purely scientific problem, arising out of the fact that scientists do not understand some particular ecological phenomenon, how, for example, DDT finds its way into the fat of Antarctic birds. Its solution brings them understanding. An ecological problem, in contrast, is a special type of social problem. (We can easily be led to suppose otherwise because most books on ecological problems are written by scientists.) To speak of a phenomenon as a 'social problem' is not to suggest merely, or perhaps at all, that we do not understand how it comes about; it is labelled a problem not because, like a scientific problem, it presents an obstacle to our understanding of the world but rather because—consider alcoholism, crime, deaths on the road—we believe that our society would be better off without it.

In calling a social situation a 'problem', then, we are evaluating it. Hitler was obsessed with what he called 'the Jewish problem'; most of us do not believe that there was any such problem. Or take a more controversial case. In countries like Australia, although not in the United States, an unemployment rate of 2 per cent is commonly described as a social problem. But in his *The Costs of Economic Growth*, E. J. Mishan argues that a rate of unemployment of these proportions is a cost democratic societies ought to be prepared to pay for the sake of price-stability, that to think of it as something they would be better off without—to think of it, that is, as a problem rather than as an inevitable cost—is quite to misunderstand the economic situation.[1] Not every social cost constitutes a problem; if the cost is an inevitable consequence of an otherwise desirable state of affairs, only the silliest sort of Utopian would treat its existence as a problem. Obviously, however, men can disagree both about the desirability of the state of affairs and the inevitability of the cost. They may not value price stability highly, or they may not believe that it can be preserved only at the cost of a 2 per cent unemployment rate.

This explains why the very existence of ecological problems is sometimes disputed. Even pollution, it is sometimes argued, is simply a price which has to be paid for the maintenance of a high standard of living. Developing countries are not deterred from industrial expansion by the reflection that it would increase the level—or perhaps, rather, alter the type—of pollution. Pollution is a cost they are prepared to meet—not, in their eyes, a problem.

Clearly, however, there are limits to this attitude. Not even in the least developed country can the reduction of human beings to a vegetable condition by mercuric wastes or the birth of malformed children as a consequence of nuclear fall-out be set aside as a 'cost'. Pollution of this sort is not just an inconvenience, not just an unfortunate consequence of industrial activity. It threatens the very existence of human society. So much we can now take for granted; so far we can safely assume that there is a 'problem of pollution'. It is not so easy to establish, as we shall see later, that other forms of contemporary concern—the rate at which the population is growing, resources are being depleted or wildernesses destroyed— constitute a problem, or even a cost.

So much for the nature of ecological problems. They are features of our society, arising out of our dealings with nature, from which we should like to free ourselves, and which we do not regard as inevitable consequences of what is good in that society. What would it be like to solve such a problem? To solve an ecological problem, as to solve any sort of social problem, is to describe a satisfactory way of reducing the incidence or the severity of the phenomenon stigmatised as a problem. To solve the problem of alcoholism is to describe a satisfactory way of reducing the number of alcoholics; to solve the problem of traffic accidents is to describe a satisfactory way of reducing the number and the severity of such accidents; to solve the problem of pollution is to describe a satisfactory way of reducing the total volume of pollutants or diminishing their harmfulness. 'Satisfactory way' is, of course, vague. The conclusion that a social problem has been solved, as we shall see, involves an evaluation just as much as does the decision that the problem exists.

Note, too, the words 'reducing', 'diminishing'. Why not, rather, 'abolishing'? In the case of a particular pollutant, DDT for example, abolition may be feasible. In general, however, to demand the abolition of pollution would be to set before ourselves an impossibly high, and perhaps disastrous, ideal: very few, if any, social problems can be entirely wiped out. And the refusal to admit that this is so often distracts attention from a perfectly satisfactory method of reducing their incidence and their severity. At a certain point, a problem fades into a cost, acceptable even if unpleasant. (A Utopian, we suggested, finds *any* cost intolerable. A Conservative, in contrast, is too ready to dismiss problems as costs.)

That will suffice for ecological problems and the form of their solution in general. Now to consider them in detail. I shall begin with pollution. Not because it is the most intellectually interesting or the most difficult of ecological problems but for precisely the opposite reason: it is the simplest to analyse and the most manageable of them all. To try to say anything about pollution which is not now trite and commonplace is next to impossible. But by looking at it in detail we may be able to bring out the complexity of even what is (relatively) a simple problem. And that will help us when we come to consider problems which are rather more difficult to analyse.

First, a definition. The classical definition of dirt is 'matter in the wrong place'; pollution is simply the process of putting matter in such a place in quantities that are too large. Or, more broadly, matter and physical processes—allowing, for our present purposes, that everyday distinction—since radiation and noise now commonly count as pollutants. (Compare the concept of 'clean' and 'dirty' atomic bombs.) In the right place, and in the right quantity, the substance or the process may be not only harmless but even beneficial; phosphate fertilisers are beneficial in a potato field but not in a lake or river, salt is harmless in the seas but not in irrigated fields.

What makes a place 'wrong'? It may be wrong 'aesthetically' in something like the original sense of that word, displeasing to the senses. Oil in an estuary, soot on a building, beer cans in a park, are all, for this reason, in the wrong place. No doubt, aesthetic tastes differ and a smoggy sky can have its own peculiar beauty. Some would resent the pollution of the Kamagawa in Kyoto by cloth-dyers, others rejoice in the multi-coloured stream. But few human beings enjoy swimming in sewage however 'treated'; the Rhine as it now looks and smells at Cologne has few admirers. Secondly, a place may be 'wrong' because the substance or the process in that place in a certain quantity is dangerous to human health, or will eventually move into places in which it will be dangerous. Finally, a place may be 'wrong' because the substance or the process in that place in a certain quantity will destroy wild-life, plants or animals. (That is an aspect of pollution I shall set aside until I come to discuss preservation.)

Solving the problem of pollution, then, means reducing the flow of substances or processes into places which are 'wrong', in one of these three senses.* Successfully to undertake this task one must first know what substances are in fact harmful and by what means and in what quantity they produce their deleterious effects. Many of these substances are in the wrong place only as a result of scientific and technological developments. The temptation, there-fore, is to resist the view—as comparable with calling in the devil to exorcise—that we can solve our ecological problems only with the help of more science and more technology. But in the situation in which we now find ourselves, that is obviously the case. The scientists and the technologists first drew our attention to the ecological problems which confront us, and without their aid we cannot hope to solve them, even if they, in turn, cannot solve them by their own efforts.

I distinguished between ecological problems and problems in ecology. And indeed it is vital not to confuse them, not to suppose that scientific discoveries can by themselves solve our ecological problems. Nevertheless the solution of an ecological problem will *normally* depend on the prior solution of problems in ecology, or, more generally, of scientific problems—not always, for sometimes we can deal effectively with a problem without having much understanding of it, as when we take an aspirin for a headache although we do not know how it reduces the level of pain. It will depend, in fact, upon the solution of a sub-set of problems—scientific, technological, economic, moral, political, administrative—each with its own style of solution. The solution of any member of this sub-set is necessary but not sufficient for the solution of the ecological problem. It is not sufficient, at least, unless it is the only problem remaining, the problems constituting the rest of the sub-set having already been solved. By considering these problems in turn, we can hope to analyse out the ingredients in a satisfactory solution to pollution-problems. At the same time we shall then be in a much stronger position to consider whether they are soluble

* There is, no doubt, a further sense of 'wrong place'; it sometimes means 'the place in which the substance or process would be dangerous to me personally'. So in the thirteenth century Parliament forbade the burning of coal-fires in London while it was in session, i.e. while Parliamentarians were living in London rather than on their country estates. Until quite recently 'men of substance' have always found it possible to escape to private retreats. That may explain why they are only now agitated about ecological problems. (The Earl of Leicester recently broke a four-generation silence in the House of Lords. His subject: pollution and its effect on the countryside. His ancestors might have spoken out against conditions in the new industrial cities. They did not do so.) I have presumed that the reformer's object is to reduce the total volume of pollution, not simply its incidence in the particular place in which he happens to live.

at all within the framework of existing Western institutions and traditions.

Take first the scientific sub-set. Much has still to be learnt about pollution.[2] The scientist is partly guessing when he lays down 'acceptable levels' of pollution; he cannot predict with any assurance, for example, the long-term effects of DDT. Indeed, the environmentalist Charles Wurster condemns the tolerances laid down by the American Food and Drug Administration as 'hocus-pocus', derived by quite illegitimate means from experiments on test animals.[3] Scientists find it difficult to decide on standards which governments can incorporate into anti-pollution legislation. Such legislation has been successfully challenged in the courts of Pennsylvania because the standards it laid down were 'confusing and inadequate'. There may well be important pollution-problems, too, which have not yet emerged. On the other side, scientists sometimes reduce their effectiveness as ecological reformers by proclaiming the danger of levels of radiation, let us say, which have existed in many areas of the world over millennia, without, so far as is known, having done any particular harm. The 'so far as is known', however, is important. These natural processes may in fact be quite harmful, so that, let us say, oysters from granite regions ought to be condemned for human consumption. The 'natural' is not necessarily harmless, let alone beneficial, to man. Quite certainly, too, the fact that such processes already exist in nature gives us not the least reason for believing that we can safely increase their level of intensity, even slightly. Human beings may have gradually evolved a degree of resistance to 'natural' levels of radio-activity, but not to any increase in that level by however low a percentage. The 'only a hundred extra deaths' resulting from a nuclear test are not purely statistical entities; they are children dying in misery. But the fact remains that until they know more about the actual effects of pollutants and the mechanisms through which they work, ecological reformers are in some measure crippled. (Compare the way in which tobacco-manufacturers have been able to make use of scientific ignorance about the precise manner in which cigarette-smoking increases the risk of cancer.)

More scientific investigation, then, is certainly needed. But, as we have already suggested, this investigation will sometimes have to assume a rather novel form. Any scientific contribution to the solution of ecological problems depends upon the discovery of relationships between physical processes which are ordinarily investigated by quite separate sciences. To appreciate the effects of nuclear fall-out, for example, it is necessary to investigate, first, the type of chemical substance a nuclear explosion releases; secondly, the mode of its distribution by atmospheric forces; thirdly, the manner in which it is taken up by the human body; fourthly, its effects on the body, including the body's genetic mechanisms. It is not the business of any one university department, to put the point crudely, to look at this whole complex of relationships, and what is not the business of any one department tends to get ignored. Everybody who writes about ecological problems is, in respect to certain of the topics he is discussing, an amateur. So far as the Western tradition discourages communication between specialists, it presents an obstacle to the adequate examination of ecological problems. Inter-disciplinary investigations are in this area not a luxury, but a necessity.*

Once the scientific problems have been solved, once it is understood how a particular form of pollution arises and in what its danger consists, the next problem is technological: to discover a method of reducing its incidence. That involves deciding, in the first place, which of the causative factors it will be easiest to control. Knowing, for example, that the Los Angeles smog is a joint product of the siting of Los Angeles, its hours of sunlight and the exhaust fumes from the internal combustion engine, it is at once apparent that only the third of these is controllable at a tolerable cost. So what has to be invented is a device which will reduce the output of hydrocarbons in exhaust fumes. This constitutes a technological problem, the solution to which lies in the invention of a device which would satisfy particular technical specifications. (The word 'device' is here being used in a very broad sense; an insecticide is a 'device' and so is the sterilising of insects as a means of biological control.)

The idea of a 'technological solution' is, however, a good deal less straightforward than it at first appears to be, as the phrase I used above 'at a tolerable cost' already hints. It is very easy to think up technical solutions of ecological problems if we consider them in isolation, and if we define a technical solution, without any reference to costs, as one which describes a way of freeing ourselves from the ecological condition which concerns us. Such a solution is sometimes said to be 'practical' but not 'operational'.[4] So Los Angeles' smog could be reduced in intensity by roofing over the entire city, or by making everybody use public transport, or by substituting fuel-cells, in their present state of development, for internal combustion engines. But few would seriously advance these proposals as 'solutions', as *satisfactory* ways of dealing with

---

* In Australia, the three Academies—Science, Social Science and Humanities—have set up a joint project to explore the ecological problems of the Botany Bay region. Part of the object is to get scientists and scholars with very different backgrounds working alongside one another in the exploration of particular problems. How it will work, remains to be seen. But this is at least the right way of proceeding. Close communication between specialists is a more effective procedure than the attempt to rely on 'generalists'.

the smog problem. Why not? Simply because the costs, or so it is widely believed, would be too great, costs of various sorts, social, ecological, economic and political.

In so far as ecological problems can be solved only with the help of scientific discovery and technological invention, they can be solved only within the Western rational tradition. That much is obvious. Mystical contemplation will not reveal to the chemist the origins of the Los Angeles smog nor enable the engineer to design an effective device for reducing its intensity. But it is a proper criticism of Western society that, in its—often childish—enthusiasm for technological 'advance', it has failed adequately to consider the costs of introducing new devices and has defined 'costs' far too narrowly.

This objection can be directed, even, against anti-pollution devices. The manufacture of such devices will normally create more pollution. It may, by modifying the character of the pollutant, introduce new dangers—reducing the percentage of carbon monoxide in exhaust fumes while increasing the percentage of the no less dangerous nitrogen dioxide. Or it may shift the incidence of the pollution from a wealthier to a poorer community—manufacturing smokeless fuels in an industrial town to make the London air cleaner—without reducing its total volume. Any technological innovation, furthermore, involves an element of ecological risk; it is impossible to calculate all its consequences in every possible circumstance. The best the technologist can do is to exclude effects which are already known to be dangerous and to investigate further effects which are suspect. That is why, as I said earlier, calling upon the technologist to save us is so often equated with calling in the devil as an exorcist.

But it would be quite wrong to conclude that for the reasons just advanced the technological method of overcoming ecological problems should be abandoned, that what Western societies should do is to shut down factories, let us say, rather than insist on their reducing, by technological means, their emission of pollutants. For that, too, involves risks. Closing down a factory may involve great economic and social risks—and, in the end, greater ecological risks if the social resentment engendered by the closure is directed against the whole system of ecological controls. It, too, may do no more than shift the incidence of pollution from richer to poorer regions, as the factory-owner takes his capital elsewhere. To give up taking any risks would be to give up acting. Every action costs something, risks something. What can properly be demanded is not that men should cease to act in ways which involve ecological risks— there are no such ways, as matters now stand, whatever the situation in the Garden of Eden—but rather that they should take more account of the ecological costs and benefits of their actions. And this means, once again, that they will have to make fuller use of rational Western-type methods, cost-benefit analyses or decision-procedures.[5] It is at this point that the economist enters the picture, as a specialist in the use of such methods. And so we come to the third sub-set of problems.

An engineer ought to be able to determine whether a particular technological innovation will in fact increase or reduce the rate and quantity of pollution-emissions. A cost-surveyor ought to be able to calculate its cost of production. But neither is accustomed to consider, or has any proficiency in estimating, its ecological costs. On the other side, the ecologist has had no experience in estimating either manufacturing or social costs. The economist is helpless unless information flows to him from the engineer, the cost-surveyor, the ecologist. But he has methods of conjoining and comparing costs and methods of calculating those costs which do not enter the market. Ecologists and economists ought to be friends. They are both interested in the allocation of scarce resources in the most effective possible manner. And each has methods at his disposal which the other needs.*

Cost-benefit analyses, however, have their difficulties, of which the first is ignorance. In a few special cases, the effects of pollution can be accurately estimated. But nobody really knows just what damage New York air pollution, let us say, does to human health.[6] Estimates of infant and foetal deaths resulting from nuclear tests in the United States range from four thousand (Tamplin) to four hundred thousand (Sternglass).[7] These uncertainties do not justify inaction. Nor do such reflections as that by choosing to smoke tobacco, or to drive cars, individuals run a greater risk than they are subjected to by any save quite exceptional industrial pollution, including nuclear fallout. The principle is quite widely accepted in our society, and it seems sound enough, that it is one thing to take risks on one's own behalf, quite another to be subjected to risk-taking by the actions of other people. (Industrial pollution is something 'they' do, smoking is something 'we' do, just as setting up nuclear power stations is something 'they' do, driving cars is something 'we' do.) The precise degree of the risk, furthermore, is often unimportant: if we are convinced that nuclear tests which kill four thousand people cannot be justified by considerations of national security, the question whether the number is four thousand or four hundred thousand is quite irrelevant. There are certainly

---

* Cost-benefit analyses of technological innovation are now taking shape as 'technology assessment', with its emphasis on the importance of studying alternative proposals in an all-embracing way. See the articles in *New Scientist*, 58: 847 (24 May 1973). The difficulties to which I draw attention in what follows still apply.

many cases, all the same, in which anti-pollution policies are frustrated by the fact that the costs and benefits of alternative courses of action—or of inaction—are largely unknown. And that is not the only difficulty.

Costs and benefits can be hard to quantify. And it is a proper objection to traditional cost-benefit analyses that they have tended to ignore costs, even when the economist recognised their importance, which are not readily quantifiable. This, the critics of Western civilisation might argue, is a product of the perverted Western attitude to life, its overemphasis on quantity, its neglect of what has recently come to be described, if more than a little obscurely, as 'the quality of life'—so described in deliberate contrast to the familiar emphasis on quantity. Over the last century, certainly, the West, especially in rapidly developing countries like the United States, Australia, the Soviet Union, has emphasised the size of a bridge rather than the aesthetic delights it offers, the magnitude of a city rather than the quality of its theatres, its restaurants, its schools. Too commonly, it has been supposed that biggest, brightest and best—even in the case of fruit and vegetables— naturally coincide. This attitude is not peculiar, of course, either to modern times or to the West.* In the contemporary West, however, it has reached its apogee. That no doubt is one reason why quantitative factors have so often been emphasised, qualitative factors ignored. If the bigger is *automatically* the better, one does not need to take separate account of them.

But the problem goes deeper. If economists have tended to ignore non-quantifiable costs, this is mainly on account of the extreme difficulty of handling and comparing them. As I said earlier, they have tried to develop methods of overcoming this problem, but they have a long way to go. And this is a serious handicap to the rational consideration of alternative courses of action. One of the most important indices of the quality of life in a community, to take an example, is the degree of suspicion with which human beings regard one another. It is intuitively obvious that New York would score very high on any such an index; Canberra relatively low. One can think of ways of quantifying the scale: the percentage of houses and cars left unlocked, number and type of locks on the doors, rate of ownership of bed-side pistols, percentage of shops accepting personal cheques, and so on. But certainly it is not an easy task; one can see why it is more attractive to compare *per capita* gross national income, wholly inadequate as this is as a guide to the relative advantages and disadvantages of

---

* Roman megalomania is notorious; the collapsed cathedral of Beauvais, the ruined temples of India, Cambodia, Ceylon, bear witness to a similar attitude. Even the Japanese— more often micromaniacs—have occasionally succumbed to it, with their 'biggest Buddha'.

living in a particular country. Similarly, it is easier to quantify the percentage of sulphur dioxide in the smoke from a factory than the rise in the suspicion-index resulting from an enlargement of the number of anti-pollution informers and inspectors. As this example illustrates, difficulties in quantifying by no means tell entirely against anti-pollution policies. The costs of at least certain forms of pollution can be easier to quantify than the costs of anti-pollution measures.

More information cannot overcome the wider difficulty affecting cost-benefit analyses and particularly obvious in the case of nuclear pollution, that men differ so notably in their estimates of costs and benefits, in the comparative value they attach, for example, to human life and to national security, over a spectrum ranging from the absolute pacifist for whom not a single life ought to be sacrificed in the interests of national survival to the no less absolute nationalist for whom individual lives are of value only as instruments of national destiny. Some of the proponents of ecological reform are primitivists or at least ruralists. They dislike big cities, they dislike industrialisation, for their own sakes. As the 'Blueprint for survival' prepared by a group of English scientists for *The Ecologist* makes apparent—a representative document to which we shall often have occasion to revert—their ideal is quasi-Arcadian, the small town set in the countryside.[8] So they would not regard it as a cost of a pollution-control system that it destroyed our large cities but rather as a benefit. Some of us, in contrast, would think of the destruction of cities, although not necessarily their reduction in size, as a very serious cost.

Within a given society at a particular period of its history such differences may scarcely exist or may be of very slight importance. In universities during the nineteen-fifties, for example, there was sufficiently general agreement that an increase in budget, in staff and even in students constituted a benefit; the dissentients were so few in number as not to amount, from the point of view of policy-making, to a significant minority. When the 'end of ideology' was announced in that same decade, this substantially meant that the community was no longer divided about costs and benefits. But that is far from being the case now; it is deeply divided, precisely on the issues which most closely touch ecological problems.

This need not be an absolute impasse. By spelling out the costs, or the benefits, in greater detail the 'Blueprint' authors, for example, might persuade their critics that a particular policy is the right one to adopt—that it is not, as their critics at first thought, undesirable to destroy our large cities. Indeed, the 'Blueprint' attempts to achieve this end by drawing attention to the crime-rate in large cities; it tries to convince us, too, that 'only in a small community can a man or a woman be an individual'. (Why, one wonders, are the streets of London and Boston, Tokyo and Sydney, awash with refugees from the narrowmindedness, the conventionality, the constant surveillance of small towns? When the authors of the 'Blueprint' write in praise of 'small towns', their minds, one suspects, turn to the highly selective and untypical Cambridge.) At the same time arguments of this sort often strike one as curiously artificial, the 'finding of bad reasons for what we believe on instinct', as Bradley said of metaphysics. The conflict between those who condemn and those who defend industrial growth, or cities, or the centralisation of authority, cuts very deep indeed. It is not, generally speaking, to be resolved by the discovery of new facts—facts, let us say, about the higher crime rate in the city. The city-lover might excuse this, in part, as an inevitable cost of the attractiveness of the city to young people in the crime-minded 18–24 year-old group and to every kind of deviant, good or bad, and in part ascribe the blame for it to social problems which could be solved by more vigorous and effective urban policies.

Taken together, these reflections may tempt us to set aside cost-benefit analyses as wholly useless, a consoling rigmarole which men use to disguise the arbitrariness of their choices. But at worst to try to construct such an analysis clears one's mind, drawing attention to costs and benefits one might otherwise have overlooked. And when a form of action is limited in character and narrow in its effects, its costs and benefits can be calculated with a relatively high degree of precision. No one seriously doubts that a rise in the death-rate from lung cancer is a cost, and its reduction a benefit. The real danger in cost-benefit analyses is that non-quantified costs will be left out of the picture, as interfering with the neat professional character of the analysis. These considerations entitle us to be wary of governments which announce that decisions can safely be left in their hands, that *they* have conducted cost-benefit analyses, too confidential to be submitted to the public gaze, which make it perfectly clear that their favourite projects will be to the public advantage. Unless we know what they have counted in and what they have left out and how they have calculated costs and benefits we cannot afford to accept their assurances that all is well.

So far, to summarise, I have been trying to make three points, each of which applies to anti-pollution measures but also has a wider significance. The first is that ecological problems are social problems, not scientific problems; to solve them satisfactorily is, in most instances, to be faced by a sub-set of problems, scientific, technological, economic, moral, political, administrative. The second is that scientific ignorance and technological incapacity may profoundly affect, in a variety of ways, our ability to solve ecological problems. The third is that any proposed solution, to be satisfactory, to be 'operational', must take into account, on a wider scale than has normally been attempted, the costs and the benefits resulting from the use of that, or another, method of control.

Our task is still by no means completed. There are further subsets of problems to be considered—moral, political, administrative—before we are in a position to assert that we know what it would be like to solve the problem of pollution. A proposed solution to an ecological problem may be objected to not only on the ground that its undesirable effects out-balance, on certain assumptions about relative importance, its desirable effects, but also on the more fundamental ground that however desirable its consequences its use is morally impermissible. Proposals for population control are the most obvious example. There are those who object to the hormone pill as a contraceptive agent only because they believe that it is dangerous. But others object because, they maintain, to take such a pill is morally wrong, quite independently of the physical consequences of so acting. And even those who would dispute this particular conclusion can easily imagine ways of reducing the rate of population growth—by the deliberate spreading of disease, infanticide, the cutting off of medical aid from underdeveloped countries—which, with varying degrees of conviction, they would reject as morally impermissible. We do not regard an ecological problem as satisfactorily solved merely because someone has thought up a device which would produce the desired results with a minimum of consequential disadvantages. The use of that device has also to be compatible with our moral principles. Even those who agree with Hitler that there is a Jewish problem might condemn, on moral grounds, his 'final solution'.

In this case, too, the impasse is not necessarily final. Science and technology may overcome the moralist's objections by inventing a new method which would not be incompatible with his moral principles. Or alternatively the objector might decide, as many Roman Catholics have in recent years decided, that the moral principles with which he was operating permitted exceptions, or did not rule out, as he had first thought, the adoption of the method in question.

These are conservative ways of solving the moral problems which arise out of the prima facie conflict between moral principles and the adoption of a particular course of action. They leave the moral principles intact or, at most, narrow their range of application. But the problem can also be solved in a more radical way, by rejecting the moral principles outright. It is very commonly argued nowadays, as we have already seen, that only such a radical change in the moral principles most widely prevalent in Western societies—'a new ethic for a new earth', to take over the title of a volume of ecological readings[9]—can solve our ecological problems.

In the case of pollution, one is at first inclined to reject this suggestion outright, to argue, indeed, that control over pollution, unlike control over population, presents, in principle, no moral problems. This is certainly true when the polluter is endangering the life, or damaging the health, of his neighbours. There is no novelty in the view that to endanger life and health is wrong. Like every other moral principle it admits of exceptions, and there can be disputes about what—war, for example—should be allowed to count as an exception. But to the general principle there would be, I think, no dissentients.

Even the most ardent opponent of state intervention, further-more, would agree that the state has the right to coerce its citizens to prevent them from physically harming their fellow-citizens; for John Stuart Mill, this is the pre-eminent case in which the state is justified in intervening. So action against health-endangering pollution is not only not in conflict with any widely-held, or even with any minority, moral principle; it is positively called for by such principles.

What, however, when the danger from pollution is to natural beauty or to wildlife? Wildlife I have reserved for later considera-tion; in this case the moral principles are certainly controversial. Natural beauty also has its complications. Its importance has been disputed, as the importance of life and health has not been disputed. The West certainly regards it as wrong—an occasional outburst of iconoclasm excepted—to damage works of art, and right for the State to intervene in order to protect them. No one defended the despoiler of Michelangelo's *Pietà*; his assault upon it, indeed, created more international anger than the thousands of attacks upon human beings that daily take place. The situation in respect to the destruction of natural beauty is by no means so clear.

If works of art, why not the naturally beautiful? There has been a great deal of argument about the relative value of natural beauty and works of art. Hegel thought that natural beauty was inferior; this is an inevitable consequence of his general view that nature is of value only when man has perfected it. In general, indeed, natural beauty has not figured prominently in the writings of aestheticians. Oscar Wilde's attack on nature-lovers in *The Decay of Lying* is more than a mere playing with paradoxes. 'My own experience is,' he there writes, 'that the more we study Art, the less we care for Nature. What Art really reveals to us is Nature's lack of design,

E

her curious crudities, her extraordinary monotony, her absolutely unfinished conditions. Nature has good intentions, of course, but, as Aristotle once said, she cannot carry them out.'[10] As Wilde's reference to Aristotle reminds us, this is a powerful Western tradition, by no means peculiar to Wilde or to Huysman's hero Des Esseintes, Wilde's model, for whom 'Nature has had her day; she has finally and totally exhausted the patience of all sensitive minds by the loathsome monotony of her landscapes and skies'.[11]

At the same time, Wilde and Huysmans were swimming against the stream, in opposition to the powerful tradition, never stronger than in their own nineteenth century, that nature is superior to art. 'Nature, I loved, and next to Nature, Art', as the poet Landor put it. That perfervid art-lover Bernard Berenson was prepared to wonder 'whether art has a higher function than to make us feel, appreciate and enjoy natural objects for their art value', i.e. whether the appreciation of art is anything more than a means to the appreciation of natural beauty.[12] By now, indeed, that the 'love of nature', understood as an appreciation of its beauty, is a good form of enjoyment would generally be taken for granted. And the destruction of natural beauty is the destruction of that form of enjoyment. (In G. E. Moore's *Principia Ethica*, indeed, the very existence of natural beauty is taken to be good.) So there is no striking novelty in the view that natural beauty ought to be protected against the polluter, even if the beauties of nature have, for the most part, ranked larger in the writings of poets than in the theories of moral philosophers and aestheticians. A 'new ethic' is not required to justify action against the beauty-destroying polluter; at most what is needed is a strengthening of existing moral principles.

And this is an important fact. For an ethic, as we have already suggested, is not the sort of thing one can simply decide to have; 'needing a new ethic' is not in the least like 'needing a new coat'. A 'new ethic' will arise out of existing attitudes, or not at all. (We shall look later at a case where this has actually happened—in relation to cruelty to animals.)

The fact that there is already resistance on moral grounds to the destruction of natural beauty, resistance within the Western tradition, just as there is to industrial processes which endanger human health, provides us with a foundation on which to begin work in any campaign on moral grounds against pollution. One can expect to find, indeed, that with increasing affluence men will place greater emphasis on what economists call 'superior goods'. They are suddenly awakening to the squalor which industry and scientific agriculture have created around them just as in the early nineteenth century they suddenly awakened to the fact that they were living on a vast dung-heap. Smokestacks are no longer a welcome feature on the landscape, as a symbol of prosperity and power.

One must not, of course, exaggerate the extent of this reaction. Indifference to squalor is still widespread. And more than indifference; the sight of a littered pavement or of beer cans by a desert road can afford, it would seem, positive enjoyment as signs of man's presence, testimonies to his affluence, or a non-violent protest against middle-class concepts of neatness and order.[13] But the reaction none the less exists, sufficiently to suggest that old attitudes, for a time cast aside in the interests of industrial progress, are beginning to re-emerge. The older towns, villages, even cities, reveal a clear consciousness of their surroundings; it is only in the nineteenth century that men, infected by greed, lost their capacity for harmonising their cities and their landscapes.

Moral problems, then, do not hold up the solution of pollution-problems, even if changes in our moral outlook might make them easier to solve. What of political problems? Even supposing we have satisfied ourselves that a particular device would be effective in solving a particular ecological problem, that its use is morally admissible and that, on balance, the benefits consequential upon its use outweigh its costs, we still have the task of persuading our fellow citizens that this is so. For, in general, a decision on our part to use a particular device—if that decision is unique or almost unique—would be totally ineffective. There is no point in our replacing an internal combustion car by a fuel-cell car, if we alone do so. Or perhaps it is wrong to say that there is *no* point in doing so: it may satisfy our conscience or give us a sense of moral superiority. But it will make so minimal a contribution to the problem of pollution as to be, from that point of view, meaningless.

It could happen, of course, that millions of our fellow-men quite spontaneously acted in a similar fashion. As soon as anti-pollution devices were released on the market they were immediately seized upon. This is likely enough to happen when the device, as in the case of the hormone pill, solves personal as well as social problems. But in the case of pollution it will normally be necessary, at least, for the innovators to *persuade* their fellow-men to make use of the device. And in many instances something more will be required: to persuade the State to coerce its citizens into using it. Indeed, it daily becomes more apparent that the principal obstacles to the solution of ecological problems are in fact political, to persuade or coerce citizens into action. To put forward policies which have no chance of success is not only wasteful of energy. It can engender frustration, despair and withdrawal—already in evidence after the collapse of student Utopianism; it can distract attention from proposals which *would* be feasible.

In the 'Blueprint', however, the solution of ecological problems is explicitly divorced from any consideration of political feasibility. 'We are sufficiently aware of "political reality",' its authors proudly tell us, 'to appreciate that many of the proposals we make . . . will be considered impracticable. However, we believe that if a strategy for survival is to have any chance of success, *the solutions must be formulated in the light of the problems* and not from a timorous and superficial understanding of what may or may not be immediately feasible.'[14] And, of course, no one would wish to let his problem-solving strategy be governed by a 'timorous and superficial under-standing of what may or may not be immediately feasible'. But a *serious* consideration of what is politically feasible is a different matter.

Enough has already been said to make it clear, I hope, that the idea of a 'problem' and a 'solution' is not, in the sphere of eco-logical problems, as straightforward as the 'Blueprint for survival' seems to suggest, that even to speak of a 'problem' and certainly to accept a 'solution' as such is to be committed to social judgments. So the only real question is whether to describe someone as 'knowing how to solve the problem of pollution' is to judge that what he proposes as a solution is politically feasible. (We certainly should not be prepared to accept his proposal as a solution if it were, in our opinion, not scientifically or technologically feasible.) Suppose it were to be suggested that the incidence of pollution should be lessened by making illegal the manufacture of motor-cars. It would surely be quite proper to reply: 'That's no solution, it just wouldn't be feasible politically.'

No doubt, as Mishan argues, 'ideas that seem, at first, to be doomed to political impotence may strike root in the imagination of ordinary men and women, spreading and growing in strength until ready to emerge in political form'.[15] Who would have thought, even as late as 1960, that abortion-law reformers had any chance of success in the United States? It is impossible to *demonstrate* that a proposal is not politically feasible. The suggestion that pollution-problems can be solved by deriving all our energy from perpetual motion machines can be rejected out of hand, demonstrated not to be feasible. For it is incompatible with scientific laws. The sug-gestion that they can be solved by the sort of social reconstruction sketched in 'Blueprint for Survival', involving the complete restructuring of England into communities of five thousand people is not *demonstrably* Utopian. For there is no scientific law or self-evident first principle from which it can be deduced that such a project is not politically feasible. One must admit, too, that pro-posals are often condemned as 'unworkable' or as 'Utopian' merely as a conservative defence-mechanism. It is easy to understand why

Marcuse should describe the rejection of proposals as 'Utopian' as 'vicious ideology', even if it is less easy to understand why he thinks the behaviour of French militant students in the 1968 uprisings confirms his judgment.[16]

Judgments of feasibility, furthermore, are relative. A proposal may be politically infeasible—not 'operational'—only in a particular country at a particular stage in its development, so long as a particular government remains in power. In another country, or under another government, it may be perfectly feasible. But the question of political feasibility cannot, all the same, be side-stepped. What one can grant, to avoid the objection that infeasibility is merely being used as a conservative gambit, is that the conditions under which a proposal is politically not 'operational' should be spelt out. Suppose one has as possibilities:

(*a*) this project is not feasible unless there is a change of government,
(*b*) this project is not feasible without a change in certain of our political institutions,
(*c*) this project is not feasible except in a totalitarian State.

None of these conclusions, it will then be obvious, is the 'last word.' The first may encourage us to work for a change of government, the second to seek a change in our political institutions, the third to support totalitarianism. In each case, of course, we should take into account the *other* costs of changing the government or our institutions.

So much for the general issues. A thorough study of the political feasibility of anti-pollution measures would have to consider, first, their feasibility in capitalist-democratic societies, secondly, their feasibility in communist countries, thirdly, their feasibility in developing countries. Even this, indeed, is far too schematic; Sweden is not in the same position as the United States, Russia as China, India as Malawi. Yet the success of anti-pollution measures will, in some cases, depend upon co-operation between governments so different in character. As a joint effect of ignorance and the scale of my investigation, I shall be forced to concentrate, however, except for a few side-remarks, on the democratic-capitalist countries, and then somewhat abstractly considered. The question then is: can such countries take serious action against pollution?

Political action against pollution has, in some instances, in fact been surprisingly successful; the most famous examples, although they are by no means unique, are the return of clear skies to London and of fish to the Thames. (In some ways, the cleaning up of the

Willamette River in Oregon is a more interesting example of what can be achieved by joint effort.)[17] Such political action has a good deal on its side. In the first place, pollution, historically associated with guilt, is an ominous word. Puritans knew what they were about when they labelled masturbation 'self-pollution' and wet dreams 'nocturnal pollution'. It is not without some degree of political sense, if confusingly, that noise and such aesthetic outrages as overhead electrical cables are nowadays so often condemned as auditory or visual 'pollution'. 'Noise' and 'ugliness' do not have the same emotional force as 'pollution', with its twin suggestions of sacrilege and impurity. These emotional overtones make it easier to agitate effectively against pollution—although they also increase the danger that anti-pollution measures will be overdone, that men will pay more for the reduction of pollution than, on rational consideration, they should have wished to do.*

Secondly, the struggle against pollution appeals to men's immediate interests. It is not some remote descendant, for the most part, who suffers from the effects of pollution but we ourselves: this makes the cleaning-up of pollution a more immediately appealing political slogan than the conservation of resources. Nor can men have any real doubt that it is against their interests to permit what happened in London in 1952, for example, to happen to them; they do not wish to be choked to death by smog. When the scientific evidence is clear and decisive, a government will find it very difficult *not* to take action.

What are the obstacles, even then, to anti-pollution legislation? No doubt, it will meet with opposition from those who stand to lose by the introduction of anti-pollution measures, often enough large industrial corporations. If, indeed, the naive-Marxists were right in arguing that in a capitalist democracy the government is nothing more than the executive wing of 'big business', it would follow that no such government could ever take effective action against any but the most obvious and most cheaply remediable forms of pollution.

That is not uncommonly maintained. Just as the ecological movement is sometimes converted into an attack on Western civilisation, so it is sometimes converted into an attack upon the political system of Western democratic countries. 'The ecological movement,' Marcuse tells us, 'must seek not the mere beautification

---

* That is particularly true in the case of radiation; its invisibility and its manner of penetration increase its menace, especially now that it is linked with the great shadow that lies across our age—cancer. 'Rays', it is worth noting, play a large part in the delusions of paranoids and schizophrenics. The effect may be to increase public resistance to the setting up of nuclear power stations to a degree disproportionate to their actual danger, at least as compared with other forms of fuel generation.

of the existing Establishment'—a splendid thought!—'but a radical transformation of the very institutions and enterprises which waste our resources and pollute the earth. They must be abolished and replaced by ones that drastically reduce pollution to an absolute minimum.'[18] Even in Sweden where, as one might expect, the control of pollution has been conspicuously successful, that success has been condemned by the more radical conservationists as dangerously palliative when what is needed is nothing short of a revolution.[19]

It is no doubt true that a system of absolutely free enterprise would be completely incompatible with pollution-control. In such a system, the government would stand aside to permit the industrialist to select the cheapest land in relation to the cheapest transport in order to turn the cheapest raw materials with the help of the cheapest labour into the dearest possible products, and for that purpose to make use of the cheapest manner of disposing of his wastes. The government would leave it to the 'guiding hand' of Providence to ensure that by acting thus he advanced the social welfare. But except in the United States—which has taken over from Oxford as the home of lost causes—absolute free enterprise has now very few defenders as an ideal and nowhere does it exist in practice. There is no novelty, nowadays, in a democratic state's acting, for the sake of certain of its members, in a way which increases an industry's costs. It did this when under the influence of nineteenth-century humanitarianism it prohibited child labour, limited hours of work, laid down minimum wages, insisted on industrial safety measures, introduced workers' compensation. There is no novelty, even, in the state's regulating the siting of an industry, the quality and character of its buildings or the methods of its waste disposal, all in the interests of amenity. Such moral and political issues as this sort of state intervention involves, the nineteenth century long ago fought out. Nor has the industrialist been left free to produce contaminated foods or dangerous drugs. Control over pollution, that is, involves no form of political action unfamiliar to a Western-type society.

Intent on maximising their profits, particular industries will certainly do what they can to prevent or to render ineffective anti-pollution legislation, just as they opposed laws laying down minimum sanitary or safety measures in factories. In so far as they restrict themselves to argument, one might even say that it is their *responsibility* to oppose; if a society is to arrive at the optimal situation at which pollution is reduced to a tolerable level at the minimum cost, someone needs to emphasise the costs, as distinct from the benefits, of anti-pollution measures. (It is not inhumanly complacent to be content with a 'tolerable level' of pollution; to demand that the Thames or the Rhine be drinkable without filtration would be, at least in my judgment, totally absurd.)*

Sometimes, furthermore, polluting industries will exert a disproportionate influence on governments, more especially on those local governments in relation to which they are major employers or major taxpayers or on governments which are emotionally committed to economic growth. They do not always confine themselves to lobbying; sometimes they will employ whatever pressure they can, including bribery and blackmail. They have large funds at their disposal; they can buy space in newspapers and on television programmes; they belong to a network of cross-connected institutions. Reformers and large corporations do not, in consequence, compete on even terms. In a particular case, however, they can come close to doing so, if large corporations are suspect, if there is a high level of honesty in the civil service, if the risk is to health rather than to landscape, and if the corporation is unable to base its counter-campaign on a crucial issue, for example, the risk of serious unemployment.[20]

The corporation, too, is a powerful and permanent institution; anti-pollution campaigns depend on the energy and zeal of a few energetic people, often enthusiasts who have not the patience to conduct a long campaign. The corporations often lose the initial battles but win the war.[21] It would be wrong to be either complacent or cynical about the outcome of anti-pollution campaigns. The prospects are at their worst when corporations and trade unions share the opposition.† Particular battles will certainly be lost. But at least democratic societies provide mechanisms of protest and agitation which are wholly absent in any of their actual alternatives. And can we even imagine a society so constituted that within it no anti-pollution battle could ever be lost? (Not to raise the further question whether there is any ground whatever for

---

* The opposite view is sometimes taken; I have just glanced at a publication on pollution prepared for schools by Ambassador College in the United States, a religious organisation. It is content with nothing less than 'absolute cleanliness'; the religious conception of pollution as 'impurity' runs through the brochure. But although it would be very nice to be able safely to dip a glass into the lower Rhine and drink its water, the cost would be enormous. At a certain level, as I have suggested, pollution becomes a cost rather than a problem.

† This is just one illustration of the difficulty in generalising, even from one democratic-capitalist country to another. The English trade-union leader George Woodcock recently told an environment conference in Finland that 'in most situations a trade union . . . would be more concerned about opportunities for employment than environmental considerations', and that 'it is most unlikely any trade union would declare a proposed development "black" on those environmental grounds—except where the health of their members was directly endangered' (*Environmental Future*, p. 513). In Australia, in contrast, trade unions declared oil drilling in the Barrier Reef 'black', because it endangered not their jobs but the Reef. The great risk always is of a coalition between 'hard-hat' trades-union members and the extreme right, whose attitudes—racialism, nationalism, anti-intellectualism—they not uncommonly share. (Note for American readers: no trade-unionist will work on a project declared 'black' or for suppliers of goods to the project.)

believing that such a society, were it imaginable, would in fact arise out of the flames of our present society.)

Political resistance to anti-pollution programmes, it is worth observing in this context, does not only come from 'big corporations'. The history of aborted anti-pollution measures in the United States—as told in James Ridgeway's *The Politics of Ecology*[22] —is basically a tale of political manoeuvres, of battles between the Federal Government and the States, between Congress and the White House, of the influence exerted by government agencies, especially the Corps of Army Engineers. Such power conflicts are not confined to democracies; as so often, the striking thing about the United States is the degree to which conflicts are there made public which in other societies are successfully concealed behind closed doors. The disappearance of large corporations, then, would not necessarily bring with it the death of all opposition to anti-pollution measures: conflicts between government agencies can be quite as significant as conflicts between reformers and corporations, a National Electricity Board quite as given to polluting as a private corporation. (It may nevertheless be true, as Ridgeway's analysis rather suggests, that to take ecological problems seriously is to be committed to the advocacy of considerable political changes; that even if they can be solved within the Western tradition, broadly considered, they may not be solvable within democratic states which are organised in particular ways, with particular systems of local government or particular state-federal constitutions. That is an important point to which we shall have to return.)

The main political obstacles to reform, however, derive not from organisations, governmental or private, but from established habits and expectations, which anti-pollution measures would compel us to abandon. The first of these is that we have all been accustomed to thinking of the air and the water as existing, most obviously, only in order to serve us, as practically infinite and as self-repairing. So without any consciousness of acting wrongly, we have let fumes escape into the air, or waste products into river, lake or sea. Air, in particular, has been the classical example of a 'free good', free because its supply is so great that it did not enter any market as a commodity.[23] But the same has been true, for the most part, of seas and lakes, rivers and estuaries. This way of thinking of air and water was, until recently, unimportant in its consequences. But fundamental changes have taken place: changes in the volume of pollutants, changes in their character.

In this situation there arises what Garrett Hardin has called 'the tragedy of the commons'.[24] A system of common lands for pasture works quite effectively so long as the number of beasts grazing on the land is below its carrying-capacity. But suppose the herd increases to a point beyond the carrying-capacity of the land. Then each individual herdsman can still calculate that it will pay him as an individual to add another animal to his flock: the profits accruing to him from his so doing are his personal profits, the deterioration of the land is a cost shared by all the herdsmen. So as the result of a series of rational decisions by individuals, the land is over-grazed and exhausted.

Similarly, it has paid each individual industrialist—and, indeed, each boat-owner, each householder, each farmer—to make use of the atmosphere, the seas, the rivers, as a way of disposing of his waste. And each individual can rightly argue, except in extreme instances, that the contribution made to pollution by his car, his incinerator, his waste-water and his sewage is negligible. If he were to desist, the effect would be indiscernible. In such circumstances, appeals to the individual not to pollute are almost certain to be unavailing: coercion is inevitable. What does this entail?

Coercion in such cases has to be based on some measure of general acquiescence, an agreement on the part of the citizens that what each of them would continue to do as an individual without any feeling of moral guilt he ought none the less to be prevented from doing—the kind of unwilling acquiescence, at the very least, that citizens give to laws regulating the parking of cars in public places. The acquiescence must be not only to the need for the legislation but to the appropriateness of the penalties attached to it. No government, one may feel confident, could now follow the example of Edward I in laying down torture and execution as the penalty for burning coal-fires. Unless such acquiescence is widespread, either the law will be a dead letter, or, in the attempt to enforce the law, the democracy will be gradually converted into a police state, or there will be widespread bribery and corruption. (These last two alternatives are far from being incompatible.)

But to secure the acquiescence when it cuts across established habits and expectations is no easy matter. That is a very important factor in explaining the slowness with which Chadwick's 1842 report on 'the sanitary conditions of the labouring classes in Great Britain' produced any real effects, for all that it drew attention to present dangers. It was not just that landlords found cess-pits cheaper than sewers. The 'labouring classes' resented the sanitary inspector, they objected to any interference with their excretory habits; they wanted to bury their dead, and to be buried themselves, in the familiar surroundings of the local churchyard.

A second, closely connected, expectation relates to costs. In estimating the costs of running a factory, the owner's expectation has been that he will only have to meet such costs as directly arise from his particular enterprise, such costs as raw materials, labour, machinery, depreciation, taxation, insurance. He does not expect to meet the cost of replacing Mrs Jones' curtains, even if it is the smoke from his factory that causes them to rot. Pigou, writing less than half a century ago, was perhaps the first economist to emphasise that 'smoke in large towns inflicts a heavy uncharged loss on the community, in injury to buildings and vegetables, expenses for washing clothes and cleaning rooms, expenses for the provision of extra artificial light, and in many other ways'.[25] Since Pigou, and more especially in the last decade or so, economists have paid a good deal of attention to such 'external' costs and the best way of reducing them to their optimum level—whether by taxes, by subsidies, or by fines.[26] The way was prepared for such action when industry was compelled to pay taxes in order to meet the costs of public services and to insure against certain forms of damage to others, e.g. to the workmen in their employ. As we said, there is no moral innovation in the view that one ought to pay for damages to one's neighbour; all that is new is the wider application of the ideas both of 'damage' and of 'neighbours'. But to legislate in order to compel individuals to meet external costs, or to restrict the use of air and water, is to encounter resistance not only from large corporations but from a wide variety of individuals. It adds to a motor-boat owner's costs to install a new type of waste-disposal apparatus, and this is a type of cost he has not been accustomed to meet.

A third expectation, of more recent origin, presents even greater difficulties, the expectation that there will be a constant flow of 'improved' commodities, replacing the 'out-of-date' and the 'old-fashioned'. Many of these novel goods do not present any pollution problem, but a great many of them involve at the very least a pollution-risk. For they are the products of the chemical industry; they introduce into the biosphere molecules which have never previously appeared there, or which if they were ever naturally synthesised rapidly vanished just on account of their toxic effects. (Commoner suggests that during the long course of evolution cells must at one time or another have synthesised very many of these molecules, which do not survive only because the cells which synthesised them immediately perished.) Only the nature-mystic would suggest that 'natural' products are always bound to be harmless, and the new artificial products to be harmful. Food which human beings have eaten ever since their hunting and fruit-collecting days may well be largely responsible for the majority of their major ills. But the fact remains that vast quantities of new, and conceivably dangerous, chemical products are accumulating in a biosphere which contains no enzymes capable of breaking them down. There is a very great risk inherent in this fact.

The only satisfactory method of dealing with certain forms of pollution may be to revert to the older products; recent experience with detergents suggests that the attempt to produce new trouble-free detergents, for example, only creates fresh problems. Such a reversion, one is inclined at once to argue with relief, would also be of great assistance to the less developed countries, many of whose products the new synthetics have displaced. But the situation is not as simple as that. Here we see how the sub-sets of problems can interact. For a sudden increase in the demand for tropical products could have disastrous ecological effects by encouraging the greater use of fertilisers and insecticides and the clearing of unsuitable land for agriculture. Furthermore the replacement of detergents by soap, for example, could adversely affect the world's food supply: natural fats and oils, needed as food in the less developed countries, would make their way to the affluent countries for use as soap. The pollution of American rivers is a small price to pay if the alternative is increased starvation in developing countries.[27] This is just one example of the complexity of anti-pollution policies, unless we are prepared simply to forget the fate of a vast segment of the world's population.

It is certainly true that governments or, more desirably, independent government research institutes need to insist on much more rigorous ecological policing of new products. This does not, in principle, present insuperable difficulties. The policing of drugs is now a familiar procedure; governments and industry alike are very conscious of the outcry, and the costs, resulting from the release of drugs which turn out to have thalidomide-type consequences. Political resistance can no doubt be expected. But experience suggests that this type of resistance can be overcome, given a government which is subject to a variety of public pressures and is not wholly corrupt. In all I see no good reason for believing, then, that a capitalist-democratic society *cannot* act effectively against pollution—indeed to say that it cannot do so would be to fly in the face of the facts. But I see every reason for believing that public pressure for it so to act cannot safely be relaxed.

Further political problems arise as soon as we ask who is to legislate against pollution. Pollution, as we noted above, is no respecter of boundaries. Yet legislative competence halts at boundaries. The multiplicity of municipal and other governing bodies surrounding an area like Botany Bay in Australia—local councils, airport authorities, port authorities—like the multiplicity of nations whose effluents flow into the Mediterranean or the North and Baltic Seas, can be a real obstacle to effective action.[28] The introduction of effective anti-pollution measures may depend on achieving an agreement between a number of political authorities with conflicting interests and conflicting political systems, varying greatly in their degree of industrialisation and in their willingness to take into account long-range consequences as distinct from immediate profits. To that extent, the recent political traditions of the West, with their emphasis both on the nation-state and on local government authorities, can constitute a considerable political obstacle to legislative action.

Some of the anti-pollution campaigners would welcome this conclusion, as a demonstration that all power should reside in a centralised supra-national government—or at the very least in a centralised government. That is far from being my own conclusion. No doubt, one could *imagine* a powerful supra-national government, under whose benign rule all men were free and equal citizens. No doubt, too, there are a great many defects in any actual local government system and any actual nation-state. There is room for argument, furthermore, about the powers which should be entrusted to particular legislative bodies, national or international. New forms of local government—corresponding in type to the Thames Conservancy and cutting across municipal boundaries—may well be desirable; international organisations will play an essential part in much anti-pollution legislation. But our political experience does not suggest that a highly centralised system, communicating with the general public only at the bureaucratic level—so that in practice one encounters government only as a face at the window—is a desirable form of government.

No doubt it can legislate firmly but it has an enormous inertia; it is highly resistant to change. To change, unless it is going to act tyrannically, it has first to secure agreement across an immense variety of conflicting interests. Experiments at the local government or at the national level can and do spread, should they be successful. But it is hard enough to get them accepted in the first place even at that level. Imagine the situation if the whole of Europe to say nothing of the rest of the world, had first to be convinced that censorship should be abolished, before it could anywhere be abolished. A small community can be tyrannical in the extreme, hostile to any form of enterprise or experiment. But at least there is some hope of escaping from it; the thought of a world government, from whose rules there was *no* escape, must fill anyone who cares about freedom with horror. Better a polluted world than this!

But, as I have already suggested, these are not the options; the setting up of an agreement on pollution in the Baltic does not have the consequence that in future Denmark will be indistinguishable from the Soviet Union. There will be problems in satisfying the diversity of interests involved, but there will be problems however we act. The important fact is that the issue will to some degree have to be fought out in public, not in the back rooms of a centralised government or a supranational Ministry. The record of international agreement on such subjects as health—as distinct from peace and war—is by no means such as to cause one to despair.[29]

To turn now to the last of the areas we discriminated: executive problems, decisions about the best method of implementing policies. This is not just a matter of detail. The choice of a particular method can have broad social effects. Sometimes, of course, there is no real option. It may be essential to prohibit entirely the use of a particular pollutant—an insecticide, let us say—and the normal apparatus of coercion is called into operation. But more often the objective is to lower the level of pollution and the choice lies between subsidies, the selling of rights, fines and taxes. Let us look at each of them in turn.

The thought of subsidising the polluter, paying him to make use of substitute materials or to install anti-pollution devices, horrifies the more extreme sort of retributionist. The polluter, as the retributionist sees the situation, has wickedly poisoned the air and the sea; let him now pay for his misdeeds. But moral indignation, although it can be politically effective, is a poor substitute for the rational consideration of executive alternatives. The factory-owner may be so far innocent, that he did not realise the consequences of his actions; nobody knew that the mercuric salts the Swedish papermills were pouring into the ocean would, as a result of the action of algae and the consumption of algae by fish, find their way back into human bodies. To shut down such an industry, or to impose upon it costs it simply cannot meet, may not be the justest way of dealing with the problems. And the same applies when an impoverished upstream town is found to be polluting the water supply of a downstream town. It may be better, in a particular case, for all of us to meet the costs of anti-pollution measures out of taxation rather than to make them fall on the polluting agent. There may be absolutely no option to this policy if there is to be any hope of reducing the use of polluting insecticides by under-developing countries.*

A major difficulty, of course, is that the agent is not then under pressure to develop the cheapest possible method of pollution control. He may in fact take advantage of the situation in order to introduce more productive machinery under the pretence of taking

---

* If safer insecticides were substituted for DDT in spraying against malaria, the cost, it has been estimated, would be raised from sixty million dollars to five hundred and ten million dollars. Compare 'Blueprint for survival' (p. 9, sect. 222) quoting from a 1971 World Health Organisation report.

steps against pollution. And industries which are uneconomical when their real costs are taken into account may survive with the aid of subsidies. But at least during a period of transition neither of these considerations is decisive. Morally, too, it does seem inequitable for a government to close down an industry because the government has suddenly introduced new standards of pollution.[30]

A modification of the subsidy plan has been proposed by Buchanan and Tullock. Let us take the classical case of a smoking chimney. Then, they argue, if this is a real cost to the nearby residents, it ought to be possible to draw up a scheme under which they are taxed in order to provide funds with which to compensate the factory owner for the cost of installing anti-smoke machinery; if the residents refuse to agree to any such arrangement, they cannot really be suffering from the effects of the smoke.[31] On this view, similarly, a downstream town should contribute to the costs of reducing upstream pollution.

Brian Barry has attacked the Buchanan-Tullock proposal on the sufficiently obvious ground that it provides no incentive for anyone establishing a new factory or a new town to choose this site for it rather than that, even when a less polluting site could easily be found. Then, too, it is inequitable, he argues, for those who happen to live near a factory to be called upon to subsidise the shareholders of that factory and the consumers of its products.[32]

In an existing situation, however, the Buchanan-Tullock solution is not wholly inequitable. That the polluter should pay is not, or so we have suggested, always an appropriate principle. There is no reason why a group of persons particularly affected by a pollutant— or their landlords—should not be called upon to help pay the costs of reducing its effects. Quite certainly, however, the Buchanan-Tullock proposals cannot serve as a general solution. Apart from questions of equity, it is often not possible to determine, except by expensive investigations, who in fact suffers from the fallout of a particular factory. It is often a far simpler solution for the State directly to subsidise the polluter, not attempting to meet the costs of doing so by taxing a particular class of taxpayer. A great deal of pollution, as we have already suggested, crosses local and national boundaries; the Buchanan-Tullock solution would involve complicated international negotiation. But there is no absurdity, no moral impropriety, in their proposals, if they are limited to a particular class of cases.

Another possibility is that the governing authority, whatever it may be, regards itself as selling rights, the right to pollute a river or the atmosphere to a particular degree. (I am assuming, of course, that we are prepared to accept a 'tolerable level' of pollution.) This implies that the government should regard itself as the owner of what has up till now been regarded as a 'free good', much as land-owners took over the commons in the eighteenth-century enclosure acts—although, of course, it is not possible for a government *physically* to fence off the air. In general, when a purchaser nowadays buys land, what he buys is the right to use it in certain ways. Unless it lies in a certain region, he will find that he cannot use it for industry, or high-rise housing, or for a multitude of other purposes. If it is farm land, he may be restricted in respect to what he is allowed to grow on it; if it is needed by a state instrumentality or a public utility it may be taken from him; in Sweden he will have to permit others to wander over it. So we can think of buying a piece of land as being, in essence, the buying of certain rights: the right to construct on that area a building for a particular purpose, built of particular materials at a particular cost. The sale of rights over water or air would be in some respects parallel to this; it is not unlike, too, the sale of fishing rights in England.[33]

Policing would be necessary, to ensure that the rights were not infringed. But the industries which have bought their rights could be expected, in part, to do their own policing, assuming that the cost of rights would be heavily increased if the pollution level rose beyond a certain point. The revenue from rights might be used to subsidise, where that is desirable, or to compensate—to compensate, for example, landowners near a new airport. If the right were fixed at a price which would permit such compensation, this would encourage the search for an airport which will affect fewer people. And something similar is true of the sale of rights generally.

A further possibility, and the one which most naturally occurs to us—partly because it satisfies our zeal for retribution—is the fining of polluters. One major objection to this method is that it requires extensive policing, a very marked increase in the number of confrontations between police and citizen and between police and informer. This is a very serious consequence, as is evidenced in the deterioration of police-citizen relationships since the intro-duction of traffic controls. If our legal system is not entirely to break down, there is good reason for believing that we need to reduce rather than to increase, as we have steadily been doing, the number of actions that are accounted crimes.

The final possibility, the taxing of polluters, is comparable in many respects to the selling of rights. It does not treat the polluter as a criminal, but as doing something for which he can be forced to pay. Unlike subsidisation, it encourages the discovery of cheap anti-pollution devices; unlike fining, it does not affect police-citizen relationships—although it may, of course, arouse considerable resentment and attempts at tax dodging.

I have done no more than sketch alternatives. Each alternative involves difficulties I have not so much as mentioned, e.g. the selling of rights may set up a competitive international market, spreading pollution more broadly if more thinly. Some methods are not applicable at all to pollution from a particular source: the large factory is more easily dealt with by one method, the motor-boat owner by another. Except when, as in the case of automobile exhausts, action can be taken at the supply-level, it is hard to see any way of dealing with the minor polluters—you and I—except by fines (or the exercise of moral pressure by our fellow-citizens). My concern was only to make two points: first, that governments ought not to think in terms of retribution, and, secondly, that the choice between methods of combating pollution is not simply a matter of detail.

To sum up, a successful attack on pollution involves the solution of a great variety of problems, not only scientific and technological but moral, political, economic, administrative. We ought not to pretend to know the solution to a pollution problem until we know how to reduce the incidence of that form of pollution by the use of a method the costs of which are not greater than the resulting benefits, which is politically feasible, and which can be effectively administered without intolerable disadvantages, economic or social. Total agreement that a proposed solution is satisfactory is not to be expected; there will be disagreements about costs and benefits and about political feasibility. The immediate *moral* problems are not, in the case of pollution, overwhelming—at least so far as we have yet explored them. For there is general agreement that nobody ought to be allowed to poison his neighbour. There are, however, considerable *political* difficulties in effectively legislating against pollution, in so far as such legislation not only attempts to restrain what are often very powerful interests but cuts across habits and expectations we all share. These flow, in part, from metaphysical beliefs, the belief that nature exists to serve us. But they also include more prosaic habits deriving from such facts as that we have not up to now been called upon to meet external costs and have become accustomed to a constant flow of novel products. Other political problems arise because pollution has no respect for local, or national, boundaries. There is no reason in principle, however, why international agreements should not be arrived at, or municipal boundaries reconsidered.

It would be quite foolish to be complacent about pollution, to suppose that its world-wide incidence is at all an easy problem to solve. If I spoke of it as the *easiest* of ecological problems to solve, this was not to suggest that it is easy. But it has in some measure been successfully tackled, and there is no reason to suppose that all that can be done has now been done. There is certainly nothing in the moral, the political or the metaphysical tradition of the West to inhibit appropriate action.

CHAPTER FOUR CONSERVATION

To conserve is to save, and the word 'conservation' is sometimes so used as to include every form of saving, the saving of species from extinction or of wildernesses from land-developers as much as the saving of fossil fuels or metals for future use. Such organisations as the Australian Conservation Society, indeed, focus their attention on kangaroos and the Barrier Reef, not on Australia's reserves of oil and fuel. In accordance with what is coming to be the common practice, however, I shall use the word to cover only the saving of natural resources for later consumption. Where the saving is primarily a saving *from* rather than a saving *for*, the saving of species and wildernesses from damage or destruction, I shall speak, rather, of 'preservation'. My concern in the present chapter is solely with conservation, in the sense in which I have just defined it.

On a particular issue, conservationists and preservationists can no doubt join hands, as they did to prevent the destruction of forests on the West Coast of the United States. But their motives are quite different: the conserver of forests has his eye on the fact that posterity, too, will need timber, the preserver hopes to keep large areas of forest forever untouched by human hands. They soon part company, therefore, and often with that special degree of hostility reserved for former allies.[1] So it is as well that they should be clearly distinguished from the outset.

The conservationist movement is now no novelty. It dates back in the United States to the latter half of the nineteenth century, although it suffered a marked decline in importance during the period 1920–60 when, under the influence of technological and industrial advance, men were particularly disinclined to believe that natural resources were to any degree limited. Its spirit and ideals are summed up in the Declaration prepared in 1908 by a Conference of United States governors:

> We agree that the land should be so used that erosion and soil wash shall cease; and that there should be reclamation of arid and semi-arid regions by means of irrigation, and of swamp and overflowed regions by means of drainage; that the waters should be so conserved and used as to promote navigation, to enable the arid regions to be reclaimed by irrigation, and to develop power in the interests of the people; that the forests which regulate our rivers, support our industries, and promote the

fertility and productiveness of the soil should be preserved and perpetuated; that the minerals found so abundantly beneath the surface should be so used as to prolong their utility; that the beauty, healthfulness, and habitability of our country should be preserved and increased; that sources of national wealth exist for the benefit of the people, and that monopoly thereof should not be tolerated.[2]

The conservationist, so much will be apparent, has no doubt that civilisation ought to continue; he fully accepts the general principle that it is man's task to make of the world a better place for men to live in. Admittedly, the governors' declaration includes a side-reference to the need, in order to achieve that end, to preserve as well as to remake. But its main emphasis is on re-making, on the draining of swamps and the irrigating of deserts, the damming of rivers. The governors would have been astonished to hear the preservationist argue that deserts ought sometimes to be left unirrigated, rivers left undammed and swamps left un-drained. What the conservationist opposes is not the harnessing of nature for man's economic purposes but carelessness and wasteful-ness in doing so. The many American conservationist acts of the late nineteenth century were largely directed against wasteful methods of oil-drilling or coal extraction. Conservation was identified with 'careful husbandry'.[3]

One might describe anti-pollution measures as a form of con-servation. For air, water, lakes, rivers, the sea, are all of them economic resources. To pollute them is to use them wastefully; to cause them seriously to deteriorate is to make it impossible for posterity to continue to civilise the world—or perhaps, to continue to survive. There is, however, a fundamental difference between pollution and the exhaustion of resources, considered as ecological problems—a difference which profoundly affects our willingness to make sacrifices in order to solve them. Pollution is something we should like to get rid of in our own immediate interests; our doing so will benefit posterity, no doubt, but it will also benefit us, quite directly. Only in a few special cases—such as the storage of atomic wastes—does the campaigner against pollution call upon us to act solely for the benefit of posterity. There is no incompatibility between our enjoying and posterity's enjoying clean water, fresh air, open spaces, the company of birds and animals. The cleansing of the Pittsburgh air or the Willamette river are gains not only for posterity but for the present generation. In contrast, it is in the interest of posterity, not in our own interest, that we are called upon to diminish the rate at which we are depleting our natural resources.

So the conservationist programme confronts us with a fundamental moral issue: ought we to pay any attention to the needs of posterity?* To answer this question affirmatively is to make two assumptions: first, that posterity will suffer unless we do so; secondly that if it will suffer, it is our duty so to act as to prevent or mitigate its sufferings. Both assumptions can be, and have been, denied. To accept them does not, of course, do anything to solve the problem of conservation, but to reject them is to deny that there is any such problem, to deny that our society would be a better one—morally better—if it were to halt the rate at which it is at present exhausting its resources. Or it is to deny this, at least, in so far as the arguments in favour of slowing-down are purely conservationist in character—ignoring for the moment, that is, such facts as that the lowering of the consumption-rate is one way of reducing the incidence of pollution and that a high rate of consumption of metals and fossil fuels makes it impossible to preserve untouched the wildernesses in which they are so often located.

To begin with the assumption that posterity will suffer unless we alter our ways, it is still often suggested that, on the contrary, posterity can safely be left to look after itself, provided only that science and technology continue to flourish. This optimistic interpretation of the situation comes especially from economists and from nuclear physicists. So Norman McRae, writing in the *Economist*, happily informs us that with the aid of the new sensors, carried by satellites, which are now available to geologists, vastly increased reserves of fossil fuels and minerals will soon be available for man's use. (They would certainly have to be vast: if our rate of consumption increases at the rate at which it has been increasing over the last decade even resources five times as great as those already known would be exhausted within the life-time of most children now less than ten years old.)[4] 'My own guess,' he writes of fossil fuel in particular, 'is that we will have an embarrassingly large fuel surplus'—this by the year 2012, when so many calculations predict the exhaustion of petroleum. 'And nuclear fusion . . . should [by that time]', he continues, 'give to mankind a virtually unlimited source of industrial power, with the oceans serving as a boundless reservoir of fuel—even for a world population far

* Neither 'posterity' nor 'the present generation' are, of course, sharp-edged concepts. By 'the present generation' I mean 'those who are now in a position to reduce or to increase the rate at which they are exhausting natural resources'; by 'posterity' those who will, or allegedly will, suffer unless that reduction takes place. But if the conservationists are right, this 'posterity' will include many who are now alive. Compare, on the vagueness of these concepts, Peter Laslett: 'The conversation between the generations' in *The Proper Study*, Royal Institute of Philosophy Lectures, vol. 4 (London, 1971).

larger and many times richer than today's.' If there is a problem, on his view, it lies only in the disposal of wastes—a pollution rather than a conservation problem.[5] The nuclear physicist Alvin Weinburg is no less confident that 'the problem of source depletion is a phony'. With the exception of phosphorus, he tells us, 'the most essential resources are virtually inexhaustible'.[6] The physical chemist Eugene Rabinowitch, editor of *The Bulletin of Atomic Scientists*, is equally reassuring. Modern science, he informs his readers, is 'showing us ways to create wealth from widely available raw materials—common minerals, air, sea water—with the aid of potentially unlimited sources of energy (fusion power, solar energy)'.[7] If these scientists, these economists, are right, there simply is no 'problem of conservation'.

Very many scientists, of course, take the opposite view, especially if they are biologists. Expert committees set up by such scientific bodies as the American National Academy of Sciences have, in fact, been prepared to commit themselves to definite estimates of the dates at which this resource or that will be exhausted.[8] This is always, however, on certain assumptions. It makes a considerable difference whether one supposes or denies that rates of consumption will continue to increase exponentially as they have done since 1960; it makes a very great—in many cases an overwhelming—difference whether one supposes or denies that substitutes will be discovered for our major resources. The Academy's extrapolations are best read as a *reductio ad absurdum* of the supposition that our present patterns of resource consumption can continue even over the next century.

The possibility that substitutes will be discovered introduces a note of uncertainty into the whole discussion, an uncertainty which cannot be simply set aside as irrelevant to our moral and political decisions about conservation, which it inevitably and properly influences. At the moment, for example, the prospect of developing a fuel-cell to serve as a substitute for petrol is anything but bright; confident predictions that by 1972 nuclear fusion would be available as an energy source have proved to be unrealistic. But who can say what the situation will be in twenty years time?[9] The now common-place comparison of earth to a space-ship is thus far misleading: the space-ship astronaut does not have the facilities to invent new techniques, nor can he fundamentally modify his habits of consumption. Any adequate extrapolation would also have to extrapolate technological advances. But by the nature of the case—although technologists have a bad habit of trying to persuade us otherwise—we cannot be at all certain when and whether those advances will take place, or what form they will assume, especially when, unlike the moonshots, they involve fundamental technological innovations such as the containing of nuclear fusion within a magnetic field.

No doubt, the space-ship analogy is justified as a protest against the pronouncements of nineteenth-century rhetoricians that the earth's resources are 'limitless' or 'boundless'. (It was often supposed, one must recall, that oil was being produced underground as fast as it was being consumed.) Fuel-cells, nuclear fusion reactors, machinery for harnessing solar energy all have to be built out of materials, including, as often as not, extremely rare metals. Men can learn to substitute one source of energy or one metallic alloy for another, the more plentiful for the less plentiful. But that is the most they can do. They cannot harness energy without machines, without radiating heat, without creating wastes. Nor can they safely presume that no source of energy, no metal, is indispensable; there is nothing either in the structure of nature or in the structure of human intelligence to ensure that new resources will *always* be available to replace old resources. Think how dependent we still are on the crops our remote agriculture-creating forefathers chose to cultivate; we have not found substitutes for wheat, or barley, or oats, or rice. Nor have we domesticated new animals as beasts of burden. So, quite properly, the conservationist points out.

The uncertainties, however, remain. We can be confident that some day our society will run out of resources, but we do not know when it will do so or what resources it will continue to demand. The Premier of Queensland recently swept aside the protests of conservationists by arguing that Queensland's oil and coal resources should be fully utilised now, since posterity may have no need for them. This is not a wholly irrational attitude. One can readily see the force of an argument which would run thus: we are entitled, given the uncertainty of the future, wholly to ignore the interests of posterity, a posterity whose very existence is hypothetical—granted the possibility of a nuclear disaster—and whose needs, except for such fundamentals as air and water, we cannot possibly anticipate.

Let us begin by supposing, for the sake of argument, that the optimists* are right, that we have no good ground for believing that any particular resource will still be in demand at any particular time in the future, that all we can say with certainty is that sooner or later, at some very remote epoch, civilisation will run out of resources. That is as far as the space-ship analogy can carry us. Should we then set aside 'the problem of resource depletion' as a

* 'Optimists', if all we take into account is the depletion of resources. From a broader point of view, of course, the depletion of resources might be the only thing that can save the world from dying either from over-population or from pollution.

mere pseudo-problem, on the ground that so distant a posterity is no concern of ours?

Kant thought it was *impossible* for us to do so. 'Human nature,' he once wrote, 'is such that it cannot be indifferent even to the most remote epoch which may eventually affect our species, so long as this epoch can be expected with certainty.'[10] And other philosophers have demonstrated a similar concern for their most distant descendants. That 'the Universe is running down', as the theory of entropy was at one time interpreted as demonstrating, is a conclusion William James found intolerable; only a faith in God, he thought, could deliver men from 'the nightmare of entropy'.[11] John Stuart Mill was reduced to a state of profound melancholy by the reflection that since there is a limited number of musical combinations, music will some day come to a standstill.[12] (This is an illuminating example; Mill did not, of course, envisage electronic music.) Similarly, there are some who felt a sense of relief when astronauts reached the moon; it kept open the possibility, they thought, that men would one day be able to leave a planet made inhospitable by decay to continue the human race on some other shore. But for myself, I more than doubt whether a concern for the ultimate future of the human race forms an essential part of human nature. Kant notwithstanding, a man is not a *lusus naturae* or a moral monster because his sleep is undisturbed by the prospect that human beings will at some infinitely remote date run out of resources or that, however they behave, they will eventually be destroyed by cosmological convulsions.

But even if this is not so, even if men are inevitably perturbed by the reflection that in some remote epoch their race will be extinct, their perturbation does not, of itself, generate any sort of responsibility towards a posterity whose fate they may lament but cannot prevent. The case is no doubt rather different when what is involved is the long-term exhaustion of resources rather than what James had in mind—the 'running down of the Universe'. For men can, in principle, so act as to delay that exhaustion whereas they cannot delay the earth's cosmological destruction. But if all that can be predicted—the hypothesis I have for the moment adopted— is a very long-term exhaustion of resources, no *immediate* action on our part seems to be called for. Anything we can do would, over millions of years, be infinitesimal in its effects; not even by reducing our consumption of petrol to a thimbleful apiece could we ensure the availability of a similar quantity to our remotest descendants.*

* To draw attention to the long-term problem, furthermore, can have effects the reverse of what conservationists would hope for; I have heard an economist argue that since the human race is in any case destined to extinction, it is absurd to pay any attention to the needs of our more immediate posterity. Compare R. D. Laing (*L'Express*, 29 July 1973).

If the exhaustion of resources is really, as the more optimistic scientists assert, a problem only for a future so distant as to be scarcely imaginable, then I do not think there is any good reason for our troubling our heads about it.

Should we, then, move to the opposite extreme and leave the future to look after itself, concentrating all our efforts on making the best we can of today? Then it would not matter whether the scientists are right or wrong in predicting an early exhaustion of resources. For the future would be none of our business. This, according to Matthew (6: 34), is what Jesus taught: 'Take therefore no thought for the morrow; for the morrow shall take thought for the things of itself. Sufficient unto the day is the evil thereof.' Nor is it by any means a preposterous attitude. We are confronted, in the present, by evils of every kind: in some of the developing countries by precisely the starvation, the illiteracy, the abysmal housing, the filth and disease which we fear for posterity; in many of our own cities by urban decay, impoverished schools, rising tides of crime and violence. It might well seem odd that the conservationist—and this is an argument not uncommonly directed against him—is so confident that he knows how to save posterity when he cannot even save his own contemporaries. Over a large part of the globe, too, the 'needs of posterity' are already being used to justify not only tyranny but a conspicuous failure to meet the needs of the present. One can easily be led to the conclusion that it would be better to let the morrow look after itself and to concentrate, as more than sufficient, upon the evils of our own time.

The view that men ought to concern themselves about the fate of posterity as such—as distinct from the fate of their children, their reputation, their property—is a peculiarly Western one, characteristic, even then, only of the last two centuries. It arises out of a uniquely modern view about the nature of the world, man's place in it, and man's capacities. A Stoic confronting our present situation might well believe that we were nearing the end of a cycle, that there would shortly be a vast conflagration after which everything would begin again. Within such a cycle, men could help to make the world a better place, but they could not possibly, on the Stoic view, arrest its cyclical course. For theological reasons, Augustine rejected the cyclical conception of history; Christians, he was confident, are saved or damned for eternity, not only for a particular cycle of existence. It was he who introduced into Western thought the idea of 'the future of mankind'.[13] Augustine did not suggest, however, that human beings could in any way determine in what that future would consist: the future lay in God's hands. God, so Matthew (6: 3) tells us, knows that men have need of food, of drink, of clothing; he will provide. Francis Bacon, writing late in the sixteenth century, was still of that opinion. 'Men must pursue things which are just in [the] present,' he wrote, 'and leave the future to the divine Providence.'[14] Although the lineal view of history left room for, it did not of itself entail, the doctrine that each generation should regard the future of mankind as its responsibility.

In Kant's philosophy, the idea of a duty to posterity assumes, perhaps for the first time, a central place. But although he exhorted men to sacrifice themselves for a posterity which would enjoy the fruits of their toil—thus initiating what Herzen was illuminatingly to call the 'caryatid' theory of history, according to which man, like the figures on a baroque façade, bears the burden of the future on his shoulders—Kant had too little confidence in man to suggest that the future is entirely of his making.[15] Providence, working through laws of progress, is still for Kant the principal historical agent. And even when philosophers began to argue, against Kant, that secular, rather than supernatural, forces would determine the future of mankind, they still did not suggest that man's deliberate decisions could wholly determine the future course of history. Progress, Engels for example thought, was inevitable; men can co-operate with, or resist, the forces that will bring about a better society but they cannot in the end thwart its emergence.

Had Western man been able to continue to believe either that the future of the world lies in the hands of Providence or that progress is inevitable he would not feel his present qualms about the future; the problem of conservation would not exist for him. But while a belief in the inevitability of progress still affects the thinking of a great many of the world's inhabitants—not only, but most obviously, in Marxist countries—amongst Western intellectuals it tends now to be replaced by the quite opposite view that unless men change their ways, catastrophe is inevitable. Such prophecies are often conjoined with the assumption that simply by *deciding* to change their ways men can create a better world. This is the fullest expression of the activist side of the Western tradition, its Pelagianism, what its nineteenth-century critics called its 'voluntarism'. Men are now being called upon, entirely without help, to save the future. The future, it is presumed, lies entirely in their hands; tomorrow *cannot* take thought of itself; it is they, now, who have to save tomorrow, without any help either from Providence or from History. No previous generation has thought of itself as being confronted by so Herculean a task.

How far is such a picture of man's relation to the future acceptable? Obviously, this is a highly controversial matter, entangled, in the last resort, in the old dispute between determinism and free-will. For my part, I am perfectly willing to accept what is negative in it: there is no guiding hand, secular or supernatural, which will ensure that man is bound to flourish, let alone survive. But it is a different matter to suppose that the future lies entirely in men's own hands, if this is taken to imply that, given sufficient goodwill, men need not fear for the future—or, more generally, that once men decide what they want the future to be like they can bring it to pass.

Some of the difficulties in this view emerge from the simulation studies of Jay Forrester and his associates.[16] Supporting his case by reference to the dismal record of good intentions in the field of urban renewal Forrester argues that what happens in society as a result of man's deliberate intervention is counter-intuitive. With great goodwill, men may conserve resources for posterity only to leave it worse off, in respect to both pollution and excessive population and so in the long run to resources, than it would have been had they been less generous. Forrester nevertheless extracts a programme for the future from his simulation-models. The computer can, he thinks, do what unaided intuition cannot; it can calculate the consequences of social actions. The present generation can save mankind from calamity, he suggests, by simultaneously and substantially reducing its capital investment, the birth rate, the generation of pollution, while holding the standard of living to a point not higher than its present level.

These predictions depend, however, on a number of assumptions. It has to be presumed, for example, that the *direction* of investment will remain constant, that individual preference scales will not profoundly alter, so that peace and quiet, or freedom from pollution, come to be more highly valued than the possession of consumer goods. But an even more serious point—for this presumption is not totally implausible—is that Forrester does not consider whether the policies he suggests could be implemented without social and political disruption, including the risk of civil and nuclear war. Relationships between economic restraints and war are not sufficiently precise to be fed into his model. At best, his policies would be effective only in an industrial community hermetically sealed off from the rest of the world.

But even if, for such reasons, we can be more than doubtful about the policies he advocates, Forrester's analysis helps us to see first, that goodwill is not enough and, secondly, that men cannot, in the social any more than in the ecological sphere, do one thing at a time, that their actions have consequences which flow from the character of their society and which operate quite independently of their wishes. It is scarcely a modern discovery, of course, that the road to hell is paved with good intentions. Both Kant and Hegel drew forcible attention to the fact that men's vices, their greed, their ferocity, what Kant calls their 'unsociableness', have as a matter of history done more to advance civilisation, however unintentionally, than their sacrificial virtues. And Marx long ago rejected as 'Utopianism' the supposition that good intentions are either necessary or sufficient to bring about desirable social changes.

The supposition, indeed, that history lies entirely in man's hands, that men can deliberately create the world of their choice, will not stand up to historical scrutiny. The Soviet Union and the United States are both of them sad reminders of that fact. Nor can it truly be replied that now we know better. Our knowledge of the social consequences of even so limited a form of action as the devaluation of a currency is extremely imperfect; an arms agreement, a rapprochement, plunge us into a sea of uncertainty. Against this background, it might be argued, to trouble ourselves about the needs of even a relatively near posterity is wholly absurd. Our ignorance is too great, our capacity is too limited.

We know at least this much, however. Men will need the biosphere. And it is sometimes suggested that our present level of industrial activity is so heating up the atmosphere that large parts of the earth's surface will—as a result of the melting of polar ice— eventually be rendered uninhabitable. So, it is concluded, we ought at once, for the sake of posterity, to reduce the level of that activity. Once again, of course, the facts are in dispute. The Royal Commission on Environmental Pollution concluded that 'such eventualities are not only remote: they are conjectural'.[17] But this case serves as a sort of touchstone, an example extreme both in its uncertainty and in the disastrousness of the consequences it envisages, were they to eventuate.

Let us now approach our problem from the opposite point of view. What positive arguments are there to justify the conclusion, so often taken for granted, that we ought to be prepared to make sacrifices for posterity, that we ought to take thought for posterity's morrow? It is sometimes suggested, as by Montefiore, that 'until men come to believe in their hearts that all life is held in trust from God, there can be no valid ethical reason why we should owe a duty to posterity'.[18] If Montefiore is right, this would certainly be unfortunate, since the greater part of the human race does not 'believe in its heart' that it is a trustee of God. As I have already pointed out, this is not even standard Christian doctrine. The conclusion would thus follow that only Christians of a certain persuasion have any valid ethical reason for concerning themselves in the slightest degree about the fate of posterity.

That is not a conclusion we should readily be prepared to accept. But what are the alternatives? How can men justify their concern for posterity, if not on the ground that it arises out of a duty imposed upon them by God?

This is a question that has seldom been asked. For the common assumption has been, as we saw, that what happens to posterity will depend scarcely at all on how men choose to act. Only very recently, indeed, have men thought it possible to engage in any kind of economic or social planning. But although Kant, for example, is mainly concerned to find good reasons for believing that the world, however men behave, is bound someday to be a better place than it now is, we can construct out of his political writings an important argument for thinking of ourselves as having a duty to posterity. It would run thus: men have not yet achieved all that they have it in them to achieve. They live in a society which is far from ideal. But they are capable of something much better than this. Their reaction to the French Revolution—their open expression of universal but disinterested sympathy when the expression of that sympathy involved them in considerable risk— was sufficient to demonstrate, Kant thought, that men possess a moral enthusiasm for the ideal, however greedy and violent their history might show them to be.[19] They have a duty to posterity simply because only posterity can realise that ideal.

This argument, as will at once be obvious, treats man's duty to posterity as an instance of his more general duty to sacrifice himself in the attempt to construct an ideal society—a duty which, Kant thought, survives the discovery that in trying to construct such a society the well-intentioned man will almost certainly do the wrong thing, whereas the greedy and the violent, as a result of what Hegel was to call 'the cunning of history' may well, however unwillingly and unwittingly, act as the agents of progress. Fichte, equally convinced on this point, offers, as Kant does not, the well-intentioned sacrificer a solace; he will go to heaven for *trying* to do the right thing even if, objectively considered, it is quite the wrong thing to do—so that, to return to Forrester's analysis, the anti-pollution campaigner will go to heaven even if by fighting for anti-pollution measures he is working against, rather than for, a better future.[20] That large segment of the world, however, which does not believe in supernatural rewards, has simply to recognise, on the Kant-Fichte view, that it is its duty to try to work for a better society—in the long run for an ideal society—even when it has become conscious that the actual effects of its actions may well be to hinder rather than to advance the emergence of such a society. This is not a very encouraging line of reasoning. Yet perhaps in the long run we shall not be able to come up with anything much more attractive. It is at least realistic, firmly based on human history, in its recognition that the unintended consequences of men's actions are more important, for the most part, than the consequences they intend.

Another possible line of argument is utilitarian. If, as Bentham tells us, in deciding how to act men ought to take account of the effects of their action upon every sentient being, they obviously ought to take account of the pleasures and pains of the as yet unborn. Sidgwick, writing in this same utilitarian tradition, explicitly formulates a principle of impartiality: 'Hereafter *as such* is to be regarded neither less nor more than Now.'[21]

In general terms, this seems sound enough. If the general maxim is that I ought not to act in a way which will do more harm than good, then the question whether the person I am harming or benefiting is yet alive is, on the face of it, morally irrelevant. Notice, however, Sidgwick's phrase 'hereafter *as such*'. If we were to adopt the principle never to act until we were quite sure that in so acting we would not do more harm than good, we could never act at all. We cannot be *quite* sure that a beggar will not choke on the bread we offer him. Obviously, we have to think in terms of probabilities. Bentham and Sidgwick after him were fully prepared to admit that we ought to take into account both the probability of the effects of our actions and also their remoteness; in general we should place the greater emphasis on effects which are near at hand. Although the hereafter *as such* has the same moral importance as the *now*, this is not true when account is taken of its uncertainty. As Sidgwick sums up: 'It seems clear that the time at which a man exists cannot affect the value of his happiness from a universal point of view; and that the interests of posterity must concern a Utilitarian . . . *except in so far as the effect of his actions on posterity— and even the existence of human beings to be affected—must necessarily be more uncertain.*'[22] A more recent utilitarian, T. L. Sprigge, makes the same point: the happiness we ought to take into account in determining how to act must be reasonably predictable and 'has a weight according to its degree of probability'.[23]

In the present case, this is a large part of the difficulty. As we have already seen, we cannot be at all certain that posterity will need the resources we propose to save for them more badly than they are needed now. Nor do we find it easy to assign probabilities. How probable is it that the more optimistic nuclear physicists are right in their estimate of the probability that in twenty years time nuclear fission, or solar energy, will be mastered? Or even accepting the argument put forward in *Limits to Growth* that the discovery of new energy sources would not solve posterity's problems, how confident can we be that in attempting to cut down on growth in order to save the biosphere we would not provoke social and political upheavals of the first order, upheavals culminating, perhaps, in the setting up of a rigidly totalitarian state?

So even if we accept the principle of impartiality and the utilitarian framework in which it is embedded, even if we accept the view that we ought not so to act as *certainly* to harm posterity, this does not appear to be a principle strong enough to justify the kinds of sacrifice some conservationists now call upon us to make. The uncertainty of the harms we are hoping to prevent would, in general, entitle us to ignore them, especially if we have good grounds for believing that the harm we could do to ourselves in trying to prevent them is considerable. We might be able to use possible damage to the biosphere as an additional argument against flying supersonic planes, when the benefits are minimal and the present damage considerable. But utilitarian principles are not strong enough to justify the cutting down of industrial growth merely *in case* posterity should run out of petrol, or merely because industrial growth *might* be heating up the atmosphere.

A general consequence of this analysis is that it would be useless to rely upon the market as an agent of conservation. We cannot assume that increases in prices, with rising demand, will suffice adequately to conserve resources. The market acts on principles even more restricted than Bentham's; each operator in the market is interested only in his personal gains, not in the greatest happiness of the greatest number. But, like Bentham, the market places great emphasis on certainty and propinquity. Demand for it means *present* demand; supply *present* supply. (Or if this is not quite true, at least it does not look far ahead—only reluctantly so far as to supply capital for, say, afforestation.) That is why although the total volume of the earth's resources—as distinct from the total volume of resources available at a particular time—is obviously diminishing, up till now their cost has for the most part declined. Some forecasters predict that supplies of mercury will be totally exhausted as early as the nineteen-eighties, yet its price (in 1972) is falling sharply.[24] Any tendency for costs to rise in the face of rising demands has been more than outweighed, whether because developing countries have sought to build up exports by the sale of raw materials or because technologists have invented more technologically advanced extractive mechanisms.[25] No doubt, unless substitutes are found, the cost of raw materials will eventually rise in a way that will reflect their scarcity—we shall not wake up on 1 July 2026 to find that there is not a drop of oil left, as the more picturesque extrapolations rather suggest—but this will not happen so long as the scarcity is potential rather than actual. The market approach can at most justify, in fact, relatively short-term savings of resources, and then only if there are good grounds for expecting that prices will rise sufficiently to compensate for the loss of interest on the income which is foregone by not exploiting them now.*

Man considered as a pure consumer or a pure producer, economic man, has, indeed, only a very limited concern for posterity. As the economist Joan Robinson has freely admitted: 'This problem [of sacrifices for posterity] cannot be resolved by any kind of calculation based on "discounting the future", for the individuals concerned in the loss and gain are different. . . . The benefit from their sacrifices will come later and they may not survive to see it. The choice must be taken somehow or other, but the principles of Welfare Economics do not help to settle it.'[26]

A somewhat different line of argument—which takes justice rather than happiness as its starting point—has been put forward by John Rawls. He does not so much as mention the saving of natural resources. (How rare it is for moral philosophers to pay any attention to the world around them!) But he has a good deal to say about the general concept of saving for posterity; that we ought to save for posterity, he in general argues, is a consequence of the fact that we ought to act justly, to posterity as to our contemporaries. The utilitarian principle of impartiality, taken literally, demands too much from us; we cannot reasonably be expected to share our resources between ourselves and the whole of posterity. What we can reasonably be expected to do is to hand on to our immediate posterity a rather better situation than we have ourselves inherited. Anything less than this would be unfair to them, anything more would be unfair to the present generation. Rawls is Kantian in so far as he presumes that the final aim of our efforts is an ideal society we shall not live to see realised. But he so far compromises with such of Kant's critics as Herder and Herzen as to argue that we can best work towards that society by improving the conditions of life *now* and passing on the results to our immediate descendants, for them to do likewise. Exactly to what degree we should save for posterity, it is not possible, he admits, accurately to determine. But about the general character of what we ought to do he has no doubts. 'Each generation,' he writes, 'must not only preserve the gains of culture and civilisation, and maintain intact those just institutions that have been established, but it must also put aside in each period of time a suitable amount of real capital

---

* Economists, quite unlike biologists, inevitably think in short terms. This is one reason why, in debates about the need for conserving raw materials, they so often sound optimistic. From their point of view it is quite absurd to worry about what may happen thirty years hence. An economist, indeed, thinks of himself as soothing our conservationist qualms if he tells us that supplies of a particular mineral will last until the year 2000—less than thirty years off!

accumulation.'²⁷ The 'capital accumulation' may take various forms—investment in learning and education as well as in machinery, factories, agriculture.

Note that, as Rawls sees the situation, we have a threefold task: first to 'preserve the gains of our civilisation'; secondly to 'maintain intact' our 'just institutions'; thirdly to hand over to posterity an accumulation of capital greater than we received from our ancestors. Many nowadays would, of course, challenge the assumptions inherent in this conception of our task. What we have been accustomed to call 'gains', they would argue, are not really such; none of our institutions are just; we should be doing no kindness to posterity by handing over to them a greater capital accumulation. But for my part, I am prepared to accept the view, at least, that if our situation were a normal one, Rawls has accurately described what posterity would expect, and all it could properly expect, from us. So far, so good. But it is not very far.

Each generation, Rawls is suggesting, should decide what it ought to save for posterity by answering in particular terms a general question: what is it reasonable for a society to expect, at the stage of development it has reached, from its predecessor? If it then acts upon the answer at which it arrives, each generation will be better off than its predecessor but no generation will be called upon to make an exceptional sacrifice. This is as far as we can go, I should agree, if our relationship with succeeding generations is to be governed by the principle of justice. The consequence is that each generation is concerned, when it is considering what sacrifices it should make, only with the next succeeding generation, not with some remote posterity. And this, as contrasted with classical utilitarianism, presents it with an easier set of calculations to make, difficult although they still are.

But although this means that, up to a point, each generation is in a unique position, unique in respect both to exactly what it inherits and exactly what it has a duty to hand on, it does not allow for the position of a generation which is unique in a quite different sense: it cannot calculate what it should do for posterity by reflecting on what its predecessors did for it. The sacrifice required of such a generation may be heroic, and Rawls's theory is based on the concept of justice, fairness, equal shares; it leaves no room for the heroic sacrifice. Yet if the conservationists are right it is precisely such a heroic sacrifice we are now called upon to make, a sacrifice far beyond anything our ancestors had to make. And this transforms the situation.

Now, in fact, men quite often do make heroic sacrifices. They make them out of love. It is as lovers that they make sacrifices for the future more extensive than any a Benthamite calculus would admit to be rational. When men act for the sake of a future they will not live to see, it is for the most part out of love for persons, places and forms of activity, a cherishing of them, nothing more grandiose. It is indeed self-contradictory to say: 'I love him or her or that place or that institution or that activity, but I don't care what happens to it after my death.' To love is, amongst other things, to care about the future of what we love.[28] (Of course, the word 'love' is used in many different ways. I have in mind the sense in which to love is to cherish. I can 'love ice-cream' without caring about what happens to it after I die.) This is most obvious when we love our wife, our children, our grand-children. But it is also true in the case of our more impersonal loves: our love for places, institutions and forms of activity. To love philosophy—to philosophise with joy—is to care about its future as a form of activity: to maintain that what happens to it after our death is of no consequence would be a clear indication that our 'love of philosophy' is nothing more than a form of self-love. The tourist who writes his name on a tree or rock-face in a 'beloved beauty spot' makes it only too clear what *he* loves. To love a place is to wish it to survive unspoiled.

Sometimes, one must grant to the Augustinian moralist, what is involved in a concern for posterity is a form of self-love, the desire to win 'immortality'. An institution, a person, is then thought of as carrying forward into the future at least one's name and perhaps some dim memory of one's character and achievements. So a grandfather may wish to have a grandchild named after him, or a municipal councillor a street or park. An author may be content to have his name inscribed on a catalogue card in the British Museum; an Ozymandias may have his statue set up for the admiration of all who pass by. In a way this is pitiable, as Shelley saw, but perhaps it is essential to the continuance of civilisation. That 'love of literary fame' with which Hume, he tells us, was consumed is at worst harmless, and at best can help men to write great works. It is only when self-love is substituted for love for an object, as distinct from being conjoined with it, that it is destructive.

Love, no doubt, extends only for a limited distance in time. Men do not love their grand-children's grand-children. They cannot love what they do not know. But in loving their grand-children—a love which already carries them a not inconsiderable distance into the future—they hope that those grand-children, too, will have grand-children to love. They are *concerned*, to that degree, about their grand-children's grand-children. 'For myself,' writes Macfarlane Burnet, 'I want to spare my grand-children from chaos and to hope that they will live to see *their* grand-children getting ready to bring a stable ecosystem into being.'[29] Such a degree of concern for one's grand-children's grand-children is a natural consequence of one's love for one's grand-children; it is, as it were, an anticipation of *their* love. And so is a concern for the future of art, of science, of one's own town or country or university. By this means there is established a chain of love and concern running throughout the remote future.

Of course, a particular chain may be broken; not every parent loves his children, not every pupil of a philosopher loves philosophy. But such links are sufficiently common and persistent to lend continuity to a civilisation. They serve to explain sacrifices beyond the call of a Benthamite calculation or a sense of justice. There is, then, no novelty in a concern for posterity, when posterity is thought of not abstractly—as 'the future of mankind'—but as a world inhabited by individuals we love or feel a special interest in, a world containing institutions, social movements, forms of life to which we are devoted—or, even, a world made up of persons some of whom might admire us.

No doubt, this concern has often been made worthless by ignorance or outweighed by greed. But the new settlers in America or in Australia were not, for the most part, *deliberately* disregarding, when they destroyed the countryside, the interests of posterity. Many of them believed that the resources of the new countries were endless. As late as 1909, it is worth recalling, the United States Bureau of Soils officially committed itself to the view that the soil, at least, was an infinite resource. ('The soil,' so the Bureau pronounced, 'is the one indestructible, immutable asset that the nation possesses. It is the one resource that cannot be exhausted; that cannot be used up.'[30]) The best of the new settlers—others, of course, were obsessed by greed—were convinced that they were building a better country for posterity to inherit. Total indifference to posterity has not been a leading characteristic of Western civilisation over the last few centuries; much of what has been most devastating has been sincerely done for posterity's sake. Jesus's 'take no thought of the morrow' has not served as a guiding principle in the West, not even in monastic orders. In general, men have sought to create a better world for those persons and activities they love.

I admitted, however, that chains of love might be disrupted. What is usually called the 'generation gap' is often not so much a 'gap' as an active hostility, a form of hatred, a kind of civil war. It is easy to imagine it accentuated, so that parents ceased, in general, to love their children. Then, too, it is often suggested that we are approaching a period in which the major activities and institutions we have learned to love will perish. 'It seems clear,' writes Harrison Brown, 'that the first major penalty man will have to pay for his rapid consumption of the earth's non-renewable resources will be that of having to live in a world where his thoughts and actions are ever more strongly limited, where social organisation has become all-pervasive, complex, and inflexible and where the state completely dominates the actions of the individual.'[31] One hopes he is wrong; one fears that he might be right. Suppose we accept his view and push it a little further, to its gloomiest extremes. For, on the face of it, this possibility greatly affects the kind and the degree of sacrifice we ought to be prepared to make.

Let us suppose that we have good ground for fearing that men can continue to survive as a species only within a wholly tyrannical society, dimly foreshadowed by Hitler's Germany or Stalin's Russia, in which the rulers, aided by modern observation-devices, will succeed in utterly destroying personal affection or any form of human enterprise. In such a society art survives only as a form of flattery, science as monitorial technology, philosophy as ideology. Suppose, furthermore, that we also have good ground for believing that a society of this sort will cover the entire surface of the earth and that there is no possibility of its ever changing. From such a world, everything some of us love would have disappeared, not for millennia, but for ever. In terms of Rawls's account, this would be a posterity which would *not* hand on what we had handed on to it. We should be unique in being the last generation to be free. Should we not then content ourselves with doing the best we can in the present, leaving posterity to stew in its own juice?

This point has been raised quite sharply by M. P. Golding, in an article in which—unlike Rawls—he shows himself very conscious of the contemporary moral situation, the emphasis on the future written into proposals to control the use of resources, the growth of population. He entirely excludes from his purview that class of cases in which the idea of a duty to posterity is linked with the concept of love, as well as any case in which what we supposedly owe to posterity 'is identical with (or overlaps) what we owe to the present generation'.[32] For in such cases, he argues, we share a common life with those to whom we owe an obligation, the sort of common life which engenders obligations.

When the posterity in question is remote, in contrast, we can have no assurance whatsoever that they will form with us a single moral community, that what they take as good we should also take as good. (Or, in my own language, that they will cherish what we cherish.) Men may in fact be converted into beings of a quite different character: the man of the future may well be 'Programmed Man, fabricated to order, with his finger constantly on the Delgado button that stimulates the pleasure centres of the brain'. Towards such a being we should have no obligations.[33] In the end, indeed,

Golding and Rawls come to something like the same practical conclusion: we should, Golding says, be reluctant to act on the predictions of what he calls 'crisis ecologists', who would have us plan for mere survival. We should do better, in his words, 'to confine ourselves to removing the obstacles that stand in the way of posterity's realising the social ideal'.[34]

So whether we approach the problem of obligations to posterity by way of Bentham and Sidgwick, Rawls or Golding, we are led to something like the same conclusion: our obligations are to *immediate* posterity, we ought to try to improve the world so that we shall be able to hand it over to our immediate successors in a better condition, and that is all. And this, of course, is a very familiar principle: it represents accurately enough what, over the last two centuries, men have seen as their duty to posterity as a whole, as distinct from the objects of their special affection. This would still imply that we are called upon not to waste those resources our successors will certainly need. But it means that we ought not to act, out of concern for posterity's survival, in ways which are likely to destroy the civilised ideals we hope posterity will share with us. We should try so to act that our successors will not be wholly without electricity, but we need not, should not, close down our civilisation merely in the hope that a remote posterity will have some hope of surviving.

At least, this much follows, too, from my own analysis in terms of loves. Obligations deriving from loves relate us to posterity just in so far as we have some grounds for believing that the future will contain what we love. But love, we also suggested, carries us beyond 'good grounds', at least in the most calculating sense of that phrase. It is certainly not possible to *demonstrate* that the kind of society, the kind of human being, both Golding and I dread will in fact come into existence. And so long as the possibility remains that men will continue to be what they have been in the past—cruel but gentle, destructive but creative, hating but loving—and will continue to carry on the activities we love, we shall not wish to take the risk that by failing to make sufficient sacrifices now we shall jeopardise their survival. This is so even when the risk is a slight one.

But what sort of sacrifices ought we to make? It follows from what I have already said that we ought not to be prepared, in the supposed interests of posterity, to surrender our loves or the freedom which makes their exercise possible, to give up art, or philosophy, or science, or personal relationships, in order to conserve resources for posterity. Posterity will need our loves as much as we need them; it needs chains of love running to and through it. (Developing these loves will also necessarily involve, of course, developing *in those we love* the idea of a duty to posterity.) So far Herder was right to rebel against Kant's emphasis on sacrifices for posterity, right in arguing that the greatest service we can perform for posterity is to do what we can to make the world a better place *now*. And that, as we saw, is substantially the conclusion both Rawls and Golding also come to. Those who urge us to surrender our freedom and to abandon our loves so that posterity can enjoy a 'true freedom' and a 'true love' ought never to be trusted. No doubt, as individuals, we might sometimes have to sacrifice our freedom or certain of our loves. But only to ensure their maintenance and development by others. And this is true, I should argue, even if they can be maintained only at the cost of human suffering—although there is in fact no evidence to suggest that we shall save posterity from suffering by surrendering our freedoms.

The surrender of forms of enjoyment is a different matter. What we would be called upon to do, at this level, is to reduce the consumption of certain goods—those which depend on raw materials which cannot be effectively recycled—and to recycle whenever that is possible, even although the costs of doing so would involve the sacrifice of other goods. That is the kind of sacrifice we ought to be prepared to make, if there is a real risk that it is essential for the continued existence of a posterity able to carry on the activities we love. It is, indeed, the kind of sacrifice we are quite accustomed to making, the deferring of consumption for the sake of the future of our children or of our impersonal loves. Nor does it rest on a concern for a remote posterity, with unguessable needs and resources: it is our grand-children who will have to make their way in a world, if the forecasters are correct, denuded of resources. A Benthamite might be prepared to take that risk; a lover will not.

Whether the forecasters of scarcity are right, as we have already seen, is by no means clear. Let us suppose that, after inspection of the evidence, we come to the following relatively modest conclusion: the rate of consumption of fossil fuels and minerals ought not to be allowed to exceed its present point. (The more dismal extrapolations all assume a constant *increase* in the rate of consumption.) With population increasing as it is, that by itself implies a considerable diminution in the use per head of at least some materials—those which cannot be recycled—and a considerable rise in the cost of all of them. Furthermore, the developing countries are unlikely to acquiesce in a situation in which they are called upon to content themselves with their present, extremely low, rate of consumption. So in practice there are only two possibilities: either the more developed countries reduce their rate of consumption very considerably; or alternatively, with all the political and moral difficulties this presents, they refuse to permit any rise in the rate of consumption of natural resources in the less developed countries. How great a sacrifice would this entail?

In the ideal society depicted in the 'Blueprint for survival' craftsmanship, cookery and the arts 'would earn both money and prestige'.[35] What disappear are such consumption goods as motor-cars. Citing as its authority the biologist Stephen Boyden, the 'Blueprint' tells us that cars are used for four main reasons: 'to go to work, to go to the countryside, to visit friends and relations, and to show off'. And since in the ideal society everybody will work in the small town in which he lives, the countryside lies around him, his friends and relations live in the same town, and there will be more reliable and satisfying ways of showing off, the car will be entirely pointless.[36] As for other consumption goods, the 'Blueprint' assumes that the reward of living in a small community, of knowing and being known, will be an adequate compensation for the lowered consumption of material goods.

Now, many of us would regard the abolition of private cars and a reduction in the flow of consumption goods generally with perfect equanimity—however little desire we might have to live in a society in which we were never anonymous. We middle-class intellectuals are often so little attracted by the consumption goods characteristic of modern society, the automobile or the television, to say nothing of the beer-can and the packaged goods of the supermarket that we greatly underestimate the degree to which they bring enjoyment to others. Boyden's comments on the car, for example, quite fail to recognise the very great enjoyment some people, young people especially, derive from driving and looking after cars.* (I shall refrain from commenting on the question whether even an inveterate car-hater like myself would not long for one, to get out of the tightly-knit small communities the 'Blueprint' envisages.) We do not seriously contemplate the possibility that, let us say, the conserving of forests might make it necessary to reduce the publication of learned books and periodicals; we assume that pretentious packaging is what would have to go—superfluous on our view, more than ready as we are to go back to newspapers and brown paper bags as wrapping, but adding, in the eyes of many consumers, a touch of instantaneous gratification to the drabness of shopping for meat and groceries. It is easy for us to accept Ehrlich's prescription for a car limited in power and weight when the car we freely choose for ourselves is of lesser

---

* Our novelists, literary rather than mechanical by training, have been singularly blind to the passions which now rule men's conduct. Only in a rare American film—especially the 'underground' films of Kenneth Anger—does the love of a man for his bike, or his car, find expression. The extraordinarily large number of automobile journals, however, bears witness to its prevalence.

power and lesser weight, or if the car plays a part in our lives only when we are living under circumstances in which public transport is impossibly inadequate. I could read Mishan's *The Costs of Economic Growth* with almost complete sympathy until I suddenly encountered his proposal that all international air travel should be banned; if I lived in London I suppose I could accept that proposal readily enough. 'Who benefits,' Ehrlich rhetorically asks, 'from the garish use of electric signs that deface the night-time sky of our cities?'[37] They have in fact given me great pleasure, from childhood on; they do not, so many people would think, 'deface' but rather embellish the darkened cities.

It is scarcely surprising, then, that conservationists are often condemned as middle-class, elitist, attempting to impose sacrifices on a working class which is enjoying for the first time in human history a degree of affluence sufficient to permit them, for example, to take holidays in resorts which were once the unique possession of their betters. So the British Labour politician, Anthony Crosland, has argued that the ecological movement is 'indifferent to the needs of the ordinary people', that 'it has a manifest class bias, and reflects a set of middle- and upper-class value judgments', that it is no more than a horrified reaction to the spread of affluence amongst the working classes and the resulting loss of amenities to the middle-classes.[38]

The situation would be simpler if we could persuade ourselves that purchasers do not really want the goods they buy, that they are deluded into buying them as a result of the deceptions of advertisers, so that we are not really calling upon them to make a sacrifice. Certainly, this sometimes happens, as Mishan is right to emphasise. We can define 'really want' in the following way: a person really wants something—as distinct from being persuaded into believing he wants it—only if he enjoys his possession of it once he owns it. And he 'really wants' one thing more than another only if he enjoys it more—as measured by his greater reluctance to surrender it. (This is too crude an analysis; for one thing many people enjoy buying *as such* rather than their ownership of the goods they buy. But for our present purposes it will suffice.) On that interpretation of the situation, many people buy objects— encyclopedias, for example—which they do not 'really want', and would never have bought were it not for their inability to resist the efforts of salesmen. It would be difficult to determine, however, what percentage of goods bought fall into that class, to what degree, therefore, a lower production of consumption goods would involve no genuine sacrifice on the part of consumers. I suspect the percentage would be relatively small.

Of course, there would be compensating benefits; the level of pollution would, at least, not continue to increase. And the productive energies of the community could be directed to service industries, with their relatively low rate of consumption. Some might find, as the 'Blueprint' supposes, that once they no longer felt that they ought to possess this or that as a visible sign that they were rising in the world, they were able to live more enjoyable lives. A changing society might offer them alternative sources of enjoyment. Even if they now 'really want' consumption goods, there are other things they might enjoy more once they were introduced to them. (Our education system attempts so to introduce them, and sometimes succeeds. In a vast number of cases, however, it fails.) But I do not think we ought to pretend that to cut down on the use of resources is not to demand considerable sacrifices from a society accustomed to enjoying the pleasures of ownership and consumption. And the sacrifice would fall very unevenly.

This is a consequence we might be prepared to accept; unequal sacrifices, we might say, are inevitable. It is just bad luck that those who find their main enjoyment in driving cars or who are used to air-conditioning or who are employed in resource-using industries or who like, or need, to travel internationally will be called upon to make more sacrifices than a professor who, like Mishan, works in London. Everybody, certainly, would have to make *some* sacrifices; costs will in some measure rise and taxation with them. But everybody, our argument might continue, will make some gains— and perhaps more gains than they at present realise—in a world in which, let us say, much less electricity and less petrol are consumed. If we are really convinced that unless we take steps *now* to recycle metals and to cut down the consumption of fossil fuels, freedom will not survive, then we can fairly easily persuade ourselves, without invoking any novel moral principles, that we ought to be prepared to make such sacrifices and to demand them from others.

Pretty obviously, our decisions about what sacrifices we *ought* to be prepared to make for posterity will depend on what we think of as constituting a sacrifice and what we are not prepared to risk, as well as on our estimate of the risk we are taking when we make, or refuse to make, a particular sacrifice. But obviously, too, our personal decision on this point by no means solves the conservation problem: all it does is to answer the *moral* question what sacrifices we ought to be prepared to make and to demand from our fellow-citizens. We still have *political* problems to face, the problem of persuading others to accept our conclusion and the state to act accordingly. Only the state—or some body set up by the state— could possibly act as a trustee over resources.

It is sometimes taken to be self-evident that this automatically forms part of the state's responsibility. 'Nobody . . . holds,' writes

Pigou, 'that the State should force its citizens to act as though so much objective wealth now and in the future were of exactly equal importance. In view of the uncertainty of productive developments, to say nothing of the mortality of nations and eventually of the human race itself, this would not, even in extremest theory, be sound policy. But there is wide agreement that the State should protect the interests of the future *in some degree* against the effects of our irrational discounting and of our preference for ourselves over our descendants.'[39] And certainly, the state's own future may well depend on the extent to which it can persuade its citizens to conserve resources. Unlike individual human beings, it looks forward to a life of indefinite length; there is no equivalent, in the history of a state, to 'three score years and ten'.

At the same time, the state is not an impartial entity, making its decisions with a wisdom and sureness to which its citizens cannot possibly aspire. In fact, no state can be as wise as the wisest of its citizens; it is subject to, and must in some measure allow for, the pressures from the most foolish. Its own discounting may easily be 'irrational', as it seeks votes from supporters whose only concern it is to maximise present gains. Quite contrary to Pigou, C. P. Snow suggests, indeed, that 'it is in the nature of politics that the short-term duties come first'.[40]*

That is why some scientists—Macfarlane Burnet, for example—argue that the liberal democratic tradition is the greatest obstacle to decisive action in such areas as the control of economic growth.[41] States which accept that tradition are too subject, they suggest, to the influence of pressure groups. But there is no good ground for believing that an autocratic state would be more far-sighted. Burnet recognises, indeed, that the Soviet Union is in this respect by no means superior to the capitalist societies. Conservationists are themselves pressure groups; in a liberal-democratic society they have an opportunity, even if they are a small minority, to obtain a hearing through press and television, to modify public opinion, to persuade governments to change their ways and to prefer long-term to short-term gains. 'Public opinion,' the first report of the British Royal Commission on Environmental Pollution tells us, 'must be mobilised in such a way that elected representatives regard themselves as trustees for the quality of air, water and the landscape.'[42] This implies, if it is to be anything more than a pious hope,

---

* That they ought, indeed, to come first was explicitly argued in 1896 by the young Winston Churchill: 'The duty of governments is to be first of all practical . . . I would like to make the people who live on this world at the same time as I do better fed and happier generally. If incidentally I benefit posterity—so much the better—but I would not sacrifice my own generation to a principle however high or a truth however great.' This, certainly, is a long way from Kant. The passage from Churchill is quoted by M. J. Lasky as an epigraph to 'The English ideology', *Encounter* (December 1972), p. 25.

first that there is a class of mobilisers, secondly, that they have some prospect of influencing the bulk of the electors and, thirdly, that the elected representatives are responsive to the views of those who elect them. These assumptions are not, in a democracy, absurd. One way and another, we have had a not inconsiderable experience of autocratic governments: our experience does not suggest that they are more sensible, more open to conviction, more sensitive to ecological issues than liberal democratic governments.

No doubt, Burnet is envisaging a society which would have the same shape as a benevolently-despotic scientific research institute, in which the only pressure groups would be scientific. Leaving aside whatever qualms we may have about this type of institutional pattern, it is not the form which any autocratic substitute for the liberal-democratic state is at all likely to take. The primary question for such a state, quite certainly, will be in what ways it can reinforce its power. Nor are clashes of interests, battles for power, any less familiar in autocratic than in liberal democratic states. The difference is that in liberal democratic states they are conducted—at least to some degree—openly in public, not in secret conclave, and that they do not terminate in the imprisonment or execution or excommunication of the losing side. Defeats are not final: questions can be raised again, as the situation alters, without provoking the cry of heresy.

Whatever the character of the state, there are bound to be differences of opinion about the extent to which it should save its resources. Some of the parties to such disagreements will be mainly concerned to protect the immediate interests of the particular groups on which they are dependent for political or financial support. Yet, as we have already suggested in regard to pollution, in so far as they are forced to state a case, as distinct from employing such methods as bribery and corruption, they may draw our attention to considerations we might otherwise have overlooked. It must not be presumed—it would indeed be absurd to presume—that those who advocate, with whatever an eye on their immediate interests, the opening up of new mines always have a worse case than the conservationists who oppose them.

The importance of the state in disputes of this sort is not that it has a method at its disposal, unavailable to its citizens, for determining how it is rational to act. What it may have—in virtue of its nature as a democratic state—are mechanisms of inquiry and debate which should ensure, at least, that such issues are properly considered. And then also it alone can initiate systems of legal control over the use of resources. It can establish institutions, too, which are relatively free from the pressures of day-to-day politics—let us say a National Resources Council which, rather than the legislature, would determine the year-by-year consumption of natural resources.*

Finally, how exactly is the state to act? At the administrative level, pollution and conservation run parallel. The choice, once more, lies between such devices as prohibition, taxation and subsidisation: men can be prohibited from using particular resources, taxed heavily if they use them, subsidised if they use substitutes. Any estimate of the advantages and disadvantages of these methods must, as in the case of pollution controls, take into account their general political consequences as well as their administrative effectiveness.

Now to sum up. Whether there is a problem of conservation is warmly disputed; our conclusion on that point will depend on whether or not we are convinced that certain technological devices will be available for use in the very near future. And the grounds on which most of us have to come to a decision on this point are anything but adequate. We cannot be certain that posterity will need what we save—or on the other side that it will not need what we should not think of saving. There is always the risk, too, that our well-intentioned sacrifices will have the long-term effect of making the situation of posterity worse than it would otherwise be. That is the case for simply ignoring posterity, and doing what we can to repair present evils.

On the other side, this is not our ordinary moral practice. We love, and in virtue of that fact we are prepared to make sacrifices for the future and are not prepared to take risks, arising out of uncertainties, which would otherwise strike us as being rational. No doubt, we often make the wrong decisions; trying to protect what we love we in fact destroy it. Over-protection can be as damaging as neglect. But these uncertainties do not justify negligence. Furthermore, we now stand, if the more pessimistic scientists are right, in a special relationship to the future; unless we act, posterity will be helpless to do so. This imposes duties on us which would not otherwise fall to our lot.

But granted that it ought to do so, is any democratic-capitalist state likely to introduce effective measures to conserve resources? Conservation has not the same popular appeal as pollution; especially when it involves genuine sacrifices. Even those who are in favour of it in principle may still find it hard to accept the view that they must, for example, reduce the level of winter heating to

---

* The suggestion for such a Council is made by H. C. Coombs in 'Matching ecological and economic realities', delivered to the Twelfth Pacific Science Congress, 23 August 1971. As a former Governor of the Reserve Bank of Australia, to say nothing of his other responsibilities, Dr Coombs must be presumed to have had considerable experience of the degree to which government instrumentalities can resist short-term political pressures.

which they have been accustomed. Indeed, if conservation were an isolated issue, one might be inclined to doubt whether the conservationist programme would ever win widespread support. Admittedly it has already had its successes. Afforestation and the control of soil erosion were both of them conservationist programmes which have more than occasionally, if by no means universally, been implemented. But they involved far less, and less widespread, sacrifice than would the adoption of a policy of conserving fossil fuels. Furthermore, they were often accompanied by a degree of subsidisation which more than compensated for temporary losses and which could not be matched in a thorough-going conservationist programme.

The fact is, however, that conservationism is not an isolated issue. By 'doing what is just in the present', we may be doing what is best for posterity to a degree somewhat greater than is ordinarily allowed. If we were to concentrate on improving public facilities as distinct from private wealth, on diminishing noise and air pollution by substantially reducing automobile traffic, we might find that we have in the process decreased the level of industrial activity to a relatively harmless point. In general, people do not seem to find their present mode of life particularly enjoyable; we certainly need to experiment with alternatives which are at the same time less polluting and less wasteful of resources. The recycling of resources both benefits us, as helping to solve the problem of wastes, and would, we hope, also benefit posterity. The extension of public transport will help our cities as well as reducing the use of fossil fuels. Education, which certainly needs improvement, is not a great polluter, or a great user of scarce resources. In the uncertainties in which we find ourselves, it is perhaps on these double-benefit forms of action that we should concentrate our principal efforts. Certainly we shall have set up objectives which are hard enough to realise, but the benefits of which are immediately obvious—or obvious to those who are not enamoured of squalor, decaying schools, over-crowded cities, inadequate hospitals and nursing homes, crime or official violence. If they are hard to realise, it is because the ownership of commodities, private affluence, is in fact generally preferred, when the crunch comes, to the improvement of the public conditions of life.

There is also the question of time. The degree of urgency, on the views of some scientists, is very great; political action is generally speaking slow, and in this case is subjected to an enormous range of special interests. In these circumstances there is a strong temptation to fall back on the ideal of the strong man, who could conserve by the direct exercise of coercion. I have refused to accept this as a 'solution' for the conservation problem, partly because I do not think there is any good reason for believing that any 'strong man' who is likely to emerge after the collapse of democracy would be primarily concerned with conservation and partly because I do not believe this to be the kind of cost we ought to be prepared to meet, for posterity's sake as well as for our own. Much the same is true of the suggestion that what we should work for is the collapse, as rapidly as possible, of our entire civilisation, as the only way of conserving resources. The cost would be enormous; the benefit more than dubious.

My conclusions are limited and uncertain. That is how it should be; as Socrates liked to point out, confidence based on ignorance is not a virtue. Nor is there any point in turning to religion in an attempt to bolster up our confidence. Men do not need religion, or so I have argued against Montefiore, to justify their concern for the future. That concern arises out of their character as loving human beings; religion, indeed, often tells its adherents—whether in the accents of the East or of the West—to set such concern aside, to 'take no thought of the morrow'. If Allah, as the proponents of stewardship now like to emphasise, is represented in the Koran as setting up men on earth as his 'deputy', it by no means follows that a Muslim ruler can be rebuked for heresy when he sells off the oil which Allah has hidden beneath the desert sands. In short, the faithful cannot hope by recourse to Revelation, Christian or Muslim, to solve the problems which now confront them. Nor will mysticism help them. There is no substitute for hard thinking, thinking which cuts clean across the traditional disciplines. But intellectuals, no less than the religious, have their delusions of grandeur. Society, as much as nature, resists men's plans; it is not wax at the hands of the scientist, the planner, the legislator. To forget that fact, as a result of conservationist enthusiasm, is to provoke rather than to forestall disaster.

CHAPTER FIVE   PRESERVATION

By 'preservation' I mean the attempt to maintain in their present condition such areas of the earth's surface as do not yet bear the obvious marks of man's handiwork and to protect from the risk of extinction those species of living beings which man has not yet destroyed. The word is often used rather more widely, as when we speak of 'preserving' buildings or villages, stretches of urbanised landscape like Tuscany, cities like Venice. For my present purposes, however, I shall exclude from consideration the preservation of artifacts; the case for preserving them overlaps, but does not coincide, with the case for preserving what human beings have not created. As we have seen, it is generally agreed that works of art ought not to be destroyed; there is no such agreement that it is wrong to destroy wildernesses or undomesticated species. Should there be? This is the first issue we have to consider. We have seriously to ask ourselves whether it constitutes a genuine problem that at an ever-increasing rate men are converting wildernesses into tamed landscape—into farms, towns, suburbs, tourist resorts— and destroying the plants and animals which once shared the earth with him. Does it really matter that the moa no longer stalks the New Zealand plain? Does it really matter that tourist resorts have been set up in the remotest corners of New Cale- donia? In his 'Song of the Redwood Tree' Walt Whitman asserts that the redwood tree must 'abdicate' his forest-kingship so that man can 'build a grander future'. What, if anything, is wrong with this attitude?

There are two different ways of trying to answer these questions; we can think of wildernesses and of species as having either a purely instrumental or an intrinsic value. On the first view, wildernesses and species ought to be preserved only if, and in so far as, they are useful to man. On the second view, they ought to be preserved even if their continued existence were demonstrably harmful to human interests. As it is sometimes put, they have a 'right to exist'. The first view can easily be incorporated within the traditional Graeco-Christian picture of the world, the second view presents greater difficulties.

'Usefulness' need not be narrowly interpreted: wildernesses and species, it might be argued, are valuable not only as economic resources, actual and potential, but as providing opportunities for the pursuit of science, for recreation and retreat, as sources of moral renewal and aesthetic delight. Let us look at each of these in turn. Take first the economic value of wildernesses and wild species. Biologists have now demonstrated that wet-lands, mangrove swamps, are not infertile appendages to the shore, fit candidates for draining and levelling, but hospitable providers of food and lodging for the young of economically valuable fish. This is only one illustration of the manner in which the preservation of a wilderness can be economically profitable. Somewhat less directly, by studying the behaviour of trees and plants in wild conditions, biologists can hope to discover why the yield gradually falls off under cultivation; the wilderness acts as a norm.

Something similar is true of wild species, whether plant or animal. Cultivated plants and animals have been bred for special purposes; they are liable, in consequence of their breeding, to diseases which could in principle entirely wipe them out. Men need a reservoir of wild species, with their greater genetic diversity, to protect them against this eventuality. Species once destroyed cannot be replaced: to destroy a species is a peculiarly irreversible act, which may well have quite calamitous long-term ecological consequences. To attempt totally to wipe out dangerous species of viruses and bacteria, even, might encourage the emergence of still more dangerous mutants. A species often turns out to be unexpectedly useful, a tropical plant to contain pharmacologically valuable substances. There are good economic and biological arguments, then, essentially conservationist in character, for thinking much more carefully than we ordinarily do—obsessed as we are with the 'conquest', the 'development', the 'perfecting' of nature—about the total effects of transforming a patch of wild country, whether swamp or mountain, or acting in a way which may lead to the extinction of species. No doubt, the human race has survived without apparent harm the disappearance of the moa and the dinosaur, the transformation of Europe into a tamed landscape. But a purely economic argument will suffice to establish at least a prima facie case against the clearing of wildernesses, the destruction of species.

To turn now to the scientific value of wildernesses. I have already drawn attention to the utility of biological investigations in nature reserves. But biological inquiry has a value in itself as a form of human enterprise, quite apart from its utility. We should not think it right to destroy a scientist's laboratory; for the same good reason we should try to preserve areas in which the biologist —or the geologist—can work, even when his investigations have no immediate practical value. There is then, taking together the economic and the scientific value of biological inquiry, a strong case for setting up what in South Africa are known as 'Strict Nature Reserves' which only scientists would be permitted to enter—reserves differing in their rock-structure, climate, flora, fauna, and big enough to permit those large animals to roam whose role in the preservation of eco-systems is so often vital.

Then there is the need for recreation. Recreations are not all, of course, of equal value. Few of us, nowadays, would be impressed by the argument that cocks ought to be preserved since otherwise cockfighting will die out. The case of hunting is more difficult. In the nineteenth century, 'preservation' meant in fact the preservation of game—the cutting off of rivers and moors and woodland from public access so that landed proprietors and their friends could enjoy the sport of hunting. The enthusiasm for killing, purely for sport, is a form of enjoyment the West sometimes carries to the point of mania, whether it be the small bird or the elephant which is the victim. (The explorer Speke, to take only one instance, counted any day a loss on which he did not have unfamiliar game to shoot.) In such Eastern books of moral instruction as the Chinese *Concerning Rewards and Punishments* (Kang Yiu Pieu) hunting is, in contrast, condemned as wholly perverse. There is something more than a little odd, certainly, about the view that wild species ought to be preserved in their wild conditions because some men enjoy killing them. For my part, I should agree with Plutarch that 'sport should be joyful and between playmates who are merry on both sides'.[1] And I am unable to persuade myself that the kangaroo enjoys being hunted. (On purely preservationist grounds, herds may have to be culled; that is a different matter.)

Yet even for so ardent a preservationist as Aldo Leopold hunting obviously meant a great deal: in his eyes, 'public wilderness areas are, first of all, a means of perpetuating, in sport form, the more virile and primitive skills in pioneering travel and subsistence'.[2] For most of his long history, man has been a hunter; we should not lightly assume, whatever our personal distaste for hunting, that he can now set that legacy aside. But at best the recreational value of hunting will justify the preservation of only a relatively few species of animals and those plants that give them sustenance. At worst, as Leopold himself fully recognises, it leads to the destruction of those species which limit the success of hunting, the acclimatisation of species which are destructive of wildernesses, and the opening up of hunting grounds, in a manner which destroys their original character, to make them more accessible to hunters.

Something the same is true of other, morally less dubious, forms of recreation. 'Even the purest of nature lovers,' it has been pointed out, 'has physical weight and boots on his feet.' Assured of his total innocence, he can yet destroy the sparse grass of mountain

H

heights or so firm the trails that trees and shrubs can no longer survive around them.[3] In search of a wilderness, he by his very presence converts it into a man-made landscape. It was for long supposed that in National Parks the interests of the hunter, the tourist, the biologist, could all be reconciled. In *The Earth as Modified by Human Action* Marsh had set out thus attractively his policy for national parks:

> It is desirable that some large and easily accessible region of American soil should remain, as far as possible, in its primitive condition, at once a museum for the instruction of the student, a garden for the recreation of the lover of nature, and an asylum where indigenous tree . . . plant . . . beast, may dwell and perpetuate their kind.[4]

But we have now discovered that neither a museum nor an asylum can be at the same time a 'garden for recreation'.

The seeker after recreation does not for the most part want wildernesses in the strict sense of that word. His conception of wilderness 'subsumes the existence of picnic tables, wells, toilets, washrooms, and the like'.[5] What he is looking for are pleasant surroundings in which to enjoy forms of recreation which are not available to him in cities. The decision to open up the National Parks by building roads into them has been described as 'one of the great statesman-like acts of American history'.[6] But it was a decision to put recreation first, the preservation of wildernesses second —and therefore nowhere. For a wilderness opened up to all comers is rapidly converted into a tamed and as often as not a degraded landscape.

Garrett Hardin has suggested that wildernesses should be specially reserved for the use of those who are fit enough to enjoy a sojourn in untouched wildernesses. 'A wilderness that can be entered only by a few of the most physically fit,' he has argued, 'will act as an incentive to myriads more to improve their physical condition.'[7] As it stands, however, this is a paradoxical policy: if the myriads were in fact to improve their condition they would be able to enter the wildernesses and the whole object of the exercise would be subverted. That is why Hardin is obliged to suggest that this restrictive policy should be supplemented by a lottery.

The general principle that so far as possible forms of enjoyment should be preserved, provided only that they are not morally objectionable, is a sound one. But the real problem is that there are in this case conflicting interests: what Hardin is in fact proposing is that people who do not fit into a very limited category—physically fit lottery-winners—should not be permitted to enter wildernesses.

And it is not *obviously* apparent why they should be kept out: there is not the same obvious value in preserving wildernesses for a very limited class of recreationists as there is in preserving them for scientific or for economic reasons. Hardin's view that the state will thus encourage physical fitness is more than dubious; the existence of such wildernesses as the Antarctic, with admittance restricted to a selected few of the physically fit, has certainly done less for physical fitness than the opening up of civilised walks through the Swiss mountains. Taken in all the arguments, on purely recreational grounds, for preserving wildernesses as distinct from public parks is by no means a strong one—at least in those areas of the world where there is a pressing need for recreational facilities.

What about the need for solitude? Do men need places where they can be totally alone? John Stuart Mill's argument for preserving wildernesses rested in large part on this assumption that 'it is not good for man to be kept perforce . . . in the presence of his species'. 'A world from which solitude is extirpated,' he continues, 'is a very poor ideal.'[8] The enjoyment of solitude is, however, something of a paradox. A peculiarly human enjoyment, it yet depends, for its very existence, on the absence of human beings. It is the enjoyment, one might even say, of human absence. The virtues of solitude are by no means universally recognised. The inhabitants of a crowded camping ground and the solitary walker over the mountain look at one another with incomprehension, distaste, and even fear. That is why the searcher after solitude is often resented, and the preservation of wildernesses—as distinct from 'opening them up to tourists'—condemned as the attempt of a misanthropic few to limit the enjoyment of the gregarious many. 'A conservationist [preservationist],' Galbraith has ironically remarked, 'is a man who concerns himself with the beauties of nature in roughly inverse proportion to the number of people who can enjoy them.'[9] Or as the point has been more savagely put: he wishes 'to keep nature locked up as a private preserve, to be enjoyed only by those with a great deal of money or free time'.[10]

The arguments of preservationists on this point are sometimes more than a little disingenuous. Not long ago the government of Tasmania decided to flood a lake in a remote part of that island as an element in a hydro-electric scheme. As part of their case, in many respects a strong one, against that decision, the preservationists argued that 'man has a need to know himself', and that this self-knowledge he can achieve through adventures with nature in the country around Lake Pedder. 'Its appeal,' the argument admits 'is specific and selective. It is not for everyman's taste but for those who would make the effort to know themselves. *In this sense it is everyman's opportunity.*'[11] There could scarcely be a better example of the illicit use, in such arguments, of the general concept of 'Man'. Instead of saying frankly, and being content with this, that a very small percentage of the population obtains not only enjoyment but a special sort of spiritual refreshment out of Lake Pedder, the pretence is that somehow Lake Pedder is, in the last resort, for everyman, in spite of the fact that 'its appeal' is—and this puts the matter mildly—'specific and selective'. Such sophistry cannot in the end do preservationism any good, even if it is easy to understand the political motives which lie behind it.

The mere fact that, like the enjoyment of poetry, the enjoyment of solitude or private meditation is a minority enjoyment does nothing to suggest, of course, that there is no virtue in trying to ensure its continuance. Human beings differ greatly in their sources of enjoyment, minorities have their rights; the preservation of these rights is what democracy is about. But the special consideration that the enjoyment of solitary wildernesses may only be possible at the cost of greatly restricting the recreation of others raises problems not only about its political feasibility but even about its moral desirability—unless a case can be made out for its being a form of enjoyment of such value and importance that other forms of enjoyment ought to be sacrificed to it, that just as none but biologists should be allowed into strict Nature Reserves so other wildernesses should be reserved as places of recreation for the meditative solitary-loving few. (Lotteries for mystics?)

This is a claim often made: it is strongly suggested in the Lake Pedder manifesto. Arguing in support of the view that Niagara Falls ought to be preserved from industrial development, Charles Eliot Norton described the falls as 'one of those works of Nature which is fitted to elevate and refine the character and to quicken the true sense of the relations of man with that Nature of which he is a part'.[12] What force is there in this claim? Some force, I think. Nature, on this scale, helps to preserve men from *hubris*, to make them more conscious that things go in their own way, indifferent to man and man's concerns: it encourages a kind of humility which has in it nothing of servility.

It helps to free men, too, from the bondage of Philistinism. 'We city-dwellers,' as Brecht's Herr Keuner puts it, 'get dazed from never seeing anything but use-objects; . . . trees, at any rate for me, have something independent about them outside myself.'[13] Even more is this true of waterfalls and mountain crags, of the life of animals and birds in a wilderness, of the desert and the swamp. Here, if anywhere, we escape from the 'What's in it for me?' attitude so characteristic of our society.

Yet doubts remain. 'Any protracted, genuine association with nature,' so a writer in the *Yale Review* once argued, 'means a reversion to a state of brutal savagery.'[14] This objection cannot be lightly dismissed. Thoreau tells us—and Garrett Hardin quotes the passage with approval—that what men learn in the wilderness is 'that Nature is so rife with life that myriads can afford to be sacrificed and suffered to prey on one another; that tender organisations can be so serenely squashed out of existence like pulp'.[15] Is this the sort of moral lesson which we need to learn from nature? It is a lesson, certainly, that more than a few inhabitants of the wilderness carry away from it and apply to human life.

Herder had qualms of a rather different sort. 'It appears,' he writes, 'among what people the imagination is most highly strained: among those namely, who love solitude, and inhabit the wild regions of nature, deserts, rocks, the stormy shores of the sea, the feet of volcanoes, or other moving and astonishing scenes.'[16] And this highly strained imagination, he goes on to argue, has been the source of fanatical religions, of superstitious terrors.

It would appear, then, that the moral advantages of wilderness-experiences are by no means indisputable; quite the contary. I have suggested, and many of us will know from our own experience, that there is refreshment as well as enjoyment to be found in wandering through wild country. (Not only recreation but re-creation; it renews one's sense of proportion.) But it is not at all clear that to sustain this experience the wild country needs to be a wilderness in the full sense of the word: were it, for example, to be purged of flies I, for one, would not find the refreshment diminished. It is much easier to state a case for the preservation of humanised wildernesses as places of recreation than for the preservation of wildernesses proper.

Finally, let us look briefly at the aesthetic value of wildernesses. For the Graeco-Roman tradition enjoyable 'scenery' meant the olive grove, the cultivated field, the orchard, the carefully disposed villa or temple. Mountains and wildernesses were crude, unformed, inhuman, unperfected, not worth the attention of a cultivated man. The gods might make their home on mountain tops or, like Jahweh, hand down from the heights their decrees. But mountains were no place for ordinary men and women; they were dangerous, frightening, with wild animals still a serious threat. Man allowed himself the luxury of admiring them only when he was no longer intimidated by their ferocities. And only after the success of his farming ensured that he had enough to eat did he enjoy the spectacle of wasteland.

The typical classical attitude is still expressed in Charles Cotton's seventeenth-century poem, *The Wonders of the Peak* (1681). Here is his description of the Derbyshire Peak country:

> A country so deformed, the traveller
> Would swear those parts Nature's pudenda were.

Shameful, unfit for the eyes of man, so that coach-blinds should be kept drawn as it was traversed—that is a characteristic classical description of the wildernesses which in the nineteenth-century men were so extravagantly to admire.[17]

There have always been occasional exceptions, of course: that atypical Basil the Great raised Gregory of Nazianzus' eyebrows by praising the wild country in which his monastery was set. Gregory's response is typical. 'All that has escaped the rocks,' he wrote in remonstration, 'is full of gullies, and whatever is not a gully is a thicket of thorns; and whatever is above the thorns is precipice.'[18] It would not do to praise that unreformed wilderness which symbolised man's sin, a reminder of his woeful state. Eden knew no thickets, or gullies, or precipices; on Milton's account, indeed, they are what now make Eden inaccessible to man. When the hermit went into the wilderness it was not in order to enjoy it but to remove himself from all sources of worldly enjoyment: to be wholly alone with a God who was not of this world. He went there, too, to fight with the demons who inhabited the wilderness. 'By no means satisfied,' as John Cassian expressed their attitude in the fifth century, 'with that victory whereby they had trodden under foot the hidden snares of the devil (while still living among men), they were eager to fight with the devils in open conflict, and a straightforward battle, and so feared not to penetrate the vast recesses of the desert.' If in the wilderness they hoped to find perfection, this was only by first conquering, in God's name, its diabolic inhabitants. Through the desert to paradise—that was the motto for anchorite and for mystic. But only because the wilderness was the last foe which had to be conquered.[19]

It might be supposed that wild nature, as coming directly from the hands of God, ought, rather than civilisation, to be enjoyed. Christian theologians, indeed, had difficulties on this point. On the one side they felt it incumbent upon them, like the psalmist, to praise the handiwork of God; on the other side, they condemned the world as a corruption of God's original intent. Only the heavens were still pure, untouched by Adam's sin, which, so Luther argued, cursed not only the soil he was to work but the whole earth, innocent though it was. 'We must speak of the whole of Nature since its corruption,' he wrote, 'as an entirely altered face of things—a face which Nature has assumed, first, by means of sin, and secondly by the awful effects of the universal deluge.'[20] The world, so it was commonly argued, must once have been a perfect sphere; the irregularities of its surface—mountains, wildernesses—

are not God's creation but the effects of sin. Indeed, not only the earth but the 'rude and ragged moon' are, in Thomas Burnet's words, 'the image or picture of a great ruin, and have the true aspect of a world lying in its rubbish'.[21] To enjoy the wilderness, on this interpretation of the situation, is to indulge in a wholly perverted taste.

Until relatively recently, indeed, to call a place a wilderness was unmistakably to load it with abuse. Gerard Manley Hopkins' 'Long live the weeds and the wilderness yet'[22] would have seemed an absolute paradox to the first New England settlers who saw their new country as 'a hideous and desolate wilderness, full of wild beasts and wild men'.[23] Here is Tertullian, roused for once to enthusiasm: 'All places are now accessible, all are well known, all open to commerce; most pleasant farms have obliterated all traces of what were once dreary and dangerous wastes; cultivated fields have subdued forests; flocks and herds have expelled wild beasts; sandy deserts are sown; rocks are planted; marshes are drained; and where once were hardly solitary cottages, there are now large cities. No longer are [savage] islands dreaded, nor their rocky shores feared; everywhere are houses, and inhabitants, and settled government, and civilized life.'[24] Eighteenth- and nineteenth-century romanticism, with its nature-mysticism, was responsible for a transvaluation of values. God and nature were identified: and the enjoyment of nature was thereby elevated to its highest point, at the hands of such American transcendentalists as Dwight, into a religion. And on the whole that attitude of mind has persisted into the twentieth century. It is thought desirable for a house to have 'a view', rather than an enclosed garden prospect—most desirably a view of a landscape in which the hand of man is not blatantly obvious.* That it will persist into the twenty-first century, however, can certainly not be taken for granted.

It is a very considerable presumption, indeed, that our descendants will continue to admire wildernesses aesthetically, just as it is a considerable assumption that they will continue to enjoy solitude.

---

* It is worth remembering, however, that when that notorious nature-fancier William Wordsworth wrote his famous line: 'Earth has not anything to show more fair', what he was describing was not a Lake District mountain, dale or stream but the view of London from Westminster Bridge. And if looking at that view nowadays we can only sadly reflect with an older poet:

Quid non mortalia pectora cogis
Auri sacra fames!

Wordsworth's lines still come naturally into our minds as we look at the Tuscan landscape or the view of Florence from the Piazzale Michelangelo. In the United States the beauties of the wilderness have been highly esteemed, but the townscape and the rural countryside largely ignored. What the West now needs, it is by no means absurd to argue, is a revival of the classical feeling for town and rural landscape much more than the Romantic passion for wilderness. Compare David Lowenthal on 'The American scene', in *Geographical Review*, 58: 1 (January 1968), pp. 61–88.

Neither attitude of mind is at all universal; it is not in the least like assuming that they will continue to enjoy, most of them, eating or drinking or making love. This consideration, echoing a now familiar difficulty, may serve to underline what will already be obvious; the argument for preservation, as I have so far presented it, is a special case of the argument for conservation. We ought, I have so far maintained, to preserve wildernesses because they may turn out to be useful and because they may afford recreational pleasures, scientific opportunities and aesthetic delight, to our successors. The first of these considerations, our argument has suggested, is a powerful one, the others less powerful in so far as they rest on the presumption that our descendants will still delight in what now delights only some of us and did not delight our predecessors. On the other side, they do not call upon us entirely to sacrifice present enjoyments for the future; we, anyhow, can find pleasure in biological inquiry, in wilderness-recreations—even if most of us prefer the tamed to the true wilderness—and in the sight and smell and sound of wild animals, plants and birds.

The real difficulty arises, of course, out of the fact that there can be clashes of interests. These raise very sharply the question of 'rights'. We have already drawn attention to the clash of interest between the wilderness-lover and the ordinary vacationist. This conflict can be construed economically as a conflict over the best use of scarce resources. More obviously, there can be sharp conflicts between the tourist *industry* and the preservationist as also—an old battle this—between the preservationist and the miner. None of the arguments I have so far advanced is strong enough to permit the conclusion that in every such case, where a species or a wilderness is seriously threatened, the victory ought to go, on moral grounds, to the preservationist. In a particular case the interests of the tourist industry, mining, farming may be involved to such a degree that their spokesmen will certainly have the political, and may even have the moral, advantage. That is one reason why the arguments I have so far advanced would not be considered adequate by the more uncompromising preservationists.

Sometimes, indeed, such arguments are dismissed out of hand as, in a broad sense of that word, essentially economic. 'I am not greatly moved,' writes Fraser Darling, 'when I hear supporters of the national park and nature reserve movement argue that living things have educational value, that the beauties of nature give pleasure to humanity, that they are of scientific value . . . and that we cannot afford to lose them.' And this is because, he tells us, 'the essential attitude [in such arguments] is not far in advance of that of the timber merchant', i.e. it still determines what ought, or ought not, to be allowed to survive in what are substantially economic terms, by reference to human needs.[25]

It is at this point, indeed, that the cry grows loudest for a new morality, a new religion, which would transform man's attitude to nature, which would lead him to believe that it is *intrinsically* wrong to destroy a species, cut down a tree, clear a wilderness. As I have already suggested, these demands strike one, at a certain level, as merely ridiculous. One is reminded, indeed, of the exchange between Glendower and Hotspur in *Henry IV Pt. I* (III.i.53):

Glendower: I can call spirits from the vasty deep.

Hotspur: Why so can I, or so can any man,
                But will they come when you do call for them?

A morality, a religion, is not, as I have already argued, the sort of thing one can simply conjure up. It can only grow out of existing attitudes of mind, as an extension or development of them, just because, unlike a speculative hypothesis, it is pointless unless it actually governs man's conduct. But it may be true that in fact men's attitudes are already changing, that the 'new morality' would be a natural outcome of a change that is already in process, which can now be hastened by exhortation or argument. That possibility we should at least explore.

We shall look first at one change that has already taken place. Men now commonly recognise that they ought not unnecessarily to inflict pain on animals. This means that they recognise at least one point at which their relationships with nature are governed by moral principles. This has not always been so. By looking at what happened in this case we may hope to learn something of the grounds that already exist in the Western tradition for a more radical reassessment of man's relationship with nature.

In the Old Testament, men and animals have a common principle of life (*Nebesh*); as we have already seen, God is represented as caring for animals just as he does for men. At least one of the Talmudic teachers argued that 'the avoidance of suffering of dumb animals is a Biblical law'.[26] But in Christian thinking, as we have also seen, Paul's rhetorical question 'doth God take care for oxen?' was for long decisive.[27] The Stoic teaching, with which Paul concurs, that the Universe exists only for the sake of its rational members carried with it the conclusion that between men and animals—to say nothing of plants—there was no sort of moral or legal tie. Augustine lent his immense authority to this doctrine. 'Christ himself,' he writes, 'shows that to refrain from the killing of animals and the destroying of plants is the height of superstition, for, *judging that there are no common rights between us and the beasts and trees*, he sent the devils into a herd of swine and with a curse withered the tree on which he found no fruit.' 'Surely,' Augustine continues, 'the swine had not sinned, nor had the tree.'[28] Jesus, that is, was not punishing the swine when he sent devils into them, or *blaming* the barren tree. If he had sent the devils into a bystander or cursed a woman for being barren, we could only have concluded that they had sinned; otherwise Jesus's action would be morally indefensible. But he was trying to show us, according to Augustine, that we need not govern our behaviour towards animals by the moral rules which govern our behaviour towards men. That is why he deliberately transferred the devils to swine instead of destroying them, as he could easily have done.

So for centuries it came to be standard Christian teaching that men could do what they liked with animals, that their behaviour towards them need not be governed by any moral considerations whatsoever. There were, of course, occasional exceptions. Francis of Assisi is the most famous example of a Christian nature-lover, calling upon birds as his sisters in an Umbria still not entirely Christianised out of nature worship. (Modern ecologists not uncommonly proclaim him their patron saint.) But his case is anything but a clear one. Biographies by English animal-lovers, often Protestant, naturally stress his fellowship with nature; Roman Catholic biographers, in contrast, are intent on establishing his orthodoxy. They write with scorn of those who see in Francis a sentimental nature-lover, only by an accident of time ineligible for the Presidency of the Royal Society for the Prevention of Cruelty to Animals. Nor is there any hope of settling such controversies by returning to primary sources; those sources were for the most part deliberately designed to create a particular image of Francis, the image varying from chronicler to chronicler. On the face of it, however, his attitude to nature is reminiscent of the psalmist's or of that old English hymn which tells us, in a somewhat unfortunate metaphor, that 'even the worm bends his knee to God'.

Only once, however, does the question of callousness arise in the biographies of Francis written by his friends or near-contemporaries and then it does so rather disconcertingly. One of the brethren, taken ill, told Francis' disciple Jonathan that he had a longing for pigs' trotters. 'In great fervour of spirit', Jonathan cut the trotters off a living pig. Francis rebuked him, but with no reference whatsoever to his callousness. He urged him, only, to apologise to the owner of the pig for having damaged his property.

In any case, Francis had little or no influence. The Franciscan philosophers accepted the traditional Aristotelian-Stoic view of the relationship between man and animals. Pius IX refused to sanction the setting up of a Society for the Prevention of Cruelty to Animals in Rome, on the ground that it would suggest that men had duties to the animal kingdom. In so far as cruelty to animals was wrong, this was only because, so it was argued by Aquinas, by Kant, and by a multitude of lesser thinkers, it might induce a callousness towards *human* suffering. There was nothing wrong with cruelty to animals *in itself*.

These conclusions were supposed to follow automatically from the fact that animals could not reason and therefore had no rights. But there was an alternative argument, more fundamental, on which some of the Stoics particularly insisted. Human life, they contended, would become quite impossible if men thought of themselves as governed in their relationships with animals by moral considerations. It would then be quite wrong to kill animals for food, to harness them for work in the fields, to use them as beasts of burden. And that would mean the collapse of civilisation —'we shall be living the life of beasts once we give up the use of beasts'.[29] In other words, only by supposing themselves to be quite free from all moral considerations in their relationship with nature can human beings, according to the Stoics, justify their civilising of it.

In the long run, these considerations did not prevail. It is now generally agreed by moral philosophers, and has been for a century or more, that it is wrong to treat animals in such a way as to inflict on them unnecessary pain—even if the range of this principle is still disputed, how it applies, for example, to vivisection. Interestingly enough, too, moral philosophers now take it to be *obvious* that cruelty to animals is morally wrong. Such otherwise so different moral philosophers as Schopenhauer, Mill, Laird, Rashdall, Leonard Nelson all maintain that their predecessors must have been blinded by what Rashdall, himself a Dean, called 'prejudices of theological origin'.[30]

This, then, is one case in which men have experienced a change of heart; they have come, in the very long run, to accept certain moral limitations on their dealings with nature. As we have already suggested, however, this limitation has not been carried in the West very far—not, except for a relatively few, to the conclusion that it is wrong to kill animals but only to the belief that it is wrong so to act as to cause animals quite *unnecessary* suffering, suffering, that is, which is not essential for the satisfaction of fundamental human needs.

And what is the theoretical foundation of this new moral attitude? This is important, if we are to decide what the likelihood is that it might be extended to the preservation of species. In part, perhaps, a growing recognition—certainly extensible—that men and animals are more alike than Augustinian Christians were prepared to concede. The Augustinian view reached its apogee in the seventeenth century when, as we have already pointed out, Descartes and Malebranche were capable of arguing that animals not only could not reason but could not even feel.* Such sceptical thinkers as Montaigne and Hume, in contrast, insisted at once on the resemblance between men and animals and the need to treat them humanely. In his *Apology for Raimon Sebond* Montaigne argued that it is absurdly presumptuous for men to set themselves up above the animals; in his 'Essay on Cruelty' he drew the conclusion that 'we have a general duty to be humane, not only to such animals as possess life, *but even to trees and plants*'.[31] Hume, intent on arguing that human and non-human intelligence worked in the same general way, did not go so far as Montaigne in his moral conclusions. But at least he laid it down, in relation to animals, that 'we should be bound by the laws of humanity to give gentle usage to those creatures'.[32] Both Hume and Montaigne, it is necessary to observe, accept the Stoic principle that we are not called upon, and cannot be called upon, to act *justly* towards animals. But what Hume calls 'the cautious, jealous virtue of justice' is not, both he and Montaigne rightly argue, in this case the relevant one. And it is not incompatible with the preservation of civilisation, far from it, to extend humane feelings, as distinct from justice, to the animal kingdom.

This was the approach that won the day. 'The French have already discovered,' Bentham wrote, 'that the blackness of the skin is no reason why a human being should be abandoned without redress to the caprice of a tormentor. It may come one day to be recognised, that the number of the legs . . . or the termination of the *os sacrum* are reasons equally insufficient for abandoning a sensitive being to the same fate.'[33] Observe the characteristic transition from slave to animal; humane feelings towards animals arose as a development of humane feelings towards man in general—whether slaves, or criminals, or the insane. Bentham's Utilitarianism looks not to the rationality of the agent or the patient, in the Stoic manner, but to the effect of the agent's actions on all sentient

---

* Only within a theodicy does the question: 'Why do animals suffer?' so much as arise. But in the West that question rather than 'How can we reduce animal suffering?' was, for centuries, the problem of problems. It engendered fantastically elaborate solutions. So the Chevalier Ramsay suggests that the less guilty of the fallen angels were shut up in animal bodies and made men's slaves. They tempted man to fall, and as a consequence were still further degraded, losing the remnants of reason and the power of speech with which their own fall had still left them. Their sufferings as animals are at once a punishment and a means through which they might be purified and thus regain their former state. See D. P. Walker: *The Ancient Theology* (London, 1972), pp. 254–5. Ramsay's fantasy was constructed well after Descartes wrote; it suggests the extremes into which any alternative hypothesis led the justifiers of God's ways. Malebranche is quite explicit that for purely theological reasons, it is necessary to deny that animals can suffer, since all suffering is the result of Adam's sin and the animals do not descend from Adam. This is another point at which Christianity has encouraged an exploitative attitude to nature.

beings. The pains of animals, because they do not include the pains of anticipation, might be less than the pains felt by man, but that is no reason for not taking them into account. The question is neither, so Bentham argues, 'can they reason?' nor 'can they talk'? but 'can they suffer?' Basically, that is, cruelty to animals was condemned on humanitarian grounds. Just for that reason, only those animals whose suffering is most human-like were brought under the protection of the law: the 'lower' living things, such as insects, were not protected. Ants could still be killed by poisoning or by pouring hot water on their nests without fear of legal consequences or moral reprobation.

In general, then, the argument was that the deliberate infliction of pain on animals whose sufferings were obvious was a morally bad form of conduct. And it was not, in general, thought necessary to carry the argument beyond that point. But there were a few more intransigent exceptions; some of the advocates of anti-cruelty legislation argued not only that animals had feelings but that they had rights, thus setting themselves wholly at odds with the Stoic-Augustinian tradition. In 1792 the Platonist Thomas Taylor published a work entitled *A Vindication of the Rights of Brutes*. (It consists in large part of quotations from a neo-Platonic work, Porphyry's *Concerning Abstinence*.) His purpose was ironic. His title page bears the epigraph *Quid Rides?*; his work as a whole is intended as a *reductio ad absurdum* of Thomas Paine's *The Rights of Man* and Mary Wollstonecraft's just published *A Vindication of the Rights of Woman*, the latter work echoed in his title. Here, he is saying, are the conclusions to which you are driven if once you allow, with Paine, that even the least rational of men—or what is worse, with Wollstonecraft, that even women—have rights. Before you know where you are you will be treating animals as having rights.

And this prophecy was to be fulfilled in, for example, H. S. Salt's *Animals' Rights*.[34] In defence of the view that animals have rights Salt argues that they are protected by law. If that argument suffices, however, then we should have to conclude that not only animals but trees and plants and even rocks and landscapes can have rights; for they, too, can be protected by law—and not only, as Salt concedes, as *property*. Salt's view misconceives the nature of the change that has taken place in Western moral thought. What has happened over the last century and a half in the West is not that animals have been given, by law and public opinion, more power, more freedom, or anything else which might be accounted as a right. We are still perfectly free to kill them, if it suits us to do so. Rather, men have lost rights; they no longer have the same power over animals, that can no longer treat them as they choose. This is characteristic of a moral change; it follows from the fact that, in

Hart's words, 'moral rules impose obligations and withdraw certain areas of conduct from the free option of the individual to do as he likes'.[35] But that men have lost rights over them does nothing to convert animals into bearers of rights, any more than we give rights to a river by withdrawing somebody's right to pollute it.*

Disputing Salt's conclusions, D. G. Ritchie has argued, in my view correctly, that animals cannot have rights since they 'are not members of human society'.[36] We sometimes now meet with the suggestion, however, that animals do in fact form, with men, a single community, and so can properly be said to have rights. Indeed, Aldo Leopold has gone further than this: 'When we see land as a community to which we belong,' he writes, 'we may begin to use it with love and respect.'[37] (As a final absurdity, it is worth noting, Thomas Taylor's *Vindication of the Rights of Brutes* had looked forward to a time when 'even the most contemptible clod of earth' would be thought of as having rights. He was better as a prophet than as an ironist.) Ecologically, no doubt, men form a community with plants, animals, soil, in the sense that a particular life-cycle will involve all four of them. But if it is essential to a community that the members of it have common interests and recognise mutual obligations then men, plants, animals and soil do *not* form a community. Bacteria and men do not recognise mutual obligations nor do they have common interests. In the only sense in which belonging to a community generates ethical obligation, they do not belong to the same community. To suggest, then, as Fraser Darling does, that animals, plants, landscapes have a 'right to exist', is to create confusion. The idea of 'rights 'is simply not applicable to what is non-human.†

---

* In his *A System of Ethics*, Leonard Nelson argues that to establish that we have duties to animals, it is only necessary to establish—what is, he says, obviously true—that they have *interests*, which he takes immediately to entail that they have rights. It is not, however, clear to me in what sense animals have interests. If all that is meant is that unless certain things are done for them they will die, that they have *needs*, this is also true of plants. The crucial difference between plants and animals is that animals are sentient, that they suffer if those needs are not satisfied. And to justify the view that we ought not to treat them in certain ways nothing more is needed. Having interests does not entail having rights, unless 'interests' is interpreted in a sense in which animals do *not* have interests—as a person may, for example, have an interest in an estate.

† This is one of the many points at which I am troubled by the apparent dogmatism of my observations. There are some contexts in which the concept of rights is straightforward, as when someone says of a professor that he has a right to take a sabbatical and means no more than that he has a contract which lays this down. In other contexts it is relatively straightforward as in such remarks as: 'School-teachers have a right to take a sabbatical' when this means that school-teachers *ought* to have the right which a professor *actually* has, a judgment which might be supported by arguing that a school-teacher has the same need as a professor for long periods during which he can think, read, travel, gain fresh intellectual contacts. But in other cases, as when someone says that 'every man has the right to live', it becomes very difficult to know what he is claiming unless something like this: it is morally wrong for one man to take away the life or the livelihood of another. And that last utterance,

We have already suggested, however, that the condemnation of cruelty to animals does not depend on the presumption that men and animals—let alone men, animals, plants, soil—form a single moral community. It has been a movement of sensibility, a movement based on the growing recognition that not only a positive delight in suffering—so much moralists have always admitted—but even callousness, an insensibility to suffering, is a moral defect in a human being. It is one thing to say that it is wrong to treat animals cruelly, quite another to say that animals have rights.

The principle that we ought not unnecessarily to cause animals to suffer does not carry us far, no doubt, as part of a case for preservation. It does not permit of extension, although Montaigne tried so to extend it, to animals, plants, soils, which either do not suffer or do not suffer in ways which impress themselves on the consciousness of human beings. Nor does it exclude, oddly enough, the *killing* of animals. Indeed, in many ways its position in our moral code is somewhat paradoxical.[38] Its importance for us, however, is that, first, it represents a case in which Western men have come to believe that their dealings with nature can properly be subjected to moral approval or condemnation; secondly, that it is a change which grew out of certain 'seeds' in Western thought —in particular, the humanitarian 'seed'. The question now is whether we can construct a case for preservation by finding other such 'seeds', without having to fall back on such certainly non-Western principles as that 'nature is sacred'.

There is, it might be said, such a 'seed' in the Old Testament. In Genesis (7: 15) Jahweh is represented as telling Noah to take with him into the Ark 'two and two of all flesh, wherein is the breath of life'—not only the 'clean', it will be observed, but even the 'unclean'. And this shows God's concern, so it has been argued, for the preservation of animal species.* What potency has this seed? Certainly its prevalence explains why scientists were for so long reluctant to believe that fossils could be relics of species and varieties now extinct. The world, so it was thought, had been created as a perfect and complete system—a great chain of being—

or so I have suggested, is not in fact equivalent to 'every man has a right to live'. The supposition that 'it is morally wrong to treat x in the manner y' entails 'x has a right not to be treated in the manner y' initiates the sort of confusion which culminates in utterances like 'insects have a right to live'. That is what I have substantially argued. But I am only too conscious of the fact that many would wish to challenge my assumption that the proper starting-point for a theory of rights is the use of the word in legal contexts.

* Aquinas specifically argues that in the case of every species except man God cares nothing for the benefit of the individual but does watch over the species as a whole. So, without any disrespect to God's intention, man can do as he will with individual animals and plants—they form no part of God's concern. God will ensure that man's treatment of individuals does not destroy the species as a whole. See Aquinas: *Summa Contra Gentiles*, chs. CXII–III.

in which everything had a place. The destruction of a species would be the disruption of a system. The botanist John Ray, writing at the beginning of the eighteenth century, points out that if the fossil evidence were taken at its face value, 'it would follow that many species of shell-fish are lost out of the world'. But this, he says, 'philosophers hitherto have been unwilling to admit, esteeming the destruction of any one species as dismembering of the Universe, and rendering it imperfect; whereas they think the Divine Providence is especially concerned to secure and preserve the works of the creation'—a doctrine lent support, he says, by the fact that Providence 'was so careful to lodge all land-animals in the ark at the time of the general deluge'.[39] (As late as 1836, in Büchner's *Woyzeck*, the travelling artisan announces his intention of making 'a hole in nature' by destroying all fleas.)

One is sometimes reminded of this 'great chain of being' by the 'ecological niches' now such favourites with preservationists. The traditional doctrine no doubt reflected in part, as well as metaphysico-theological prepossessions, a recognition of the interdependence of species, crudely expressed in Swift's familiar lines:

> So, naturalists observe, a flea
> Hath smaller fleas that on him prey;
> And these have smaller fleas to bite 'em
> And so proceed *ad infinitum*.

Everything—plants as well as animals—lives in a particular kind of region, a region which contains both its prey and its predators, opportunities and limitations. To destroy a predator is to increase the opportunities for other predators, or to make less confined the numbers of its prey. It leaves open, that is, an 'ecological niche'.

It is no longer possible to suppose, however, that 'Nature' or 'Providence' so arranges matters that a region will never be transformed, except as a result of human interference, in such a way as to reduce the opportunities of a species to a point at which it will disappear. In the present mood of disillusionment with humanity, man the hunter, rather than the ice ages, is now often blamed for the extinction of the large species which once roamed the earth.[40] Perhaps some, at least, of these allegations will in fact turn out to be correct. Certainly, too, over the last few centuries, human beings have managed to destroy species at an unprecedented rate and are continuing to do so. The fact still remains that gradual or catastrophic changes in the biosphere of completely non-human origin have produced, and may well in the future produce, destruction as notable as, if less rapid than, any men can bring about. Man is not the only agency which destroys species. There is no ground for asserting that 'Providence' or 'Nature' always ensures the preservation of species—even if this were a satisfactory route to the conclusion that men ought to follow its example.

In search of a more viable 'seed', one might turn to Aquinas' principle of diversity. 'Although an angel, considered absolutely,' writes Aquinas, 'is better than a stone, nevertheless two natures are better than one only; and therefore a Universe containing angels and other things is better than one containing angels only.'[41] If this be so, then to destroy a species is always to diminish the value of the Universe by reducing the number of natures it contains. But this is a very hard doctrine to sustain. It means that even if I could wipe out mosquitoes merely by raising my right hand, and even if by so acting I ran no ecological risks, I should be wrong to do so, merely because I should be decreasing the number of species in the Universe. Is it so obvious that a Universe consisting of human beings and a cobra is better than a Universe consisting of men alone? Should St. Patrick be condemned if, indeed, he drove the snakes out of Ireland? And if to drive them out of Ireland is worthy of praise, should it not be equally praiseworthy to drive them out of the world? (Leaving aside, as I am doing for the sake of argument, any possible ecological side effects.)

Yet there is something to be said for Aquinas' praise of diversity, and so far a case for preservation. We are faced at this point, no doubt, with a fundamental conflict of attitudes. There are those, like Thomas Burnet, for whom every sort of diversity is intolerable, for whom the earth as a uniform sphere would be an infinitely more desirable place than our own dear warty world, a monoculture is more attractive than a diversified landscape, a grid-iron city of glass cubes more 'perfect' than one which exhibits a diversity of styles and shapes. Metaphysicians—Fichte and Teilhard de Chardin will serve as examples—have not uncommonly sung the praises of uniformity. 'The multitude of beings,' Teilhard once wrote, 'is a terrible affliction.' He was confident that the world could not remain for ever 'a huge and disparate thing, just about as coherent . . . as the surface of a rough sea'.[42] There are others for whom diversity is everything, and any kind of uniformity demonstrates a failure of imagination, the deadening of creativity. Yet, metaphysical enthusiasts like Teilhard de Chardin apart, few, I think, would wish to argue that it is always better either to reduce, or to increase, diversity. For the reduction of diversity finally issues in a pure Being which is indistinguishable from nothingness, the multiplication of diversity in a world so diversified as to be wholly unmanageable.

The acclimatisation societies which flourished in the nineteenth century were enthusiasts for diversity. They sought, in every

I

country in which they operated, to acclimatise as wide a variety as possible of exotic animals and plants. To introduce a new species was, in their eyes, a major triumph. It would now generally be agreed that this policy was a mistaken and to some degree a disastrous one; acclimatised plants and animals have provoked many an ecological calamity, as the landscape both of Australia and of New Zealand still bears witness. It is not a good thing to attempt to introduce the maximum diversity into every individual ecological system: to do so may seriously diminish the prosperity of other members of the system. Man is himself perhaps the most striking example of an acclimatised invader, and an established ecosystem can be greatly weakened by his presence. But goats or rabbits or deer or prickly pear can be scarcely less destructive. For all their intrinsic attractiveness, they can impoverish, aesthetically as well as economically, the system into which they are introduced. A countryside is not necessarily improved in appearance by the introduction of exotic trees. Wordsworth long ago condemned the introduction of the larch into the English Lake district, for all that it adds so much to the beauty of the Dolomites, and the exotic pine forests add a drab note to the Australian landscape.

This kind of diversity, then, the preservationist is almost certain to oppose. Indeed, he is likely to be if anything too rigorously puritanical in his attitude—for there can be no real doubt that, for example, such introduced trees as the elm and oak have worked wonders for the landscape of Great Britain, as has the eucalypt in California or the casuarina in Egypt. If preservation is taken to imply that no landscape should ever be modified from its original form by the introduction of exotic plants and animals then it has not, in my judgment, a leg to stand on. The introduction of such species, indeed, may be the only thing that can save a countryside from destruction or restore its fertility.

There are, then, two principles which seem to be untenable: the first, that it is always better to increase the diversity of an ecosystem; the second, that it is never better to do so. All that can be properly said is that in modifying the degree of diversity there are always inherent dangers, biological dangers, and there is also the real risk of destroying the 'character' of a landscape, the complex set of relationships which constitute its attractiveness.

This is certainly so when diversity is reduced by the destruction of species, the rooting out of hedgerows, the bulldozing of bush-land, for the sake of monoculture, whether of barley or of pine. No doubt, as we have suggested, there are those to whom the tidy rows of pine are, economics apart, infinitely superior to the un-tidiness of a snow-gum forest, an unbroken expanse of uniform crops to the uneven irregularities characteristic of mixed farming.

But Mill, scarcely an opponent of economic development, wrote with distaste of such a monocultured world, and many of us would share his feelings. 'Nor is there much satisfaction in contemplating the world with nothing left to the spontaneous activity of nature; with every rood of land brought into cultivation which is capable of producing food for human beings; every flowery waste or natural pasture ploughed up, all quadrupeds or birds which are not domesticated for man's use exterminated as his rivals for food, every hedgerow or superfluous tree rooted out, and scarcely a place left where a wild shrub or flower could grow without being eradicated in the name of improved agriculture.'[43] There are now good biological arguments, too, against extensive monocultures, arguments which draw attention to their vulnerability to disease and climatic calamity,[44] to their long-run effects on the soil, to the degree to which they have to be constantly maintained by infusions of insecticides and fertilisers which at once increase their cost and represent a danger to the wider region in which they are established, as the insecticides and fertilisers drain into rivers and thence into lakes and sea.*

What we can properly conclude, I think, is that the onus is on anyone who seeks to modify an ecosystem's degree of diversity and that he has to produce a far more elaborate and complex argument than has ordinarily been supposed. This principle does not apply only to biological systems, but also, for example, to social and political 'anomalies'. The maxim that 'the more uniform, the better' is usually defended by very short-sighted arguments. But this is not to say that it is always wrong to reduce, or always right to increase, the diversity of social institutions or biological systems. So there is no general argument from a principle of diversity to preservationist conclusions.

There is one other very broad principle which, were it acceptable, would certainly permit the conclusion that a species ought never to be destroyed. For it asserts that men ought, in general, to 'reverence life'. And this principle may be interpreted as forbidding the destruction not only of species but of any individual animal. (Indeed, in Theravada Buddhism the monk, and even the layman so far as he is able, 'does no harm to seeds or plants'.)[45] In its extremer forms, this principle has never been firmly established in the West. The poet Cowper, no doubt, would not include amongst his friends 'the man who needlessly sets foot upon a

---

* It is customary to rebuke the European farmer for inefficiency, on the ground that his crop each year is relatively light in proportion to the size of his farm, or that it demands a heavy expenditure of labour. But in many cases a farmer of this sort has been farming the same ground for some hundreds of years. His 'inefficiency' appears in a different light if we think of the production of his land over the centuries. Annual production is not the best test of efficiency—whether what is in question is a farm or a professor.

worm'.[46] Yet even Cowper was no vegetarian: and he would not condemn a man for setting foot on a worm were the worm destructive. This, in general, is as far as the West has been prepared to go. It is to the East, and in particular to the Jains, that we should have to turn for more far-reaching moral precepts. 'Tolerate living beings, do not kill them, though they eat your flesh and blood.' The Jains, indeed, took as their ideal a man who would direct his life by the objective of never killing any living thing, even by accident. 'This is the quintessence of wisdom: not to kill anything.'[47]

Nowhere in the traditional religions of the West is the killing of living things made so central a point. But in our own century the ideal of 'reverence for life' has been emphasised by Albert Schweitzer to a degree previously unprecedented; he makes it central to his ethics. Like the Jains, too, he refuses to draw the characteristic Western distinction between 'higher' (valuable) and 'lower' (valueless) forms of life. 'Who among us knows,' he asks, 'what significance any other kind of life has in itself, and as a part of the Universe?' There is no 'category of worthless life'—life which human beings are free to destroy. To a man who is truly ethical, on Schweitzer's view, every life is sacred. No doubt such a 'truly ethical' man has sometimes to sacrifice one living being to save another—to kill germs, for example, in order to save a human life. 'But all through this series of decisions,' according to Schweitzer, 'he is conscious of acting on subjective grounds and arbitrarily, and knows that he bears the responsibility for the life which is sacrificed.'[48] He will not, without a sense of guilt, pluck a leaf from a tree or pull a flower or trample on an insect: he will think of himself as having a 'responsibility without limit towards all that lives'.[49]

It is illuminating to observe Karl Barth's reaction to Schweitzer. Writing in the Calvinist tradition, Barth firmly asserts that ethical behaviour has to be defined through man's relationship to God, not through his relationship to living things. Each man, Barth tells us, is addressed by God as a member of a fellowship of men and through a particular book, God's word, the Bible. We can speculate, he allows, about the possibility that there are divine commands which apply to living beings in general, and not only to man. But we do not know of any such command, nor is it deducible from what we do know about animal and vegetable life. In the typical Christian manner, Barth insists, then, on the uniqueness of man, as the only living being to whom it is known that God addressed himself. To that extent his critique of Schweitzer would reinforce the opinion of those who see in the Christian tradition a principal obstacle to the emergence in the West of a less destructive attitude to nature.

Yet Barth is not wholly unsympathetic to Schweitzer's practical conclusions. Christianity, he admits, has failed to ask itself 'how are we to treat the strange life of beasts and plants which is all around us'. Schweitzer, as Barth reads him, is protesting against our 'astonishing indifference and thoughtlessness in this matter'.[50] He agrees with Schweitzer thus far: man has a secondary, although not a primary, responsibility to animal and vegetative life. Like the Jews, Barth insists that animals and plants do not belong to man but to God. At the same time, man, for Barth, takes precedence over them and is entitled to make use of them, by divine decree. When he harvests, he does not destroy but makes sensible use of superfluity. He is entitled to domesticate animals, but he ought to treat them in a considerate, friendly way.

But what about the *killing* of animals? Here Barth is less traditional; man must not kill, he argues, without divine authorisation. 'He is already on his way to homicide if he sins in the killing of animals, if he murders an animal.' Notice that Barth does not hesitate to speak of 'murder' in connection with man's dealings with animals. Man 'murders' when he kills except, as God has permitted him to do, in order to live. But vegetarianism Barth nevertheless condemns as 'wanton anticipation of . . . existence in the new aeon for which we hope'; inevitably, he says, it is plagued by inconsistencies, sentimentality, fanaticism.[51] To kill for food is proper, in this interim life in which men now live.

What conclusions are we to draw from this controversy? It is in the first place evident, I should say, that the Jainist principle never to act in a way which could possibly result in the death of a living thing—so that the Jain priest walks on a path only at a time when the risk is minimal that he will inadvertently kill small insects—is far too strong. This is the more obvious now that we are aware of the minute living organisms which everywhere surround us. In breathing, in drinking, in eating, in excreting, we kill. We kill by remaining alive.

Nor should we hesitate about giving precedence to human beings. Schweitzer did so in fact, as Barth pointed out, when he became a doctor. Such precedence does not depend on peculiarly Christian teachings about divine revelation or a sacrificial God. If we prefer to save the life of a fellow-man rather than of the organism responsible for yellow-fever—an organism, no doubt, of considerable interest and beauty—it is because he has potentialities the yellow-fever organism lacks, potentialities for evil, admittedly, but also for good. That is why we may well be hesitant about preserving the life of those who lack such potentialities—although we may also be hesitant about allocating to any particular person the decision whether they have, or lack, them. The yellow-fever organism cannot love, or exhibit courage, or create ideas or works of art. It does not suffer as human beings suffer, or live in fear of death. Humanistic and compassionate considerations lead us to the same conclusion.

Yet, like the principle of diversity, the idea of 'reverence for life' can serve perhaps as a guiding principle, with 'seeds' in the reverence for *human* life characteristic of the Western tradition— in its theory, if by no means always in its practice. And, if I read the signs aright, a shift in sensibility is taking place at this point not unlike the shift in sensibility which has already taken place in relation to cruelty to animals. It does not imply that the living thing has to be treated as 'sacred', as an object of worship or a source of occult powers. The new 'reverence' for life is rather the sort of reverence one feels for a great building, a great work of art.

So far we can link it with another, more explicitly Western, tradition that it is wrong unnecessarily to destroy—a principle embodied in the concept of 'vandalism'. Admittedly, the principle that it is wrong unnecessarily to destroy has not been, to my knowledge, much emphasised by Western moralists. But one certainly finds it in the Jewish tradition, which bases itself on a passage in Deuteronomy (XX: 19–20) forbidding, even in time of war, the destruction of trees which might bear fruit, but interprets it widely. 'Thou shalt not destroy' was indeed converted by Rabbinical commentators into a general moral principle.[52] The eighteenth-century philosopher, Baumgarten, writing in that same tradition, condemns in a forthright manner what he calls 'the spirit of destruction' or 'the habitual delight in the death of things' and urges that a man possessed by it be shunned.[53] One could at least go this far: the moral onus is on anyone who destroys. This is particularly so when, as in the case of species, the destruction is irreversible. We commonly speak, indeed, of 'wanton' destruction where no defence of the destruction can be offered.

How far have we got, then, in our defence of preservationism on moral grounds? We looked first of all at those defences of pre-servationism which are primarily conservationist in spirit—which emphasise the usefulness of wildernesses and species as sources of genetic diversity, of scientific understanding, of moral renewal, of recreational enjoyment, of aesthetic pleasure. The first of these arguments, we suggested, is a strong one; the others, like so many conservationist arguments, depend on the presumption that our successors will continue to delight in certain rather special forms of activity which have been by no means universally characteristic of human society.

But they are none of them 'knock-down' arguments; they all

allow that economic considerations, in a broad sense of that phrase, might under certain circumstances outweigh the case for preservation. Scientific discoveries—for example, a method of constructing 'seed-banks' so that species could always be reconstituted—or changes in tastes, could wholly undermine them. So we looked for ways of arguing that the destruction of species and wildernesses was *intrinsically* wrong. We saw that in at least one case Western men have generally come to accept a limitation on their dealings with nature; they now commonly disapprove of those ways of treating animals which involve the inflicting on them of 'unnecessary' pain. And this is because, I suggested, they have come to feel that in this case men and animals—or certain animals—so resemble one another that it is inconsistent to condemn the infliction of unnecessary pain on human beings but not to condemn its infliction on animals.

With this case in mind, we then looked for possible sources, in the Western tradition, of a more general change in moral attitudes in a preservationist direction. It would not do, we said, to argue that 'God' or 'Nature' obviously wishes to preserve species or wildernesses; many species have been destroyed, many wildernesses transformed by non-human processes. As for the view that we ought always to preserve the maximum diversity, we suggested that Western society has been divided on this point, but that we can perhaps go this far: the existing degree of diversity in an ecosystem ought not to be modified without careful consideration. The ideal of reverence for life we accepted in so far as there is a tradition in the West of hostility to vandalism, and it is very natural to extend it to the destruction of nature as well as to works of art or forms of property. The man who cuts his name on a redwood is being a vandal, just as much as the man who scratches his initials on the portico of Wells Cathedral.

If we now ask about the political feasibility of action to preserve wildernesses and species we are asking about the strength of the arguments and the feelings I have been describing, in conflict with political pressures from a multitude of interests—miners, land developers, the tourist trade—to transform wildernesses in a way that is destructive of species or to wipe them out more directly as an obstacle to development. In conflict, too, with the pressure exerted by those other Western traditions that it is man's task either to conquer nature, or to transform it—to turn the world into the sort of garden in which there are no thorns, no thistles, no destructive insects or animals. Nobody needs to be told that the outcome of any such conflict is uncertain.[54] No doubt, if nature were conceived of as sacred and any modification of it as sacrilegious, the outcome would be less uncertain (unless, in the manner I shall later describe, the mystical attitude to nature found expression as the belief that nature can and will repair itself). If, to carry the same point further, it came to be regarded as morally wicked ever, under any circumstances, to destroy so much as an individual animal or plant, let alone a species, then the preservationist could certainly feel more confident of victory.

But this would be at a very great cost to civilisation. For my part, I agree, in the long run, with the Stoics: if men were ever to decide that they ought to treat plants, animals, landscapes precisely as if they were *persons*, if they were to think of them as forming with man a moral community in a strict sense, that would make it impossible to civilise the world—or, one might add, to act at all or even to continue living.[55] The Jain priest can walk abroad only because there are other, less spiritual, men to work in the fields by day and sweep the paths for him by night. I simply do not believe that in every dispute between preservationist and miner, the preservationist ought always to win—however much one may dislike the havoc miners have created on the landscape. Of course, as in the case of pollution, one again has to admit that miners and commercial interests are often in a position to exercise a degree of influence, whether over politicians or over media, with which the preservationist cannot compete, that preservationists will lose battles they ought to win, which they would win were the issues fairly represented and fairly fought out. But in this case, too, it would be quite wrong to conclude that the preservationist will never be successful, at least in countries affluent enough to forego immediate material gains in the interest of amenity.

I have tried to show that the preservationist can appeal not only to practical consequences but to established moral principles and to changing sensibilities, which he can hope to modify in a preservationist direction. This appeal will often be, has often been, successful. The scientist and the technologist can help, not only by drawing attention to the unintended consequences of destruction, but also by finding new means of mining, new means of restoring land, new methods of coping with those predators which are particularly damaging to human interests. A wider change in attitudes can help, too—less emphasis on consumer goods, a greater appreciation of the value of contemplation, of quiet enjoyment, of simply *looking* at the world around us, as itself an object of absorbing interest, not as an instrument or a resource. The Romantic Rebels of our own time are insisting on this point. Whether what is valuable in their rebellion can be absorbed into our society, without their drug-mysticism, without their violence, without their rejection of the responsibilities inherent in love, remains to be seen.

CHAPTER SIX MULTIPLICATION

'People are pollution'. Too vicious a judgment this, reflecting the anti-human bias of so many ecologists. (That bias is even more strongly suggested in P. R. Ehrlich's comparison in *The Population Bomb* of human beings to cancer cells, as if they had suddenly begun to reproduce themselves in exceptional numbers, as distinct from having learnt partially to control their mortality.)[1] No doubt, like every other animal, human beings excrete in quantities roughly proportional to their numbers and often under circumstances in which their excretions are either offensive to the senses, or dangerous to health, or destructive of their natural environment. No doubt, too, they produce, even in their most primitive civilisations, more miscellaneous *débris* than, let us say, a mound-building turkey or a termite, to mention only two possible competitors. But the relationship between population and ecological despoliation is by no means simple and direct.[2] The distribution of the population, the size of the country it inhabits, the degree and kind of its industrialisation, the flexibility of the ecological systems in which it lives and works, the nature of its social traditions and attitudes, all of these play a notable part in determining its degree of ecological destructiveness. So the inhabitants of a lightly populated country like Australia can yet be exceptionally destructive, partly because most of its population lives in a few big industrial cities, with their attendant problems of waste disposal, partly because many of its ecological systems are precariously balanced, as the great deserts of the centre bear witness, partly because the earlier European migrants cared nothing for its landscape, so different from their homeland, and, in the manner natural to migrants, sought to maximise their living standards in the minimum of time. The invasion of Australia by nomadic hunting aboriginals, the native species could endure, although it has left its traces on the countryside; modern industry and agriculture, extensive pasturage, were a very different matter. A heavily populated, traditional, mainly rural community, as in India, living in a more flexible ecological system, may create far less devastation.

Just because the origins of ecological destructiveness are so varied, a reduction in the rate of population growth would not necessarily reduce the extent of pollution, the rate of depletion of natural resources, the rate at which species and wildernesses are disappearing. Should it give rise indeed—as in some circumstances it would—to increasing affluence, it might have exactly the opposite effect. An affluent community no longer likes to spread dung on its fields; it displays its new-won affluence in 'conspicuous consumption', to take over Veblen's phrase. It carries these new habits of consumption beyond the limited area to which poverty had confined it, proclaiming its affluence on coast and countryside. It has the capital to build new factories, to open up new mines, to 'develop' wildernesses.

Nor, on the other side, should we permit ourselves to be so hypnotised by population growth as to forget that the reduction of population is not the only means of improving our ecological condition. Human beings are always in search of the 'one thing needful', which will serve as a solution to all their problems. There is a real danger that the reduction of population will be cast in this role. The precise importance of population growth as a source of ecological destruction is highly debatable. Barry Commoner has argued that the switch to synthetics rather than population growth as such is largely responsible for the sharp post-war increase in pollution; Ehrlich remains convinced that population growth is the chief villain.[3] We can safely go only this far: within a given system of production and consumption, with established techniques and social habits, an increase in population will intensify man's ecological problems. It will be harder for him to find ways of disposing of his wastes, to cut down the rate at which he is depleting natural resources, to preserve areas of wilderness and the species which inhabit them. This is so even although a decline in the rate of population growth will not *necessarily* improve the situation in any of these respects; it may be outweighed by the effects of increasing affluence or new technological innovations. (Consider the consequences if someone were to invent a cheap, safe helicopter.)

Furthermore, even apart from its ecological consequences a rapid rate of population growth constitutes, so it is now often argued, a social problem in its own right, as bringing in its train overcrowded cities, roads, schools, increasing crime, social tension, impoverished human relationships. Just how far this is true is bitterly disputed. Take first the case of the developing countries. Their problems, it is sometimes said, arise not from overpopulation but from quite other causes. The demographic problem, according to a delegate from the Soviet Union to the United Nations Population Commission of 1963, is 'not a real one'. 'It existed only,' he contended, 'because in some countries the level of production was too low and was not rising at the same rate as the population.'[4] On the face of it, this is rather like saying that the problem of coronary occlusions is not a real one, on the ground that there would be no such problem if arteries did not become clogged. But what the delegate, of course, meant to imply is that it was a relatively easy matter, given the appropriate social changes, to raise the level of production and absurd, therefore, to concentrate attention on attempts to control population.

In reply to this line of reasoning, it is often suggested that the technological backwardness, the shortage of capital, the high level of unemployment, all of which so greatly affect the level of production in many of the developing countries, are themselves the consequences of a too rapid rate of population growth. The Prime Minister of Ghana, launching in 1970 his country's family planning programme, justified it thus: 'The present rate of growth increases our population by 5000 people every week . . . In simple terms it means that as a nation, we are increasing in number faster than we can build schools to educate our youth, faster than we can construct hospitals to cater for the health needs of the people, and faster than we can develop our economy to provide jobs for the more than 140,000 new workers who enter our labour force each year.'[5] Nor would his interpretation of the situation entirely lack expert support. The French demographer Sauvy is anything but an alarmist on the subject of population growth. Yet even he has written that 'overpopulation, underdevelopment and lack of education are, if not synonymous, at least simultaneous, and the first two derive from the third'.[6]

But this is scarcely a satisfactory statement of the use. There are, it will be observed, logical uncertainties in Sauvy's claim: the difference between synonymity, simultaneity, causal consequence ought not to be thus lightly skated over. And these logical uncertainties reflect empirical uncertainties. It is very hard to disentangle the effects of population growth as such from the effects of other social forces, so as to determine how, if at all, overpopulation, lack of capital, technical backwardness are causally related. Many economists, certainly, would now deny that a high rate of population growth necessarily brings with it economic problems. 'The economic effects of a high rate of population growth,' the economist Kuznets writes of the developing countries, 'would not constitute a major obstacle to an increase in per capita production.'[7] The main problems of the developing countries, as he sees them, arise out of their traditions, their habits, their social structures, rather than the rapid multiplication of their population. To that extent he would agree with the Soviet dismissal of 'demographic problems'.

So once again, just as in respect to the relationship between population and pollution, we encounter a head-on collision between experts, on which we cannot hope to arbitrate. In this case, too, a relatively modest conclusion is the most we can safely venture. A decline in the rate of population growth would not *necessarily* ease the problems of the developing countries. But a high rate of growth accentuates these problems, makes them more difficult to solve, even if *in principle* it does not rule out their solution.

Our experience in the developed countries bears out this modest conclusion. Many of us have lived through a period of rapid population growth. It has certainly not brought with it a decline in living standards, as these are conventionally measured. But we have witnessed over-crowded schools, urban disintegration, degenerating levels of public courtesy, an increasing rate of natural despoliation, increasing crime and mutual suspiciousness. It would be quite wrong to conclude that any of these was the consequence, solely, of the growth in population and equally absurd to deny that population growth has made them worse. The increasing crime rate, to take a case, is in part, although not entirely, a consequence of the fact that our population now contains an abnormal percentage of the adolescents and young adults who are traditionally most given to crime. And even if there are in principle other ways of alleviating the problems we have listed, a reduction in the rate of population growth may be at once the most efficacious and the most feasible of the methods available to us. Zero population growth, whether in developing or in developed countries, is not a magic cleanser, guaranteeing us cleaner, brighter, more sparkling schools, streets or adolescents. But at worst it will afford our societies a period of reflection, instead of our living in an atmosphere in which politicians and administrators are forced into making a series of *ad hoc* decisions in the manner of men swept away by a flood. And what is true of the developed countries, with their tradition of rapid adjustment, is even more true of the conservative-minded developing countries.

What of the effects of population growth on posterity as distinct from our own generation? Even those who deny that population growth *at present* creates any serious social problems might well have qualms about the future. As in the case of natural resources we find ourselves confronted, however, by a set of arguments, some of them already familiar, some novel in form, which purport to show that we need not bother our heads about posterity. Once more, for example, we are accused of being men of little faith, we are told that Providence will provide, sending with each mouth a pair of hands. This is not a new attitude. That somewhat extraordinary Lord Chief Justice, Sir Matthew Hale, whose doctrine of stewardship we have already met, had been convinced that Providence will always so act as to ensure that 'neither the excess of generations doth oppress and overcharge the world, nor the defect thereof . . . doth put a period to the species of things'.[8] (Did not God promise as much, in the covenant of the rainbow?) Nearly two centuries later, with Malthus as his target, Archibald Alison began by reminding his readers that 'to increase and multiply was the first command of God to an infant world'. 'It is in vain,' he went on to admonish them, 'that human wisdom contrasts this precept with the limited extent of the globe, and deduces imaginary dangers from its literal fulfilments.' Providence will provide; our fate does not lie in the hand of beings 'who may be influenced by worldly passions and who may err'.[9] But a generation acutely conscious, as Hale and Alison were not, that should man disappear from the face of the earth he would not be the first species to do so, a generation which is not prepared to stand by and watch Providence acting through its favoured instruments of famine, war, disease, is not readily convinced by such arguments. It does not wish to see repeated the third-century world described by Tertullian when 'pestilence, war and earthquake have come to be regarded as a blessing to the nations, pruning the luxuriant growth of the human race'.[10] The acceleration of population growth has been man's doing, a consequence of his technological proficiency, and the undoing of its consequences must also be his work.*

Nor ought we too readily accept the view that if not Providence, then technological progress will provide: The economist Colin Clark, to take an example, sets out to show that 'the full support of one person requires the continuous cultivation of an area no larger than twenty-seven square metres'—and this without taking any account of the remoter technological possibilities.[11] But it is characteristic of Clark that he pays no attention to many of the issues which perturb those who fear the outcome of the present rate of growth.† Admittedly, the question for how long men could keep alive on the planet, what is the *maximum* population the planet can support, is one the critics of population growth have often raised. Ehrlich, for one, has argued that 'some two billion

---

* I have deliberately used the phrase 'acceleration of population growth' rather than the rhetorically more effective 'population explosion'. For what we are witnessing is the acceleration of a process which has been continuous, if at an increasing tempo, since about 1650. The phrase 'population explosion', with its suggestion of sudden novelty, obscures the fundamental causes of a phenomenon which is in any case by no means easy to understand. Compare W. D. Borrie: *The Growth and Control of World Population* (London, 1970), pp. 7–10.

† Clark, of course, is a Roman Catholic, as is the poet James Macauley, whose attack on the 'Reverend Malthus' for 'killing conscience with arithmetic' Clark cites with approval. In the Western world, indeed, an extraordinarily high percentage of those who still favour population growth are Roman Catholics. This fact does not, of course, entitle us to ignore their arguments. But if we find their arguments puzzling in their insensitivity, we must recall that the Roman Catholic Church has never placed much store on the reduction, as distinct from the relief, of human suffering. Their 'conscience', so much is clear, is very different from mine.

people aren't being properly fed in 1968' and that the most optimistic view is that something like even this level of malnutrition can be sustained for as much as another two decades.[12] Clark is fully justified in regarding such estimates with suspicion: a man living in the tropics, working only sporadically, can be 'properly fed' at calorie-levels much lower than are needed to support an industrial worker in Chicago. But other opponents of population growth dismiss the whole issue of starvation as a red-herring, distracting attention from the fact that even if the world could support a much greater population than Ehrlich is prepared to admit, the maximum population for the world is by no means its optimum population.[13] For many of us the question how many people the earth could support if they were all prepared to live in the manner of battery-hens is not of the slightest interest.

Nor are we any happier with the suggestion that the world of the future could cope with its population problems by planetary or inter-stellar migration or satellite colonies. Colin Clark is prepared cheerfully to contemplate 'the problems which may face our descendants seeking to travel about the universe in large spaceships, or making their homes in air-locked domes on the surface of other planets, or on artificial satellites'.[14] Our growing knowledge of the moon, the planets and the quality of life on satellites is scarcely encouraging to such hypotheses. I, for one, should certainly not care to put my trust in a celestial bus-service, carrying excess inhabitants to distant planets. (Arithmetical exercise: calculate the number of buses and the expenditure of fuel necessary to carry even to the moon's inhospitable surface the children who will be born *each minute* by 2070 if the present rate of population growth continues.)[15] And certainly if we see in man's relationship to nature something essential to his well-being, the thought of living in an air-locked dome on the desolate surface of the moon can only provoke nausea. Once again, the real question is not whether these things *can* be done, but whether we ought so to act as to make it necessary for them to be done.

An argument of a rather different kind, demographical rather than technological, suggests that we should not directly attempt to lower the rate of population growth—the danger of which it does not deny—but should rather try to bring about conditions under which it will decline of its own accord. This argument makes use of the 'theory' of a 'demographic transition'. Roughly speaking it runs thus: in the first stages of human history, births and deaths are kept in near balance by disease and famine; in the second stage, births outpace deaths as a result of such death-controlling factors as better agriculture, better transportation, better sanitary conditions, better medicine; at the third stage, the emergence of urban-industrial life offers powerful incentives to couples to limit their fertility and a new balance is found, now by deliberate control over births. From this piece of schematised history, it is deduced that the rate of population growth will decline if and only if there is urban-industrial development.[16] And hence, as by Maddox in his *The Doomsday Syndrome*,[17] that to solve the problems of the developing countries it is only necessary to speed up their rate of economic development. (As if we knew how to do this!)

The concept of a demographic transition has recently come under considerable attack.[18] As a general account of the circumstances in which populations wax and wane it certainly will not do; it does not square with the facts. The decline of fertility in France and Ireland was not a product of industrialisation; fertility changes in the United States have not varied directly with changes in income-levels; in the developing world there is no clear correlation between fertility and the level of urbanisation or industrialisation.[19] In other words, we simply do not know enough to be able deliberately to produce a low rate of fertility by varying other social factors, even if it lay within our powers to do so.[20] The most that can be said is that once a society is *thoroughly* industrialised some degree of fertility decline commonly sets in—although isolated pockets of high fertility, like the Hutterites in North America, remind us that religious beliefs can continue to affect procreative behaviour even in an industrialised society.[21]

Furthermore, we have no clear evidence that the 'transition' can, or will, take place in the developing countries at a rate fast enough to reduce their population growth within the next few decades. Circumstances in the West were very different: there the major drop in the death rate occurred only *after* the industrialisation which in the developing countries a lowered death-rate has preceded.[22] In short, then, to leave the reduction of population rates to Providence and its four horsemen, to technological innovations, to the automatic effects of increasing industrial activity, would be to take too great a risk—assuming only, what is scarcely a stupendous assumption, that the population of the world cannot continue to double *ad infinitum*. The task of reducing the rate of population growth is one, therefore, we must deliberately take on our shoulders.

Let us look at the problems this will involve. In the first place, to what rate should we attempt to reduce it? It would be nice to be able to give a straightforward answer to this question, to be able to reply: the optimum population for the world—or even for some particular country—is so many millions and that can be achieved by such and such a rate of growth. There are not lacking those who believe that they can offer such neat answers. The literature on population growth, indeed, is littered with estimates of optimal populations. But to justify, or decide between, these estimates is quite another matter. For all the confidence with which it is wielded as a controversial cudgel by the opponents of population growth, the concept of an optimum population is an extremely obscure one, anything but easy to apply in practice.[23] If anyone doubts this he need only recall debates about the optimal size of a club, a University, a school, a town. Yet these are relatively simple issues. It will be worth examining the concept in some detail, if only to make it clear to ourselves how little use we can make of it.

Optimum population was originally an economist's concept, employed, although not so named, by Mill and made familiar to English demographers by Carr-Saunders.[24] Its great virtue, one might say, consists in its mere existence. For its existence as a concept immediately entails that a distinction can be made between optimum and maximum, that in the field of population biggest does not necessarily mean best. And this, although sufficiently familiar to Plato and Aristotle, is not something that can be taken for granted; the opposite assumption, indeed, runs through the literature.

So the seventeenth-century economist and political theorist Davenant laid it down that: 'People are the real strength and riches of a country . . . 'Tis better that a people should want [lack] country than that a country should want people. No country can be truly accounted great and powerful by the extent of its territory or fertility of its climate, but by the multitude of its inhabitants.'[25] This was in a work with the significant title *An Essay upon Ways and Means of Supplying the War*. Indeed, the advocates of a large population have not uncommonly seen in such a population the source of a nation's 'greatness', defined in military terms. This brings out one difficulty in the concept of an optimum population. It is always optimal *in respect to some particular end*; it maximises some specific property. The optimal economic population—the population which gives the highest per capita real income—will certainly not coincide with the population which gives a country its maximum power or the leaders of that country *their* maximum power. For the maintenance of power requires resources to be set aside for that purpose—an army, armaments—which will raise the numbers of the population necessary to produce any particular distributable income. That is why expansionist powers are commonly pro-natalist.[26]

When Plato and Aristotle attempted to settle on an optimal population for the Greek city state, they had in mind criteria quite different from these. They were thinking in terms of the maximum and minimum size at which the city-state type of political organisation could survive and work effectively. (In his *Laws* Plato set the maximum very precisely, if only with the aid of Pythagorean numerology, at 5040 landholders. I do not know what some modern optimalists substitute for numerology: certainly not any form of rational arithmetic.) More recently, the question has been raised what population will ensure men the greatest degree of liberty.[27] This will certainly not coincide with the population which gives maximum power to the central authorities. And just how it relates to the population which permits the highest real income per head is anything but clear. How it could possibly be calculated, in the light of our ignorance about the conditions of liberty, is even more obscure.

Most of us are not so single-minded that we would be content with maximising a particular welfare-function at whatever cost. So it is natural to try to work with something more complex. In his introduction to *The Optimum Population for Britain* L. R. Taylor tells us that an optimum population should seek to maximise:

1. the vigour and potential of individuals;
2. the currently acceptable pattern of social organisation;
3. the realisation of cultural goals which were listed as moral, political and aesthetic standards;
4. real output per head.

It should minimise:

1. pollution;
2. nutritional and
3. social stress.[28]

But the difficulties inherent in any attempt simultaneously to maximise a number of goods are sufficiently familiar: there is no pre-established harmony between them. The policy which maximises 'aesthetic standards' may be completely incompatible with the policy that maximises 'real output per head'; to maximise real output per head is certainly inconsistent with minimising pollution. It may well be incompatible with minimising 'social stress'. How, too, are we to tell when aesthetic standards have been maximised? Or human potentialities? What are our indices? The idea that an optimum population could be mathematically deduced by the use of these criteria is simply ludicrous.

No doubt, one might 'trade-off' these objectives, sacrificing so many units of pollution-control for so many units of output per head, thus arriving at a population which, although not in either respect optimal, had at once an *acceptable* level of pollution and an *acceptable* level of output. In buying a car, it is useless to look for one which simultaneously optimises all the virtues of a car, including cheapness. We seek for one which is acceptable in a number of different respects, without being totally unacceptable in any one respect. But the mere fact that there are so many different cars on the market suggests that for different purchasers the 'trade-off' level is very different. And this is even more obviously true in the case of 'optimal' populations. For Johnson, the man who is tired of London is tired of life, for Cowper he is tired of spiritual death. They would be unlikely to agree about the optimal size for a city. The idea that there is a population optimal by anyone's standards will not endure a moment's reflection.

Ehrlich, it is true, proposes something a little more definite—a negative criterion, at least. A country is over-populated, on Ehrlich's criterion, if it is not self-sufficient.[20] To anybody brought up in an atmosphere of international trade this suggestion will seem ridiculous. Its ridiculousness, Ehrlich would reply, depends on the assumption that there will always be a surplus in other food-producing countries to enable countries like England to continue to survive. And that assumption, he would maintain, is unjustifiable. But whatever the shortages which develop, no nation, certainly, will ever be in a position in which it has nothing to exchange at any price whatsoever. Any attempt to implement the idea that a country should regard itself as having passed its optimal population if it is not self-supporting in every respect—if, for example, it cannot produce all the titanium it needs—would wreak total social havoc. More generally, given those obscurities in the concept of resources which we have already sketched in discussing the need for conservation, it is impossible to use 'resources' as a mode of defining optima.[30]

A further weakness in the concept of an optimal population is that it can lead to an underestimation of the costs of population control: 'optimum' is implicitly interpreted as meaning 'best in every respect', and any attempt to draw attention to the undesired consequences of controlling population growth is dismissed as special pleading. But it certainly has such costs, difficult as it is to estimate their importance. The least disputable, perhaps, arises out of the fact that many people take a great delight in having and bringing up children. It would be a severe cost to them to give up the large family they would wish for and would enjoy. Of course, it might turn out that were the social pressure to have children no longer effective, so many people would wish to be childless that there would still be room for a certain number of large families. But childlessness, too, has its costs as well as its benefits.

Another, more disputable, cost is that population control produces undesirable changes in age distribution. In a stabilised population the percentage of aged people would increase up to a figure of about a quarter, an increase which could be made even more marked by advances in medical science if these advances were to affect, as they quite well might, only the life expectancies of the aged. And an ageing population may stand in the way of desirable social changes, out of sheer inertia.

Ehrlich, one must note, dismisses this consideration as 'perhaps the most preposterous argument against population control'.[31] He is right enough, in so far as he points out that population growth must *at some time* be reduced and that 'whenever growth is halted an increase in the average age of the population is a mathematical certainty'. (Not quite 'mathematical': the number of the aged might decline, as the result, let us say, of changing public attitudes to suicide or long-term consequences of ecological destruction. But of a high order of probability.) It must be granted, too, that those countries in which the age distribution most nearly approximates to the distribution in a stabilised society—England and Sweden—scarcely live up to Sauvy's notorious description of 'a population of old people ruminating over old ideas in old houses'.[32] Sauvy blames the French age distribution—in 1960 over twenty-seven per cent of the population was more than sixty years of age and the mean age was forty-six—for the cultural and political malaise which, in spite of its prosperity, France is at present experiencing. But it is by no means clear that the roots of that malaise do not lie elsewhere. The conservatism of the aged, furthermore, can be diminished by the sort of social changes—involving re-education—sketched by Ehrlich and by Sauvy. In a more stable society the relative slowness of their reactions might be less significant. Our experience of a youth-oriented society has not been enticing. The most reactionary movement of modern times, the Nazi movement, was essentially a youth movement. Yet all the same, as an ageing man, I cannot but feel that a society of which almost a quarter are over sixty is not the most cheerful of prospects, even if a society in which almost half are under twenty-one is also rather too much.

Other costs are even more controversial. It is sometimes maintained that small families are calamitous to the child. The only child, so it is then suggested, is 'a special kind of being' who 'cannot fail to believe himself the centre of the world'. Inevitably, 'he is destined to the disappointments and sufferings of any being ill-prepared for life'. Nor is the family of two, the argument continues, sufficient to overcome this difficulty; the optimum is three or four or five children. Since three children is also, so Sauvy maintains, the smallest that will ensure the renewal of the family there is a kind of pre-established harmony, as he sees the situation, between the 'psychological' optimum and what he takes to be the social optimum. Below the level of three children, so he writes, 'quantity and quality thus decay together: life avenges the insult directed at it'.[33]

In most modern societies, however, many of the traditional advantages of a large family are no longer significant. The sustaining role of the family has been largely taken over by the State. And necessarily so, since the family is often scattered over a wide territory. Its members live disparate and incompatible lives to a degree unknown in a more traditional, less socially mobile, society. And only a limited range of activities can successfully be carried on within a single household. The members of a large family, too, may find themselves seriously disadvantaged because their parents cannot afford to educate them adequately. If, under the pressure of population growth, the standard of public education declines, this consideration will become more, rather than less, significant.[34] Furthermore, as Pressat points out, 'a large family reduces the possibility of contacts for the child with the adult world, depriving him of the specific advantages which go with this kind of contact'.[35] In short, even although there are *possible* costs in reducing the average family size and *actual* costs in increasing the degree to which the State substitutes for the family they are scarcely sufficient to set against the consequences of a perpetually doubling population.

As for economic considerations, as we have already suggested and as even Colin Clark admits, rates of economic growth 'do not show any discernible correlation, positive or negative, with rates of population growth'.[36] Clark is convinced, however, that to lower rates of population growth would be to remove a powerful incentive to social change, and more particularly to social change in the direction of greater liberty.[37] As examples, he cites archaic Greece and the sixteenth-century Netherlands. In both cases, however, the effects of a rising population were mitigated by colonisation. (Plato takes colonisation for granted as a way of relieving population pressures.) One could readily point to other instances, as J. J. Spengler does, in which a decline in population has preceded, and apparently made possible, a flowering of economic and social growth.[38] Clark himself admits that the challenge-response mechanism does not always work: too great a challenge, of any sort, can generate apathy or a neurotic running-around in ineffective circles. (Contemporary England?)

I have been sceptical about the possibility of calculating optimal populations and, even more, optimal rates of growth. (Even more, because that involves deciding not only that, under existing circumstances, a population of a certain size is optimal, but also what *will be* the optimal population at some time in the future.) I have suggested, too, that the effects of lowering the rate of population growth are largely unknown but unlikely to be entirely desirable. But this vagueness and this guarded pessimism do not entail that the project of controlling population growth ought to be abandoned. For the fact from which we began remains: that world population simply cannot continue to increase at its present rate, that if it were to do so it would issue in a population which would be by any conceivable standards overcrowded, in which men would have neither room nor resources. The ultimate choice, as we said, lies between permitting population growth to be controlled by famine and disease or attempting deliberately to control it, fully conscious of the fact that in the process we shall make serious mistakes in our estimates of future numbers and future needs, mistakes which by their very nature cannot be corrected overnight. And conscious, too, that any reduction in rates of population growth has costs as well as benefits.

Furthermore, although one cannot expect to find men in accord about precisely what the population of Britain, let us say, ought to be, we can more realistically expect to find them in reasonable agreement that this population ought to fall somewhere within a certain range. (Just as, to revert to my previous example, few would be prepared to buy a car which had a maximum speed of ten miles an hour, however effective its brakes and steering, or a car, however speedy, with brakes that would not stand up to two successive applications.) The population of Britain is now about fifty-four million: demographic projections—though they are already proving to be unreliable—suggest that it will be sixty-six million by the turn of the century. There are those, many of them biologists, who confidently maintain that this is already too large; some of them, indeed, would set the optimal figure as low as twenty million.[39] Others would not find sixty-six million, perhaps even eighty million, too many, granted some redistribution of population *within* Britain. Few would wish the population to be more than a hundred million. At first sight, this is a large range of difference. Further discussion might reduce the gap considerably. But a population of sixty-four million would be converted into a population twice that number in little more than a century were the rate of natural increase to remain at its present 0·6 per cent and were emigration to cease. In four centuries, it would reach five hundred million. So provided only that one can set a maximum tolerable figure—and both those who believe that the optimal figure is twenty million and those who believe it to be eighty million would be prepared to agree that it ought not to reach a hundred million—one has good grounds for asserting, at least, that the present rate of growth is too high, even if not yet for determining what that rate ought to be. Something similar applies to the population of the world as a whole.

Let us presume, to make the minimum presumption, that population growth ought to be lowered to a point at which, at the very least, it will be stabilised in the twenty-second century. To many of us, it is anything but a palatable view that the world will continue to increase its population until that time. But, palatable or not, that is the most likely conclusion. Although a few optimists like Bogue are confident that 'the rate of growth will slacken at such a pace that it will be zero or near zero at about the year 2000', their optimism does not survive an examination of the facts.[40] It will be hard enough to reach that point by the year 2200. What are the principal obstacles to even so limited a lowering of the rate of population growth?

That question returns us to our central theme. So far we have done little more than set the stage. Now it is time for the principal actors to enter, the forces which tell against the reduction of population growth. In the manner of a mediaeval morality play, we can distinguish seven such actors: Ignorance, Prudishness, Religion, Ideology, Social Habits, Female Servitude, Moral Scruples. They are close relatives but it will pay us to look at them separately. The first two have roles which are important but relatively simple to comprehend; we can rapidly dismiss them. The other five, however, demand close attention. We shall have to ask how far their role in Western history is essential and to what extent therefore those critics of the West are correct who urge us entirely to recast our moral and metaphysical outlook.

Ignorance is of two sorts. First, there is *technological* ignorance. Technologists have yet to invent methods of birth control which are at once cheap, easy to use, reliable and devoid of side-effects. No device at present in use combines these qualities to a degree sufficient to ensure the success of birth-control campaigns, especially in developing countries. The defects of any such device are sufficient to lend apparent justification to exaggerations by rumour-mongers, with results that are often disastrous.[41]

Secondly, there is individual ignorance. Over considerable areas of the earth's surface, the major contraceptive devices are still quite unknown.[42] Even when they are known, furthermore, they may be feared for a variety of pseudo-medical or magical reasons. Or they may be ineffectively used, because the principle behind them is not understood. Even in the West, these factors still operate; in largely illiterate countries they are of the first importance. Neither form of ignorance, however, is either peculiar to the West or insuperable. We can safely pass ignorance by with this bare mention, to remind us of what technology and education still have to offer.

A little less obviously, prudishness can limit the spread of information. The success of the Japanese campaign to lower the birth-rate depended in large part on its capacity to use such media as television to offer explicit information about contraceptive methods. Such a degree of frankness is in many Western societies still not permissible—even if some women's papers have now broken the prudishness-barrier. Those moralists who firmly believe, for some reason totally obscure to me, that it is morally wrong accurately to describe the sexual act, even to those who are known to engage in such acts, still have the power to limit the effectiveness of contraceptive training. Their influence, for the moment at least, appears to be diminishing. But it would be foolish to ignore it; prudishness is still a potent force in the West, as it also is in some Eastern societies. It might well revive, and prove to be an even more important obstacle to the communication of contraceptive information.

Prudishness links with religion. Here we come to an agent much more complex, much more difficult accurately to describe, much more variable. It plays a quite fundamental role in determining both Eastern and Western attitudes to the control of population growth. For it has not merely, like the ignorance and prudishness so often linked with it, made more difficult the distribution of contraceptive information, it has positively set itself against the use of contraceptive methods. Such Christians as count only the Bible as an authoritative text can scarcely claim however, that it condemns population control. Take first the Old Testament. Much weight has been laid—quite recently by Pius XI in his encyclical *Casti Connubii*—on that passage in Genesis (38: 8–9) in which Onan is said to have been killed by Jahweh for spilling his seed on the ground. (It is extraordinary how wide a variety of sexual acts, from masturbation through *coitus interruptus* to the use of contraceptive devices, have been condemned on the basis of that isolated passage.) But Onan's sin seems to have consisted in his refusal to impregnate his brother's widow rather than in the contraceptive act itself. This interpretation is borne out by the fact that there is no mention of contraception in the very detailed codes of law, many of them touching on sexual questions, to be found in Leviticus.[43] The Jews certainly interpreted 'Be fruitful and multiply and replenish the earth' (Genesis 1: 28) as a positive command. But they did not take it to imply that procreation must continue *ad absurdum*. The Mishnah, for example, teaches that a man must not stop from the propagation of the race unless he already has children; the 'unless' clause is significant. With the dispersion, large families were no longer regarded, in the manner of the Psalmist, as a blessing. It was still suggested, no doubt, that a man should have at least two sons, or one son and one daughter. But even this principle was taken to apply only to men; a woman, it was generally although not universally agreed, was not under any obligation to have children.[44] So room was left for concubinage, and for contraception within concubinage.

The position in the Christian tradition, under the influence of the New Testament, was rather different. It was not incumbent on the Christian to have children. Whereas in the Old Testament virginity is represented as a calamity, the Roman Catholic Church elevated not only virginity but chastity within marriage—the 'Joseph marriage' within which, as Paul put it, men live with their wives as though they had none—to its highest point.[45] 'In these days indeed,' wrote Augustine, 'no one perfect in piety seeks to have children except spiritually.'[46] The Genesis exhortation to multiply was interpreted as a blessing on procreation and a precept to the species—not as a command directed to individuals. Tertullian, interpreting Jahweh's precept to multiply as an indulgence granted 'until the world should be replenished', was convinced that that point had been more than reached; 'Our numbers are burdensome to the world, which can hardly supply us from its natural resources.'[47] 'Why should we be eager to have children,' he elsewhere very naturally asks, 'desirous as we are ourselves to be taken out of this most wicked world?' The 'bitter, bitter, pleasure of children' is a perilous burden, he goes on to add, for the committed Christian.[48] In its early history, then, the Christian Church by no means committed itself to the view that large families were necessarily a good thing.

Aquinas set out what came to be the orthodox Roman Catholic position. 'The precept given as to generation,' he writes, 'looks to the whole multitude of men. The multitude must not only be multiplied bodily, but advanced spiritually. Therefore, sufficient provision for the human multitude is made, if some undertake the task of carnal generation.'[49] In other words, the spiritually-minded could properly leave the task of propagating the race to the carnal multitudes. 'The community of mankind,' as he elsewhere unenthusiastically puts it, 'would not be in a perfect state unless there were some people who direct their intention to generative acts.'[50] (Not everyone agreed with him: there were those within the Church for whom the perfect community would be entirely virginal.) Aquinas is not suggesting, even so, that population *growth* is itself a good thing. Heaven no doubt had to be populated,

God had to fill the places left empty by the fallen angels—but there was no great hurry about it.

Yet according to the authoritative *Dictionary of Moral Theology* 'the Catholic Church considers a large family to be the normal and natural effect of a normal conjugal life'.[51] As late as 20 January 1958, Pope Pius XII told the Association of Large Families that 'large families were those most blessed by God and specially loved and prized by the Church as its most precious treasures'.[52] Yet this is the same Pius XII who in his encyclical *Sacra Virginitas* (25 March 1954) had warmly advocated virginity, for lay and cleric alike, as the sole way of ensuring that the heart is wholly devoted to God— 'virginity is preferable to marriage, then, above all else because it has a higher aim'.[53] We can put his position thus: some human beings find it necessary to have sexual intercourse; such persons should, in general, have large families. This view *in practice*— since the appeal of virginity is somewhat limited—strongly tells against controls over population growth. 'The family,' one Roman Catholic apologist has lately argued, 'which courageously and even heroically rears a large number of people in an overpopulated area merits special praise for its virtue.'[54] From the point of view of population control, there could scarcely be a more damaging observation.

Orthodox Protestantism differed from Roman Catholicism in its estimate of celibacy. Luther, it is true, is still prepared to speak of celibacy as a 'high and rare gift'. His more influential view, however, is that 'whoever will live alone undertakes an impossible task and takes it upon himself to run counter to God's word and the nature that God has given and preserves in him'.[55] Marriage, and with marriage a large family, was, in the eyes of most Protestant thinkers, the norm. It was a Protestant parson, Malthus, who first drew attention to the dangers of population growth. But Archibald Alison was more typical when, in the passage already cited, he urged men to multiply and leave the outcome of their efforts in God's hands. An influential Lutheran theologian could still write in the 1930s that: 'Marriage is the instrument by which new life is produced—no one has the right to evade the creative will of God, who in our human situation and natural impulses commands us to be fruitful.'[56]

Both Roman Catholic and Protestant orthodoxy agreed on one fundamental point: 'The primary purpose of marriage,' in the words of the Roman Catholic Code of Canon Law (Canon 1013,1), is 'the procreation and education of children.' This was linked with their attitude to sexual intercourse. That the sexual act is 'dirty in itself' and needs to be 'justified' by being attached to an external purpose—procreation—is a view one finds running through the Roman Catholic Church* from Innocent III's 'who does not know that conjugal intercourse is never committed without itching of the flesh, and heat and foul concupiscence?'[57] to the nineteenth-century seminary text-books which bluntly lay it down that 'the sex act is a thing filthy in itself' and that marriage is an institution which gives people 'the right to perform indecent acts'.[58] Even in marriage it is morally wrong, that is, to engage in sexual intercourse for its own sake.

Nor was it only theologians who took that view. One finds something very like it in Kant, who went so far, indeed, as to argue that 'the appetite of a cannibal differs only insignificantly from that of a sexual libertine', since in both cases one person is thinking of another as an 'immediately enjoyable thing'.[59] Marriage, as Kant sees it, is directed only at 'the preservation of the species'. In Hegel, however, from the time of his earliest manuscripts, one finds a very different interpretation of marriage according to which it is essentially 'the overcoming of separateness'. In copulation, so Hegel tells us, 'what is most private to oneself is united in mutual contact and shared feeling to the point of unconsciousness, of the transcending of all distinction'.[60] (The contrast at this point between Kant and Hegel, incidentally, will serve to illustrate the difficulty philosophers have experienced in settling on an attitude to sexual relations which is neither moralistic nor mystical.)

Within the Christian Church over the last few decades something like the Hegelian view has gradually come to the fore; marital sexual intercourse is now thought of as neither, in respect to each such act, essentially procreative nor a mere remedy for concupiscence, but rather as a way in which love can affirm itself. This fact is highly important. It implies that birth control can no longer be condemned as frustrating the 'true purpose' of marriage. The most obvious change, perhaps, has taken place in the Anglican Church. In 1920 the Lambeth Conference, deeply concerned about 'a falling birth-rate and all that sinister phenomenon implies',[61] uttered 'an earnest warning against the use of any unnatural means by which conception is frustrated'. The 1958 Conference took a completely different view. 'It is utterly wrong to urge that, unless children are specifically desired, sexual intercourse is of the nature of sin. It is also wrong to say that such intercourse ought not to be engaged in except with the willing

---

* One also finds it in the writings, especially the earlier writings, of that spoiled monk Luther, whose views on matrimony are, indeed, extraordinarily complex. He sometimes writes of the love of wife and children as something beyond human power; we can love a harlot, he says, but not our wife. See on this theme Lucien Febvre: *Martin Luther* (Paris, 1928), Eng. Trans. (London, 1930), pp. 291–3. In general, the view that marriage is a 'remedy against concupiscence' has played a very large part in Protestant moral theology, as is obvious in the English Book of Prayer.

intention to procreate children.' And this is because 'husbands and wives owe to each other and to the depth and stability of their families the duty to express, in sexual intercourse, the love they bear and mean to each other . . . Sexual intercourse is not by any means the only language of earthly love, but it is, in its full and right use, the most intimate and the most revealing.'[62] Nothing could better illustrate the flexibility of Western thought—even within the framework of an Established Church.

Karl Barth, similarly, has argued that once the Messiah was born, procreation lost its old importance: 'No child conceived or born in this time will bring anything that is fundamentally and decisively new.' (In Jewish thought, this had been the justification of continued procreation. So the Talmud tells us that there is a certain number of souls waiting to be born and that the Messiah cannot be born until these are all born.)[63] Marriage and procreation are still, he says, *possibilities* for Christians, but they are no more than that. He explicitly denies that 'entrance into marriage is universally the higher way, the better possibility'.[64] And marriage itself, as Barth sees it, should be thought of as an opportunity for fellowship rather than for procreation.

Barth's theology, then, is peculiarly favourable to population control. For he denies not only that everyone is called upon to marry and produce a family but also that procreation is the primary purpose of marriage. If this were to become the standard Christian teaching—and there are some signs that it may do so—then Christian teachings on marriage, at least, would no longer be a formidable obstacle, quite the contrary, to control over population growth.

Within the Roman Catholic Church the change of heart has not won the same degree of official recognition. It is true that official approval is now extended to the idea of 'responsible parenthood' in so far as the Church—while still arguing that 'each and every marriage act must remain open to the transmission of life'[65]—permits married couples deliberately to restrict their sexual relationship to infecund periods, thus 'making legitimate use of a natural disposition'. But it still officially condemns 'the use of means directly contrary to fecundation'.[66] Yet the fact is that the papal encyclical *Humanae Vitae*, issuing from the Second Vatican Council, in which these views were laid down was in opposition to the majority judgment of the Papal Commission and to a great body of learned opinion within the Church.[67] Complicated though the whole question is by the dogma of papal infallibility, the opponents of the encyclical are able to console themselves with the reflection that the Papacy has changed its mind on more than one occasion—quite recently on the fundamental question of religious liberty—and that all that would be involved in a similar change on the question of contraception is a 'development of dogma' rather than an absolute *volte face*.[68]

The two objectives of marriage laid down in Canon Law do not necessarily harmonise with one another. One may bring so many children into the world that one cannot adequately educate them. In recent years, the double-pronged character of this criterion has been made much use of by radical Roman Catholics. Since education, they have argued, is as 'primary' as procreation, a married couple is quite entitled to decide that they already have as many children as they can educate. Given the conditions of the modern world, two may be quite enough. In defence of the orthodoxy of the view that the quality not the quantity of children is what matters the authority of Aquinas is sometimes invoked. The 'principal end of matrimony', according to Aquinas, is 'the *good* of the offspring'.[69] This is an interesting example of the way in which the complexity of Western traditions can be made use of by reformers.

There has, then, been an amazingly rapid change in the attitude of the Christian Churches to population control. But it should also be observed that individual Christians were disregarding the official teachings long before the theologians gave them any encouragement to do so. In the 1930s and 1940s it was indeed especially in predominantly Roman Catholic countries—in Belgium, in Austria—that the net reproduction rate fell to its lowest levels, as before that time in France. One more than doubts whether this reflects an exceptional degree of chastity, or a proneness to 'Joseph marriages', among the inhabitants of those countries. But they could see for themselves the economic effects of multiplication. Within Europe, only when Roman Catholics are in a minority is their fertility rate unusually high. When they are in the majority their fertility rate is often lower than that of the Protestant minority.[70] Once again changed practices are more important than changed principles, which is not to say that the two are *wholly* dissociated.

Turning to the Middle East we find a not dissimilar change of attitude. In Muslim as in Christian countries theologians are re-examining the traditional texts. Such influential theologians as the eleventh-century Al-Ghazzali, so it is now pointed out, did not prohibit contraception in all cases; the Koran's explicit precepts on this topic are, on his interpretation, counsels of perfection, not universally binding. He permitted contraception not only as a way of avoiding 'numerous anxieties on account of numerous children' but even as a means of preserving the wife's beauty and vigour 'so that she may be a perennial source of joy'.[71] In the Muslim tradition, so much the revisionist theologians are prepared to admit, the large family has generally been regarded as a blessing. But although Mahomet told men to 'marry and reproduce so that I can be proud of you before God' the Koran does not explicitly advocate large families. Large families were needed, so the argument runs, when the Muslim peoples were expanding through Europe and Asia: the situation has now completely changed.

The fact remains that in Muslim countries the old tradition is still influential. The rate of population growth continues to be high; where Muslims and non-Muslims live alongside one another in a single country the Muslims have the higher rate. This is in spite of the fact that in such countries as Pakistan infantile mortality rates are exceptionally high—higher than in India.[72] There can be no doubt that religious traditions play a large part in opposition to the dissemination of information about birth control.[73] Attempts to introduce family planning in Pakistan have met resistance from Muslim fanatics.[74]

Farther East, the situation in Hindu India is not so very different. To have a son is essential for purely religious purposes, to perform the appropriate death-rituals.[75] 'The first great law,' as the Song of Savitri puts it, is 'that a man has seed.'[76] And it was not enough simply to 'have seed': there must be sufficient children to ensure that sons would live until the father's death. In China, too, Mencius taught that 'there are three ways of being a bad son', and 'the most serious is to have no heir'.[77] Once more it is possible to argue that this does not entail having a *large* family, that the need to have a large family in order to ensure that one will have surviving sons no longer exists. But religious teachings, in both cases, have developed and encouraged a social habit. One certainly cannot hope, then, to dispel the belief that large families are good by exchanging Western for Eastern attitudes of mind: quite the contrary.

At the official level, however, the Muslim and Hindu countries are prepared to break decisively with the past. So amongst the Heads of State who signed in December 1966 a declaration that 'family planning is in the vital interests of both the nation and the family' were the Heads of State of the United Arab Republic, Tunisia, Morocco, India. Of the European States, in contrast, none signed which were either Communist or had a large Roman Catholic population, except Yugoslavia.

In all one might put the position thus: at the grass-roots level Christian opposition to population control is no longer of great significance in any country with a high level of literacy; in the East, it is precisely at grass-roots level that the old traditions are most powerful. Responsible leaders in the Arab countries or in India cannot help being conscious of the problems with which population growth confronts them. But in the West, official leaders are still afraid to commit themselves. Roman Catholics in positions of power have often been in a position to prevent programmes of family planning from being initiated by international organisations. Countries with large Roman Catholic minorities often overestimate the monolithicity of such minorities; they fear the electoral consequences of supporting family-restriction programmes. It is an interesting fact that a Roman Catholic, John F. Kennedy, was the first American President with sufficient courage to come out in favour of family planning. The situation is at its worst in countries like South America, where there is a black alliance of Roman Catholics, communists, and nationalists—the last convinced that population control is a device to prevent the development of the South American countries.[78] 'Timeo Danaos et dona ferentes' now translates 'I fear the Americans when they come bearing contraceptives'.

Ideology, especially as represented by Marxism and nationalism, is, indeed, the fourth major obstacle to birth control. To take nationalism first, the myth dies hard that population, power and security are indissolubly linked. But myth it is. Even if one defines 'greatness' solely in military terms, it is only to a limited degree that victory goes to the big battalions. The largest countries in Europe have not been the least often invaded or the most often successful in time of war. A rapidly increasing population can put internal stresses on a country which make it unfit for the conduct of a war.[79] At the moment, it is true, the 'great powers' are also countries with large populations. (Although the *dispersal* of those populations may be of more importance than their dimensions.) But considering the world as a whole, power is by no means proportionate to population.

No doubt one might argue, for example, that had France continued to increase its population at the same rate as Germany, it would have been able to put up a more powerful resistance to the German invasion. But, in the first place, it is not at all clear that what France lacked in 1939 was *numbers*. And, in the second place, one might equally argue that had Germany followed the example of France, it would never have embarked on the War or fallen into Nazism. A 'greatness' that results in such calamities is not the sort of greatness the world will wish to see pursued. And no other sort of greatness seems to be at all linked with numbers: the United States, to say nothing of the Soviet Union, is by no other standards so great as was Athens or Elizabethan England.

The dangers of identifying population and power are obvious. It would be appalling were the world to witness a breeding race parallel to its armaments race. Such power-struggles can affect a country internally as well as externally. Thus Roman Catholic apologists have sometimes looked to an increase in the Roman Catholic birthrate as a way in which the Church can regain its old dominance. A pamphlet issued in London by the Catholic Truth Society tells its readers that: 'Our faithful Catholic mothers are doing a wonderful work for God. In time if contraceptive practices continue to prevail among Protestants, their number will decrease and the Catholic race will prevail, and thus England might again become what it once was, a Catholic country.'[80] (Another interesting example of the way in which one man's 'benefits' are another man's 'costs'.) It would be wrong to suggest that this is in any way the principal motive behind the Roman Catholic Church's opposition to birth-control. That Church has, after all, opposed the dissemination of birth-control information and devices not only to its own members but to Protestants and non-Christians. Such pronouncements, however, could easily provoke a Protestant-Catholic breeding competition. In the United States, white-negro relationships still further complicate the issue. Like the South Americans, the more intransigent negroes see in laws to liberalise abortion, for example, a conspiracy against their people, designed to limit their growth. 'The abortion law,' so one Black Panther spokeswoman puts it, 'hides behind the guise of helping people, when in reality it will attempt to destroy our people.' Throughout the world, so the 1967 Black Panther Manifesto maintained, 'black people who live under imperialist governments stand at the crossroads of either an expanding revolution or ruthless extermination'.[81] Laws permitting abortion, as they see them, are the thin end of the wedge, the first stages on the path towards compulsory sterilisation. Fortunately these sentiments are not universally shared by the black peoples. But once again the potential danger is considerable, the danger of provoking a competition for numbers in which nobody stands to gain.

As for Marxism, it, like Christianity, has had second thoughts. Marx himself had condemned Malthus, the first to point unequivocally to the potential dangers of population growth even if on grounds now made inadequate by the advance of technology, not only as a plagiarist but as 'a shameless sycophant of the ruling classes', a 'bought advocate'.[82] This is not at all surprising. Malthus, it must be recalled, designed his study of population pressures as a criticism of Godwin's view that human society could be perfected by a slow process of social improvement. Men can improve society, he argued, only by weakening the natural checks on population growth, such checks as poverty, war, disease, plague and famine. But if they succeed, population growth

will inevitably outstrip the means of subsistence. He sought to
show that there is an 'iron law' of population—that population
increases geometrically and resources only arithmetically—which
makes social improvement impossible beyond a very limited point.
No Marxist can be expected to believe this. The writings of Engels
display, indeed, an unbounded confidence that science can outwit
Malthus, a confidence scarcely to be matched outside the writings
of Colin Clark. 'The productivity of the land can be *infinitely* increased,' he once wrote, 'by the application of capital, labour and
science.' Malthus's 'vile and infamous doctrine, this repulsive
blasphemy against man and nature' could be totally overthrown
by 'science, the progress of which is just as limitless and at least as
rapid as that of population'. 'What,' Engels rhetorically asks, 'is
impossible for science?'[83] 'Malthusian' functions in the Marxist
vocabulary as a term of abuse; it is comparable to 'Trotskyist'
'revisionist', 'counter-revolutionary'. We have already quoted the
delegate from the Soviet Union who denied the very existence of a
population problem. (A not unnatural attitude for delegates from
that country to take, whatever their political persuasion, when one
considers their vast territories and their heavy war losses, twice
in the century: if every human society occupied a small island, it
would be much easier to convince men of the need for population
control.) The Ukrainian delegate at that same conference, held
as late as 1963, was even more forthright: 'We do not accept that,
in this place, anyone should suggest the limitation of marriages or
births in marriage. Any such proposition must be considered
barbaric.'[84] Yet although at international conferences the Soviet
Union still (1972) refuses to support motions which incorporate a
reference to family planning, its present tendency is to abstain
from voting rather than positively to oppose. And both the Soviet
Union and its satellites allow, with a degree of latitude which
fluctuates from time to time, the practice of birth control.[85]

China, too, has not for long persisted with the traditional
Marxist doctrine that population control is a bourgeois device,
designed to conceal the fact that what the world really needs is a
social revolution. In 1959 a writer in the *Peiping Review* was prepared to assert that 'in denouncing the reactionary Malthusian
theory Marxists did not in any way exclude the necessity of the
planned limitation of population growth in the future development of society'.[86] This passage is peculiarly important just because
by separating out malthusianism from population control as such
it leaves the way open for a Marxist, without heterodoxy, to
support population control.[87]

For all the violence of his attack on Malthus Engels was prepared to recognise, even if he made little of the point, that after

the revolution 'the people in the communist society themselves' will be free to decide 'whether, when and how' population growth should be controlled.[88] And Marx's own law of population— 'every special historic mode of production has its own special laws of population, historically valid within its limits alone'— allows of infinite variety.[89] So there are sacred texts enough for the communist countries to fall back upon, should they wish to control their population growth. Population control can be 'wicked' in capitalist societies, without its being wicked once capitalism is overthrown, just as restrictions on dissentient writers are wicked under capitalism but the height of virtue in communist states.

Both Marxism and Christianity, if I have judged the signs aright, are of diminishing importance as obstacles to control over population growth in the countries in which they predominate. As I have already suggested, it is where they ally themselves with other forces, and especially with power-struggles, that their effect is most to be feared. Whenever it suits them politically, in South America, in West Bengal, communists will condemn family planning as a conspiracy 'to rob the poor of their children'. The sole question, for them, is whether at a given time and place support for family planning will advance or retard the prospects of revolution. Similarly, whenever family planning is linked, as it often is, with liberalism, anti-clericalism, the Roman Catholic Church will oppose it.[90]

It is often hard to distinguish the influence of social habits, the fifth major influence on population growth, from the influence of religion and ideology. Religion and ideology can reinforce social habits; they can, for example, encourage or discourage marriage, they can permit or forbid polygamy.(For obvious reasons, marriages in which one man marries several women, so that some men remain unmarried, are less fertile than monogamous marriages.)[91] But for theoretical purposes we can think of social habits as an independent factor.

Marriage is the most important such habit. The sharp decline in the Irish population in the nineteenth and early twentieth centuries—it halved between 1841 and 1931—was only partly a consequence of emigration; celibacy played an important part in it. The average number of children born to married women remained high, but the marriage rate was, and remained, low.[92] This is a classical example of the Roman Catholic pattern, with its alternatives of complete celibacy or a large family. But although the willingness to remain celibate was no doubt encouraged by the exceptionally puritanical character of Irish Catholicism, it primarily derived from Ireland's economic situation. The Irish example is an unusually interesting one; it illustrates just how profoundly a combination of economic decline and rising Manicheanism could affect the demographer's projections.

In most parts of the world, however, celibacy has been frowned upon except for the monk. (Even the monastery, in many instances, is only an interlude in the life of a man who is still called upon to raise a family.) And in the Western world as a whole something of the same attitude is emerging, for all Karl Barth's arguments to the contrary.* Even clerical celibacy is under fire.

Nobody knows quite why marriage, and early marriages, have now become the vogue in the West. Or perhaps we should rather say why, after centuries of being the odd man out—with important economic consequences—the West should have reverted to the pattern of conduct which has always been typical of every other region in the world—universal and early marriage.[93] Setting out to consider how this change in pattern might be reversed, it is easy to think of hypotheses about the circumstances which gave rise to it: increased employment opportunities and higher incomes for the young; a greater degree of confidence in the future resulting, in the case of the young, from a life-long experience of prosperity; more affluent parents able to offer their married children a considerable degree of material support; rising hostility between the generations and widening taste-gaps, so that parents are glad to see their children establish independent households; the fear of being accounted 'queer', in all senses of the word, if one remains unmarried; a growing competitiveness, so that a husband becomes a trophy and the unmarried man or woman a 'failure' in the battle for possessions; a dislike on the part of women for the kind of jobs which are open to them, coupled with the disappearance of the tradition that the unmarried daughter could simply live at home until marriage came her way; the belief, based on misunderstandings of Freud, that not to have sexual relations is 'unhealthy'. But it is one thing to put forward such hypotheses, quite another to decide between them, or to determine, where these factors are jointly effective, their relative strength. And our ignorance has the consequence that even although raising the conventional marriage age to, let us say, thirty for men and twenty-six for women would almost certainly act as a control on population, we have not the slightest idea how to bring about this state of affairs—except by the imposition of the sort of rigorous controls operating in mainland China. Even if we knew how to

* In England and Wales the percentage of women aged 24 who have married rose between 1920 and 1960 from 27·4% to 57%, by the age of 44 from 82% to 90%. In the United States by 1962 some 71% of women aged 24 were or had been married. Compare the situation in the Lucerne census of 1870 when 39% of women were single at the age of fifty. See van de Walle: 'Marriage and marital fertility' in Glass and Revelle, *Population and Social Change*, p. 138.

bring this change about, furthermore, we might well regard the costs of doing so as too high.

In India, the habit of marrying is even more firmly established. To quote again from the Song of Savitri:

> Daughter! 'tis time we wed thee . . .
> For this the rule is by the sages taught—
> Hear what is spoken, noble maid—'That sire
> Who giveth not his child in marriage
> Is blamable.'

And the sages are still obeyed. (At the 1961 census, less than two per cent of women were unmarried by the age of thirty and the mean age at marriage—the consummation age would be a little higher—was less than sixteen.)[94]

The Indian Government has opposed child marriages. On the face of it the success of its efforts would lessen the number of children each woman bore. But in fact child marriages are unlikely to disappear except as the result of a gradual secularisation. Such a secularisation would almost certainly have the further consequence that, in defiance of the old religious law, widows would be permitted to re-marry. Furthermore, by reducing the number of women who died as a result of too-early childbirth, it might actually increase the number of fertile women surviving. So it has been calculated that an increase of as much as five years in the average marriage age—a very considerable jump for an intensely conservative people—would reduce the number of births only by a drop-in-the-bucket ten per cent.[95] This is yet another illustration of the way in which reforms which are intuitively attractive as a solution to ecological problems can actually have the effect of intensifying them, or, at best, have only the slightest of consequences.

Another relevant habit, even more variable, is the habit of having, or not having, children and, in the latter case, in particular numbers. As we have already seen, this, too, is a matter on which religious teachers have had more than a little to say. But the change which has taken place in the United States, for example, between the pre-war and the post-war years cannot be explained as a change in religious belief. 'Voluntary childlessness is nearly extinct', so Whelpton reported in 1960.[96] The childless couple, indeed, are subject to suspicions about their ability to consummate their marriage; they find themselves, often enough, social outcasts.[97] Recent surveys report no support whatsoever for the view that the ideal number of children is none at all, a view taken by nearly ten per cent of all respondents in the nineteen-thirties.[98] Furthermore, the most favoured 'ideal family size', as reported in such surveys, rose from two to four between 1941 and 1955.[99]

A social norm emerged, indeed, in those decades which could be put thus: 'It is wrong to have more children than one can support, but one should have as many children as one can afford.'[100] If too large a family, on this criterion, was condemned as 'feckless', too small a family was no less condemned as 'selfish'. (Of course, the level of expectations in the United States being what it is, 'as many children as one can afford' did not imply a family 'large' by the standards of the developing world.)

Once more we do not know why this change in attitude took place, nor how *serious* it was, as distinct from a mere fashion—perhaps large families were 'in' as a form of conspicuous consumption, just as large cars were 'in'. In this case, too, a great many hypotheses of varying degrees of initial plausibility suggest themselves, ranging from an unconscious reaction to the threat of depopulation by the atomic bomb to the search for intimate human relations in a population dehumanised by social change.* At a somewhat less speculative level we might look upon the decision to have children as an economic one, related to the income of the parents and the costs of child-rearing, including such costs as the inroads children make on leisure time.[101] And certainly decisions about the size of an ideal family can be influenced by the cost of having children—the degree to which, for example, they provide a source of labour or, on the contrary, have to be supported throughout a longer period of education. It can be influenced, too, by the availability of pension schemes for the aged so that children are no longer a form of old-age insurance, or of grandparents and other child-minding devices to release the parents from full-time responsibility. It can be affected, too, by the strength of a woman's belief that the child is likely to survive into adulthood. So the development of medical science can affect the desired family size. It can certainly be influenced by broader social changes. Such plausible-looking hypotheses, however, as that in developing countries it is the poor peasant who wants more children and the

* The way in which modern invention after modern invention has reduced extra-familial human relations is nothing short of extraordinary. The motor-car, the drive-in cinema, television, the supermarket, the motel have all had this effect. Their influence is being accentuated by the crime-wave, which is destructive not only of life and property but, much more importantly, of trust and confidence. It is easy to understand why a large family should, under these circumstances, come to be valued as a compensation for the narrowing of human relationships. Yet the inventions mentioned above may themselves be a response to population-growth; they all of them enable one substantially to ignore one's fellow-man—as the Japanese, under similar pressure, have long since learnt to do—in one's everyday actions. If the hypothesis is correct that these inventions which cut us off from our fellow-men are a response to overcrowding, it can form the basis of a powerful argument against population growth. For a fuller study of this kind of political and social consequence of population growth see N. W. Chamberlain: *Beyond Malthus* (New York, 1970).

educated, modernised, urban woman who wants fewer will not fit the facts, unless, at least, they are subject to very considerable modifications.[102] Indeed the only policy which we can feel reasonably confident would reduce desired family size in Western countries—a sharp and permanent-looking economic decline—is, to put the matter mildly, an unattractive one. In general terms, we simply do not know how to reduce the desired family size by acceptable social policies.

In so far, however, as the recent rise in desired family size rested on the moral principle that for the rich to have a small family is selfish, for the poor to have a large family is feckless, the same principle can be used as a moral lever in an argument against population growth. For, if the ecologists are right, we are all poorer than we thought we were; the human race is poor. To have a large family is to impose a burden on one's neighbours; it is selfish. And it is also feckless. For even if the parents of the large family can afford to keep their children in comfort, the rest of us cannot afford to pay for their education, to use land and materials to build them houses, to supply them with petrol and electricity. We cannot find room for them in our countryside, on our coasts, in our cities, and we cannot cope with their wastes. The moral pressure which very recently was exerted against the 'selfish' parents of small families is now gradually being exerted against the parents of large families. This, again, is a marked and sudden change, but arising all the same out of familiar ethical principles.

A sixth factor influencing population growth is the role of women, in so far as that role has been substantially restricted to child-bearing. Christian attitudes to women are no worse than Eastern attitudes, but they are the more disgraceful because Christianity pretends, as Eastern religions do not, to rise above distinctions of class and race. 'There is neither Jew nor Greek, there is neither bond nor free, there is neither male nor female: for ye are all one in Christ Jesus.'[103] Yet in fact under the influence of Christianity the position of women dramatically worsened. At the Council of Mâcon in 585, a bishop went so far as to deny that women had souls.[104] He did not go uncorrected, but if he had been reading his Tertullian he might well have thought that this was the kindest view to take about women. 'You are the devil's gateway,' Tertullian had written, 'you are the unsealer of that [forbidden] tree; *you* are the first deserter of the divine law; *you* are she who persuaded him whom the devil was not valiant enough to attack. *You* destroyed so easily God's image, man. On account of *your* desert—that is, death—even the Son of God had to die.'[105] Better to be soulless than a dammed source of damnation.

Of particular importance in the Christian tradition has been a passage in the first epistle to Timothy.[106] Women, according to that epistle—traditionally ascribed to Paul who has thus lent the weight of his authority to it—are 'to learn in silence with all subjection'; they are not to 'usurp authority over the man'. These conclusions are derived from two premises, first, that Eve was created after Adam (it is extraordinary how, as we have already had occasion to observe, Christian apologists have emphasised the first or the second Genesis story as it has happened to suit their particular purposes) and, secondly, in Tertullian's manner, that it was Eve who was deceived by the devil. 'Notwithstanding,' the epistle ends, 'she shall be saved in child-bearing.' Some modern scholars question Paul's authorship of this epistle. And some of them retranslate this final passage—I have quoted from the authorised version—to make it say no more than that women, if they live Christian lives, will have God's help in child-bearing. But the authorised version faithfully reflects what has been Christian tradition. One finds it quoted with approval, in just this sense, in the report of the 1920 Lambeth Conference. Only now have women regained that degree of independence they had in Antonine Roman law.

It is true that the Roman Catholic Church permitted women to seek salvation in virginity rather than in child-bearing. (Aquinas's attempt to reconcile the passage in Timothy with his church's praise of virginity will delight the connoisseur of misplaced ingenuity.)[107] But it certainly did not permit them, in any respect, authority over men. Aquinas follows Aristotle in describing women as 'defective and misbegotten', in every respect except the process of generation inferior to a man as a help, and as naturally subject to man, his inferior in rationality.[108] As for Protestantism, it did not even permit the convent as an alternative to child-bearing. Luther was convinced that women should give birth to as many children as possible. 'If they become tired or even die through bearing children that does not matter. Let them die through fruitfulness—that is why they are there.'[109]

Church, kitchen, children, as a description of the role of women, is not an invention of Hitler's but a typical Christian slogan.[110] So firmly was this attitude to women embedded in Western thought that even the Enlightenment did not, in general, seriously question it. Kept in her 'rightful' place by Rousseau, severely criticised by Diderot as an inferior sex who constantly sought to dominate over men, it was only in Condorcet that she found a friend and protector, one of the first to advocate full political rights for women.[111] But not until more than a century later were these rights recognised in law. And the view that child-bearing is a woman's spiritual vocation, her route to salvation, still finds a place in papal pronouncements.

The East is in the West a by-word for its treatment of women. (Although the West should reflect on the fact that if one is to think of women Prime Ministers it is to the East and the Middle East that one has to turn.) No doubt, within Eastern cultures there is often a well-founded tradition of a time when women were the leaders: in early Japanese history this was certainly the case. But the authoritative laws of the mythical Hindu law-maker Manu are only too clear about the role of women. 'The husband,' it is there laid down, 'must constantly be worshipped as a God by the faithful wife'—even if he be 'destitute of virtue or seeking pleasure elsewhere, or devoid of good qualities'.[112] Women were not to read the Vedas; they were created wicked and can easily fall into moral ruin should they 'ramble abroad'.[113] The movement for national independence first released women from this servile state and so far prepared the way for population control.

The liberation of women is important, for our present purposes, because it increases the number of ways in which they can 'find salvation'. Their life no longer *has* to turn around child-bearing. 'Women's liberation' is an essential part, therefore, of any movement towards the reduction of population growth which takes adequate account of the needs of women.

We must now turn to the final obstacle to population control: moral objections—often, but not necessarily, linked with religious beliefs. In part, no doubt, these objections can be reduced in intensity by technological discoveries which make unnecessary the 'objectionable' methods of population-control. But only in part. Often the objection persists. Let us look at some of the most historically important methods of population-control:

(1) infanticide
(2) abortion
(3) contraception
(4) sterilisation
(5) periodic abstinence
(6) total continence
(7) legislative enactments.

Obviously we cannot explore in detail the character and the validity of the moral objections which have been raised to each and every one of these methods: that would carry us far beyond any reasonable bounds of space. We shall have to be content to comment very briefly and inadequately on the moral issues these objections raise, and the extent to which they are entailed by central Western traditions.

(1) *Infanticide*. It will be convenient to divide infanticide into two types, overt and covert. Both Plato and Aristotle support overt infanticide as a method of population control, not only as a means, the use of which they also advocate, of destroying the weakly. The Greeks feared above all else the 'growth' which has latterly become our ideal. The Romans, with their vast Empire and grandiose ambitions, were in this respect more modern: they encouraged population growth, discouraged infanticide. But it continued to be a common practice, if for personal rather than political reasons. The Senecan principle still prevailed: 'The blessing is not in living, but in living well.'

The Alexandrian Jewish philosopher Philo, so often influential in the formation of Christian ideas, attacked infanticide, however, with peculiar zeal, on grounds which combined a Jewish respect for life with a new ascetic note, a condemnation of pleasure for pleasure's sake. He attacks parents who practise infanticide as animalistic pleasure lovers: 'For they are pleasure lovers when they mate with their wives not to procreate children and perpetuate the race, but like pigs and goats in quest of the enjoyment which such intercourse gives.'[114] And one can still detect this attitude to sexual relations, on which we have already commented, behind the thin veils of many a contemporary argument against any form of population control. People who have sexual relations, the feeling is, ought to pay for their pleasure; sexual enjoyment is in itself 'animal'; it is justifiable only as a reward for procreation. This attitude no doubt grows steadily weaker: challenged in the Enlightenment, it was at its most powerful, perhaps, in nineteenth-century England and the United States, criticised even then, however, in those popular books on sex education the existence of which one tends to forget.* But it still exerts, one is inclined to think, a stronger influence than is ordinarily supposed.

Their opposition to infanticide was a point on which the early Christian fathers liked to congratulate themselves. And it certainly did distinguish them from their pagan opponents. Indeed, Christian countries were peculiarly savage in their treatment of the mother who, under whatever stress, killed or abandoned her child. She might be burned at the stake or impaled and buried alive. As so often, Christianity's high regard for 'the sanctity of life' took

* My colleague, Barry Smith, has drawn my attention to one such book written by 'a doctor of medicine', under the title *The Elements of Social Science*—'an exposition of the true cause and the only cure of the three primary social evils, poverty, prostitution and celibacy'. The only copy I have seen is the twenty-sixth edition, published in 1887; the first edition appeared in 1854. (The publisher, rather delightfully, is 'Truelove'.) 'It cannot for a moment be allowed,' writes the anonymous doctor, 'that the so-called animal passions are of an inferior kind to the spiritual. They exercise an influence on men just as diverse as any other, and shape and mould the human character as powerfully and as nobly' (p. 67). This was the extreme of heterodoxy.

strange forms. But it was rare for anyone to protest; infanticide remained a capital crime until late into modern times. This does not mean, of course, that it did not take place. But for the most part it assumed a *covert* form. 'Foundling hospitals', in which children were so neglected that they died in the first years of their life, served—and in some parts of the world still serve—as a substitute for infanticide. Mortality figures for some nineteenth-century Italian hospitals ran as high as 80 per cent to 90 per cent for the child less than a year old; in France the figures were little better. Nor was the foundling a rare exception. On the contrary, the percentage of foundlings rose to as much as 36 per cent of all births. As Malthus observed, 'considering the extraordinary mortality which occurs in these institutions . . . if a person wished to check population, and were not solicitous about the means, he could not propose a more efficient measure than the establishment of a sufficient number of foundling hospitals, unlimited as to their reception of children'.[115] There are more ways than one of killing a baby. The foundling children were baptised and that, as so often, was sufficient to salve the Christian conscience.

The general tendency of our times has been to think of infanticide as a crime a great deal less serious than murder. Bentham was in this respect a pioneer—at least in so far as Étienne Dumont's *Bentham's Theory of Legislation* can fairly be taken to represent his views. Bentham does not deny that infanticide ought to be punished; he forcibly condemns, indeed, 'the insensibility of many nations in respect to infanticide'. The normal penalty, he nonetheless argues, is grossly disproportionate to the offence: 'What is the crime? Causing the death, if so it can be called, of a babe who, in fact, ceases to breathe before knowing what it is to exist— an event which cannot arouse the smallest disquiet in the most timid mind or excite any regret save in the breast of the poor creature who, impelled by shame and pity, was unwilling to prolong a life begun under such unhappy auspices. Now what is the penalty for this crime? A barbarous punishment—an infamous death inflicted on the unfortunate mother, whose very offence displayed her excessive sensibility.'[116]

The argument is interesting: the emphasis now is on the suffering of the mother, rather than on the death of the child. And so far Bentham, writing at the end of the eighteenth century, adumbrates a change in sensibility which was to be of enormous importance in modifying attitudes to birth control. The position of the mother, not only of the baby, must be taken seriously: she, too, is a human being.

Infanticide one can think of as the extremest form of population control. No one, I imagine, would wish to advocate it—although to judge from past experience we can be pretty confident that should population pressures rise above a tolerable level, not only infanticide but the killing of the aged will once again be practised. This is a fact that has always to be kept in mind in discussing the legitimacy of birth-control methods: that if we do not control population growth now, we shall be forcing posterity to adopt much more Draconian measures. As early as 1761, Robert Wallace was already conscious of what would come to pass in an over-populated world: 'In such a [world] must there be a law to restrain marriage? Must multitudes of women, be shut up in cloisters like the ancient vestals or modern nuns? . . . or shall they . . . give a sanction to the unnatural institution of eunuchs? . . . Or, must they shorten the period of human life by a law, and condemn all to die after they had completed a certain age?'[117]

In reply, however, it not only might be but has been argued that other forms of birth control are morally quite as objectionable as infanticide and senicide, so that it would be morally absurd to advocate birth control on the ground that there is otherwise some risk that our descendants will be forced to kill off their babies and old people. Thus Tertullian wrote: 'To hinder a birth is merely a speedier man-killing; nor does it matter whether you take away a life that is born, or destroy one that is coming to the birth. That is a man which is going to be one; you have the fruit already in the seed.'[118] So we shall have to ask ourselves whether contraception and abortion are in fact equivalent to infanticide.

(2) *Abortion*. Abortion, in particular, has often been condemned as a form of infanticide. But this identification has never won much popular support. Abortion has always been common. Nowadays resistance to legalising it even in the Christian West has become steadily weaker. (Between 1965 and 1969 support for abortion on demand in the United States rose from 5 per cent to 40 per cent.)[119] It is perfectly clear, indeed, that we do not *normally* think of the foetus as an infant. The product of a miscarriage is not ordinarily buried; a miscarriage does not provoke an inquest; an abortionist is not tried for murder or manslaughter, nor is the mother who goes to an abortionist tried for conspiracy in a murder.

Modern critics of abortion sometimes take it as their point of departure, however, that our attitudes are mistaken, that 'science has now shown' that Tertullian was correct, that the fertilised ovum is already a human being. Whereas Aristotle had maintained, and after him a good many theologians, that the foetus was human only after it was 'ensouled', forty days after conception in the case of a male, eighty days after conception in the case of a female, the truth is, they argue, that from its very beginning the fertilised ovum is already 'ensouled'. So according to Paul Ramsey 'micro-genetics seems to have demonstrated what religion never could; and biological science, to have resolved an ancient theological dispute. The human individual comes into existence first as a minute information speck . . . This took place at the moment of impregnation . . . Thus it can be said that the individual is who-ever he is going to become from the moment of every impregna-tion . . . Genetics teaches us that we were from the beginning what we essentially still are in every cell and every human attribute.'[120]

But this argument simply will not do. What microgenetics has demonstrated is that the cell contains not only tissue but informa-tion, directing in some measure its later growth. But as Hardin puts the point: 'A set of blueprints is not a house; the DNA of a zygote is not a human being.'[121] What happens to the 'blueprint' in the womb has an importance which this new variety of pre-formationism does not allow. The womb is not a simple incubator; the foetus can develop into a baby only by drawing upon the resources of the mother. All we can properly say is that once there is a fertilised ovum there is something which has a statistical probability—perhaps as low as fifty per cent—of developing into a human being, provided that the mother is prepared to provide an appropriate environment for it. From an important point of view, the foetus is a part of the mother's body.*

A second point is that although the fertilised ovum is from the very beginning a *human embryo* in the sense that if it turns into an animal it will be into a human being, not into a kangaroo—it by no means follows that it is a *human being*, a person. It is not capable of making the discriminations human beings can make; there is nothing in its behaviour to distinguish it from any other living thing. That at a certain point it begins physically to resemble a human body is irrelevant. The issues would be quite unchanged if during the embryonic stage it looked more like a fish than a human being. As for the argument that it is 'arbitrary' to lay it down that at a particular point the foetus is a human being, that therefore, to be consistent, we must think of it as human from the time of conception, this is like saying that since it is arbitrary at

* It is worth adding, perhaps, that if we did think of the relationship between mother and foetus as inter-personal, it would be a relationship, in many instances, of a highly unusual kind. The foetus may be present in the womb entirely against the will of the mother, and its presence can distort the whole future life of the mother. At most, abortion would be, in these circumstances, justifiable homicide. It might be argued that the mother has a special duty to the foetus, since she alone can ensure its continued existence. But this would certainly be the heroic form of duty, not something that can properly be demanded of her—or, indeed, of the father whose life might equally be crippled by the birth of the child. She cannot be blamed for refusing to take the responsibility for the continued life of such an intruder, however blameless, in her womb. Compare Judith Jarvis Thomson: 'A defence of abortion', *Philosophy and Public Affairs* (Fall, 1971, 1:1), pp. 47–66, and the ensuing discussion in subse-quent numbers and in The *Monist* (Fall, 1972, 57:1).

what point we consider a man dead, we should think of him as being dead as soon as he is taken ill. Parallel arguments could 'demonstrate' that there ought to be no voting-age, no retiring-age, no juvenile courts. These are boundaries we have the right to decide.

There are good grounds for not welcoming abortion, at least of the traditional sort, as a method of birth control. But they are not that the fertilised ovum is already a human being, as distinct from something which, given a favourable environment, may turn into a human being. The foetus is a living thing and a living thing with special potentialities. It ought not, therefore, to be wantonly destroyed.*

But in defining 'wanton destruction', we have to take into account the woman who bears it and who *is* a human being, with all the responsibilities of a human being, as well as the life of the foetus. The effects on her largely determine on whether a destruction is wanton. To compel a woman to carry for nine months a foetus she does not wish to carry is to make an extraordinary demand upon her: those who are prepared to make this demand even when the foetus is the product of rape or is certain to be born an imbecile shock me, I confess, so profoundly that I can scarcely believe they sincerely suppose themselves to be speaking in the name of morality.

More than a few of its critics now condemn abortion as 'undemocratic'. So a traditional Roman Catholic spokesman ends his diatribe against abortion with an appeal to the 'immortal words of the American Declaration of Independence'—scarcely a declaration, I should have thought, constructed in the image of Roman Catholicism—that all men are created equal and have 'certain inalienable rights', including the 'right to life'. But it is not a triumph for democracy when, let us say, capital punishment is abolished; it is a triumph for humaneness, perhaps, but not for democracy. The Greeks were not undemocratic when they permitted infanticide. There is here a complete confusion of issues. Democracy is about *freedom*, not about being alive.

As for the notion that the foetus has an inalienable right to life, this means at most, so I have suggested, that *we* have no right to destroy it. But this is just the point at issue. It is much more obvious that a woman has the right to make major decisions which are going to affect her entire future life than it is that the needs— I shall not say the 'rights'—of the foetus have to be taken into account. Here the question of democracy, as distinct from humaneness, *does* enter the picture; a woman can scarcely be described as free if she is forced to bear children as a result, let us say, of rape,

---

* Certain types of abortion, it might further be argued, are brutalising, to the woman, the abortionist, and the public at large. This argument, even if it were sound, would certainly not apply to such abortifacients as the 'morning-after' pill.

or of a defect in her contraceptives, or a lack of consideration on the part of her husband, or an overwhelming access of affection. The East as well as the West is more and more conscious of this fact: 'It is high time,' writes Chandrasekhar, 'that women became their own masters . . . We have come a long way in emancipating our women but their emancipation cannot be complete unless we grant them the right not to have a baby they do not want.'[122]

The moral objections to legalising abortion, then, are anything but overwhelming. (One must also recall that abortion is taking place anyhow, often under deplorable conditions and in a manner calculated to maximise the shock to the woman.) One may confess to a dislike of it, to a desire that other methods should as far and as rapidly as possible take its place. It has obvious defects, of very many different kinds, although some of them may be repaired by technological advances. A situation in which every foetus was a wanted foetus would be a far preferable one. But given the inadequacies of other methods and given the fact that abortion is often the method of birth control which is most, rather than least, in conformity with the traditions of developing countries, these reservations do not suffice to justify opposition to legislation which would permit abortion. It is a particularly important form of population control in the sense that it is mainly resorted to by women who are convinced that they already have as many children as they can possibly cope with.

(3) *Contraception.* Contraception, too, was for long identified with infanticide, in Muslim—where it was described as 'small' infanticide—as well as in Christian teaching.[123] It is sometimes suggested that this way of looking at contraception derived from a false biological theory, according to which the 'male seed' was already a human being. But nobody believed that the seed was *literally* a man; it had still not been 'ensouled'. The description of contraception as infanticide was in fact, as Noonan argues, a form of moral rhetoric: it tried to attach to contraception an already existing moral condemnation—just as nowadays any sort of police action is liable to be called 'Fascist'.[124]

Modern arguments against contraception—excluding those types of contraception which involve, or may be regarded as equivalent to, early abortion—take a different form. Contraception is said to be against the natural law.[125] But this argument rests on two presumptions, the first, pseudobiological, that sexual relationships exist 'for the sake of' procreation, the second, that if they do, it is wrong to engage in them for any other purpose. It is quite impossible, however, to understand the functioning of the human sex organs on the assumption that their sole 'natural end' is procreation. There are many animal species in relation to which that view is relatively plausible, because sexual relationships are only desired, or even feasible, when the female is ready to procreate. That is not true in the case of human sexual relationships. Considering the helplessness of the new-born child, the 'bonding' of its parents is biologically quite as important as procreation. Sexual relations help to unite male and female in such bonds.

Some of the more radical Roman Catholic spokesmen are now prepared to recognise this fact. 'In creating the human female,' writes the Jesuit J. L. Thomas, 'with an ovulation cycle that renders her capable of conception during only a relatively brief period in each menstrual cycle, while at the same time endowing the human couple with no direct means of knowing when ovulation occurs, the Creator obviously intended sexual relations to serve a significant unifying (relational) function in marriage.'[126] We may not all be as ready as a Jesuit to describe with such confidence the Creator's intentions, but the general point remains a valid one, that there is no 'natural' link between sexual relationships and procreation.

But secondly, even if procreation were the 'natural end' of sexual relationships, even if, what is clearly not true, every sexual act would result in conception unless steps were taken to prevent it from doing so, it by no means follows that it would be wrong for human beings to intervene in this process. Civilisation consists, indeed, in 'frustrating natural processes'. 'Frustration of nature,' as a dissident Roman Catholic has put it, 'far from being immoral, is man's vocation.'[127] If procreation threatens civilisation there is not the slightest reason why human beings should not try to limit procreation by any means at their disposal.

One suspects, as I have already suggested, that a deeper feeling lies behind this inadequate reasoning. It comes out clearly in Bourke's statement of the traditional case: the objection is to pleasure being made the end of sexual relationships. 'I am not saying,' writes Bourke, 'that a given person should not enjoy the natural pleasure of sexual union. What I am saying is this: if he or she voluntarily seeks this pleasure, then he or she should voluntarily accept the natural resultant of such activity.'[128]

But why? Suppose I enjoy eating or drinking particular foods, but am allergic to them. If a doctor gives me medicine which will prevent the allergy is it morally wrong of me to take it? Suppose I enjoy lying in the sun but not the sun-burn which is a natural consequence of that activity. Is it wrong for me to use a cream against sun-burn? There does not seem to be the slightest force in Bourke's argument unless we fill it out, as so many Christian apologists have filled it out, by saying that sexual acts are intrinsically wrong in so far as they involve the use of one person by another. Bourke seems to presume that they are always of this latter character unless they are undertaken for the sake of pro-creation. But no one with any experience of sexual relationships as a loving bond could take that view.

(4) *Sterilisation*. The case of sterilisation is more difficult, not if the sterilisation is reversible, but if it is irreversible. We can safely neglect arguments to the effect that sterilisation is 'against nature' or that it 'destroys the integrity of the body'. Operations which, for good reason, alter the workings of the body are commonplace and unobjectionable on moral grounds.[129] But it is a serious matter when an operation limits human choice, when it has the effect that a person's future choices are determined by a single decision, made in circumstances which can change, e.g. as a result of the death of all his children in an epidemic or an accident, or the destruction of most of the world's population by some similar calamity. Of course, almost every choice we make limits in some respect choices we can subsequently make. (Even to choose a particular cake off a tray may limit our subsequent choice of cakes. Someone else may eat our second choice.) But in this case the choice is a particularly serious one, which we may live greatly to regret.

There considerations are not, however, completely decisive; in the event of a national calamity there will be others to take up the responsibility of child-bearing; the risk of finding ourselves unable to replace children we have lost by disease or accident is one we might well be prepared to take. In countries like India, where sterilisation is at the moment the most effective method, these qualms would be insufficient to justify opposition to it. But once more we might well hope, on moral grounds, that reversible sterilisation will come to be the order of the day: the popularity of sterilisation in India seems to be at least in part a product of ignorance of other methods, although its relative cheapness is also an important factor.*

(5) *Partial abstinence*. This is the name significantly preferred by Roman Catholic propagandists for what is alternatively known as the 'rhythm method'. For they see moral virtue in the fact that the use of this method involves abstaining from sexual relations on occasions when both parties desire them. Many of us, on the

* One thing it is very easy to forget, writing about these matters amid the comforts of an advanced Western civilisation, is that other methods of birth control may be, in the less developed countries, quite unworkable. Lack of running water, of privacy, of medical and health services may all have the effect that a once-and-for-all measure like sterilisation is the only reliable procedure. Compare Charles Senior: 'Sterilisation in Puerto Rico', in G. F. Main (ed.): *Studies in Population* (Princeton, 1949).

contrary, would regard the rhythm method as one of the most morally dubious of contraceptive procedures, in so far as it involves a kind of calculation which is not appropriate to loving sexual intercourse. It can in fact, so some Roman Catholic writers have argued on the basis of their experience with married couples, provoke a form of sexual obsession.[130] Even if one were to grant that periods of abstinence, based on mutual consideration, can be helpful to the maintenance of love, it is quite another matter to suggest that this is so even when they are clock-governed. The periods of abstinence entailed by the use of rhythm method are, for most couples, lengthy, and in a mobile society, in which husbands are often absent from home, can be intolerably so.

But these scruples are not powerful enough to enable us to describe the rhythm method as morally impermissible, although they may tempt us to do so. Not so very long ago a Roman Catholic priest could describe it, as Augustine would also have described it, as 'pernicious sensualism' and 'a horrible crime against nature'.[131] There was, rhetoric apart, something in this— although not for the reasons the priest would have given. But neither the principal Western nor the principal Eastern moral traditions offer, I should say, any insuperable objections to its use. In the Hindu tradition, partial abstinence has been, in fact quite normal, although the clock was set by religious rather than biological considerations.[132]

That partial abstinence should be thought legitimate by the Roman Catholic Church while other methods are condemned is thought odd by most non-Roman Catholics and by quite a few of the faithful. For certainly in both cases, as the encyclical *Humanae Vitae* (Art. 16) freely admits: 'The married couple are concordant in the positive will of avoiding children for plausible reasons, seeking the certainty that offspring will not arise.' That sexual acts which have been preceded, let us say, by taking a pill are no longer 'integral', no longer 'apt for the expression of intimate personal love', whereas acts which are deliberately confined to an infecund period retain their 'aptitude for generation' and therefore for expressing love, is certainly a doctrine which many of us find it quite impossible to comprehend.[133]

One might well think that Gandhi was more consistent when he argued for a much stronger form of partial abstinence: the married couple, on his view, ought not to engage in sexual relations except with the specific purpose of procreation; it was quite wrong to engage in them otherwise.[134]* But this is certainly to carry the

---

* This doctrine is bound up not only with Gandhi's asceticism but with his belief that 'preserving his seed' increases a man's strength and vitality; such notions, even in the West, are not confined to the mad colonel of Kubrick's *Dr Strangelove*.

ascetic streak in man's moral tradition to its wildest extremes. Whether we regard it as morally objectionable will depend on our judgment of marital relationships, and the ways in which they are fostered by sexual relationships.

(6) *Total abstinence*. Celibacy has sometimes been objected to on the ground that it is a form of homicide, preventing the birth of children who might otherwise have been born. This, for example, was the teaching of the Jewish matrimonial code Shulḥan Arukh.[135] One finds it, too, in the East, especially amongst some Hindu writers, for whom not arranging a marriage for a nubile daughter is equivalent to abortion.[136] But our argument so would lead us to reject this view. If one denies that to destroy a fertilised ovum is homicide, one will even more strongly reject the view that not to have a child which might have been—in the sense that the man could have fertilised an ovum and the woman had ova which could have been fertilised—is a form of homicide. Deliberately not to have sexual relations is, on the face of it, to have made a personal choice of a kind to which there is no moral objection.

(7) *Legislative enactments*. Let us suppose that my argument so far is correct, that there is no insuperable moral objection to the choice by individuals of any of the methods of population control I have described, except infanticide. There is still a problem to be faced. What if the question is not whether individuals can properly choose to restrict the number of children they should have, but whether the State has the right to *force* them to have no more than a fixed number of children?

This is a question we might hope to avoid as wholly speculative: family planning, we might argue, would suffice if it could be combined with other social changes affecting attitudes to marriage and childlessness. But this, so the reply might come, is too optimistic a view. Family planning is not enough: Ehrlich, indeed, heads a section of *The Population Bomb* 'family planning and other failures'. The family size which most people want and would be prepared to plan for is in most countries too large. And changes in attitudes to family size, if left to the pressure of public opinion, are altogether too slow and uncertain. The State, it is then concluded, must intervene, and decisively. That is part of its function as a trustee of resources.

Such intervention might take any of a variety of forms, each of them raising its own special moral issues.[137] At the simplest level, the State might content itself with offering incentives to its citizens to have small families. How far this would be effective is doubtful; about the degree of success of pro-natalist policies in post-war France and Russia and in pre-war Germany—so far as this is a guide to the success of policies with the opposite objective —there is considerable controversy. But we are concerned for the moment with the moral issues. There is, it might be thought, no such issue. No one raised moral objections to pro-natalist incentives: now circumstances have changed, why should they raise objections to anti-natalist incentives?

In so far as the State were to offer *pure* incentives, this might be true—if the State, for example, were to offer bonuses to couples who had no children, increasing in amount for each five years after marriage. But most 'incentives' which have actually been proposed are in fact disincentives: the withdrawal, let us say, of family allowances or maternity benefits or educational opportunities after the birth of a third child. And their effect is that *existing* children would suffer as a result of the fecklessness of their parents. Such pressures, too, are inevitably discriminatory; the wealthy can ignore financial incentives or disincentives, the poor cannot.

The moral objections multiply if we contemplate a situation in which the State would lay it down, as a law of the land, that no woman should have more than two children. Any such legislation is sometimes objected to on absolutist grounds. The parent, it is then argued—and behind this argument extends the authority of the United Nations Declaration of Human Rights—has an 'inalienable right' to determine how many children he or she will have. But a man, Ehrlich replies, no longer has the right, in most parts of the world, to determine how many wives he will have; there does not seem to be any good reason why, whatever happens, he *must* retain the right to decide how many children he will have.[138] While it is essential to the maintenance of a democracy, we might add, that every citizen shall have such rights as the right of free speech, the right of assembly, the right to participate in the political life of his community—within a democracy these rights are inalienable—it is not on the face of it in the same way essential that he retain the right to determine the number of his children.

We may more than doubt, however, whether any such policy, even although it is not in itself undemocratic, could be effectively enforced without the loss of democratic rights, whether it could be enforced except by exerting the full power of a police state. And what is to happen to those who conceive more than two children? (This is a difficulty, too, with Boulding's proposal that the State should issue licences for couples to have children, licences which could be bought or sold on the market.)[139] Is the woman to be aborted and the man sterilised? Such proposals have in fact been put forward in India. But they would involve a kind of assault on the person which, quite certainly, is morally objectionable. These, morally speaking, are the policies of last resort; I am not sure, even, that they are preferable to infanticide. It looks then as if the most the State can properly do is to adopt policies which offer positive incentives to small families. No doubt, if population pressures continue to grow, it will do a great deal more than this, at whatever cost to democratic and personal liberties. But that, once more, is an argument in favour of doing all we can to develop controls over population growth by other means.

As we have already seen, moral objections are sometimes raised even to educational programmes in favour of family planning, especially if they involve the public display of contraceptive methods. In part, this opposition rests on nothing more substantial than prudishness, in part—as the *Humanae Vitae* (article 17) makes perfectly clear—on the fact that contraception can be used by the unmarried as well as by the married. I find it difficult to take either of these moral objections seriously. But many people do; they can so limit the effectiveness of family-planning programmes as to make it hard to judge how effective these programmes would be under less limited circumstances.*

Obviously these are controversial issues, which I have dealt with more than a little dogmatically. One could not deal with them in any other way except by constructing an entire moral and political philosophy. But I think we can at least say this much: there is in the West, as also in the East, no formidable moral tradition which would suggest that it is wrong for the State or anybody else to try to *persuade* parents to have fewer or more children, or to offer them incentives for this purpose. The idea of *punishing* them for having more children is a much more controversial one. I cannot for myself see that it is incompatible with Western traditions of liberty, provided that it is introduced by due democratic processes, any more than it is incompatible with democracy to punish men for having two wives; it is not, however, to be lightly embarked upon because of its effects on already-born children. But the use of such methods of control as compulsory sterilisation would, it seems to me, threaten the Western tradition, however imperfectly it has been realised, of respect for persons.

To round off an argument which, as I read it through, offends me as much by its brevity as by its length, I should attempt to say something about the political feasibility of each method of reducing population growth and the administrative costs inherent in it. But the possibilities are so many, and so variable from culture to

---

* Just after I completed the chapter, it was reported from the Roman Catholic Philippines that a television family-planning programme was in full swing which involved showing different types of contraceptives and explaining their use. There could be no better indication of the way in which population pressures can break down pre-existing barriers, based on moral presumptions.

culture, that this task lies quite beyond my strength. Let me only say, on the matter of administrative costs, that they can be very heavy. Even if compulsory sterilisation were not morally objectionable in itself, the kind of policing it would entail, the lying, the informing, which it would bring in its train, constitute a formidable ground of objection to it. And other methods of State intervention have their costs, which ought not to be overlooked.

As for political feasibility, our ignorance is so great that it is very difficult to know what to say. Over the last few years, the state of opinion has changed with quite extraordinary rapidity. No one could have anticipated the degree to which the legalisation of abortion has come to be accepted in the Western world. In India, legislation to raise the legal age of marriage has met with great resistance, but has finally been effective. The religious obstacles to legislative action are in most parts of the world of diminishing importance. The most fundamental obstacles to control over population growth, or so I have suggested, are ideological factors like nationalism or the fear on the part of minorities of being numerically overwhelmed—and social habits. Whether, how far, and how rapidly these can be expected to change, no one can say with confidence. In general, a guarded optimism that the rate of growth will gradually decline is not totally irrational. But if one sets one's sights higher than this, if one looks, say, for a stabilisation of population growth much before the year 2200, the situation is very different. And whether in these circumstances free civilisations can survive none of us can know. There are limits to what we as a generation can do, and limits, too, to what we ought to attempt; our concern is not with the numbers of posterity as such but with their sensibility, their civilisation, their happiness. To surrender our freedom, to abandon all respect for persons, in the name of control over population growth is to make sacrifices which our proper concern for posterity cannot justify.[140]

Part Three

THE TRADITIONS RECONSIDERED

CHAPTER SEVEN   REMOVING THE RUBBISH

For me to claim that I have solved any of the world's ecological problems would be inconsistent with one of my central theses. For ecological problems, or so I have argued, can be solved only by the joint efforts of scientists, technologists, economists, statesmen, administrators. And a philosopher is none of these, let alone all of them conjointly. Then what have I done? To compare small things with great, I have sought, like John Locke, 'to be employed as an under-labourer in clearing ground a little and removing some of the rubbish that lies in the way to knowledge'—and, by way of knowledge, to effective action. Let me now look more consecutively at what I have tried to clear away.

First, mystical 'rubbish', the view that mysticism can save us, where technology cannot. Science and technology, democracy and free enterprise have always had their enemies; mysticism, primitivism, authoritarianism have always had their adherents. The ecologically-based protest—not only against shortsightedness and greed but, more fundamentally, against those attitudes to nature and society which are used to justify shortsightedness and greed—is, I have freely admitted, fully justified in itself. But it is being deployed as a new and powerful weapon in the old battle between rationality and mysticism, as when Fraser Darling tries to persuade us that the West can solve its ecological problems only by adopting 'the philosophy of wholeness', or 'the truth of Zoroastrianism . . . that we are all of one stuff, difference is only in degree, and God can be conceived as being in all and of all, the sublime and divine immanence'. (In the currently fashionable manner Darling turns to Zoroaster for what he could easily have found further West.) A moment later we find him urging us to 'exercise the ideal of our aristocratic nature, to be the servant of the planet to which we were born and to which we are still bound'.[1] His simultaneous appeal to immanence and aristocracy—his simultaneous assertion and denial, that is, of fundamental differences—is only too typical, in its intellectual incoherence, of the Western mystical tradition. And the ideal of the aristocrat who is also a servant—whether of God, of the people, or of the planet—is just as characteristic of authoritarianism. The 'philosophy of wholeness', as in classical German Idealism, serves to link the two: the 'total whole' is at once a social and a metaphysical absolute, in which the individual is totally submerged. Fraser Darling is not introducing a new element into Western civilisation; rather, he is trying to make dominant one of the most dangerous illusions to which it has been subject, the mystical, totalistic illusion. Against this attempt, I have particularly protested.

There are, of course, special reasons why ecology should so often have been thought of as being in essence mystical, as anti-scientific or as entailing 'a philosophy of wholeness'. The general tendency of Western science has been analytic, atomistic; it has explained large-scale behaviour in terms of the behaviour of particles. So classical soil-science analyses a clod of earth into a collection of molecules held together by physical forces. This way of looking at such a clod is of great importance in explaining, let us say, the behaviour of an area of land under the impact of heavy rain or of deep ploughing. The ecologist thinks of the land not as a set of clods but rather as an ingredient in an energy system, a larger whole. 'Land,' writes Aldo Leopold, 'is not merely soil; it is a fountain of energy flowing through a circuit of soils, plants, and animals. Food chains are the living channels which conduct energy upward; death and decay return it to the soil.'[2] Changes in the soil's fertility he explains by pointing to break-downs in such chains, such cycles. Similarly, whereas the atomistic biologist studies an organism as a system of cells—and, beyond that, of molecules—the ecologist looks at its place in a broader system, its habitat, and at the relationship between that organism-in-its-habitat and still wider systems.

That does not mean, however, that the ecologist can eschew laboratory studies. If he hopes to understand, let us say, the way in which mercuric salts are built up in the human organism, he needs to investigate *both* the nature of the food chain which enables mercuric salts deposited in an estuary to find their way into the brains of human beings *and* what happens in the tissues of each of the members of that food chain. Nor does the mere fact that the ecologist makes use of such concepts as energy cycles or food chains in any way suggest that ecology is supra-scientific.

This is a crucial point. Science is not *intrinsically* atomistic. It explains the behaviour of the tides, for example, by referring them to forces operating in the solar system. Sometimes, in order to explain a thing's behaviour, one needs only to look at the forms of activity which go on within it—or, as it would more commonly be put, at the particles which make it up; sometimes one needs to look, rather, at the wider forms of activity within which its own forms of activity go on. But, more often than not, one needs to look at both—explaining a person's behaviour, for example, partly in terms of his 'genetic constitution', the forms of activity he has inherited, partly in terms of the culture within which he was educated. He stammers, let us say, because he was born left-handed into a culture which demands right-handedness from its members.

No doubt, the ecologist's talk of chains and cycles may ring ancient bells by associative resonance; we think, perhaps, of the classical 'great chain of being' or of those cycles beloved by mystics—'a perpetual circle for the Good, from the Good, in the Good, and to the Good'.[3] But such associations are not justified by the actual procedures of ecologists. The 'wholes' in which ecology is interested are not mystical unities—my back garden could constitute an ecosystem—nor are they, although Fraser Darling suggests otherwise, the kind of metaphysical whole within which all differences are converted into differences in degree. Indeed, although ecology can be studied at a high level of abstractions in terms of energy transfers, one of its main contributions to human understanding lies in its emphasis on the importance of individual differences, the far-reaching consequences which can result from what at first sight appears to be a very slight change in the membership of a system. Only in so far as it has wrongly been supposed that science must be atomistic does the Western scientific tradition have any quarrel with the rise of ecology. This is not the sort of quarrel which can be resolved only by abandoning science in favour of mysticism.

Nor, to solve our ecological problems, are we forced once more to think of nature as sacred. That doctrine, too, 'lies in the way to knowledge'. So to revert, I have suggested, would be to go back on the whole tradition of Western science, perhaps the greatest of man's achievements. For to regard nature as sacred is to think of it in the manner the Jews and the Greeks deliberately rejected, as having a 'mysterious life' which it is improper, sacrilegious, to try to understand or control, a life we should submit to and worship.[4] Science, in contrast, converts mysteries into problems, to which it can hope to find solutions.

Such a reversion, furthermore, is neither necessary nor sufficient to save the biosphere. It is certainly not sufficient; societies for whom nature is sacred have nonetheless destroyed their natural habitation. A passage from Plato's *Critias* will illustrate this point. He is describing Attica: 'There are remaining only the bones of the wasted body, as they may be called . . . all the richer and softer parts of the soil having fallen away, and the mere skeleton of the land being left. But in the primitive state of the country, its mountains were high hills covered with soil, and the plains . . . were full of rich earth, and there was abundance of wood in the mountains.'[5] This decline, Plato tells us, is testified to by the fact that 'sacred memorials' remain at points, by his time dry, where once flowed rivers and streams. Man does not necessarily preserve, that is, the stream he has dedicated to a god; simple ignorance or greed can be as damaging as technological know-how. Nowhere, as we have said, is ecological destruction more apparent than in today's Japan, for all its tradition of nature-worship.

Indeed, to carry this argument further, the belief that nature is sacred can tell against attempts to preserve it. Just in virtue of its divinity, it may be argued, nature can be trusted to look after itself. Consider the case of Emerson. 'In the woods,' he tells us, 'we return to reason and faith.' 'There,' he continues, 'I feel that nothing can befall me in life,—no disgrace, no calamity . . . which nature cannot repair; . . . the currents of the Universal Being circulate through me; I am part or parcel of God.'[6] Yet Emerson was indulgent towards the plunderers of the American countryside then making their way to the American West. 'The recuperative powers of Nature' were, in his eyes, a sufficient guarantee that the self-reliance he admired would not issue in final devastation.[7] A nature which can heal men can surely heal itself, a nature that is divine men cannot destroy. To take our ecological crises seriously, so I have constantly argued, is to recognise, first, man's utter dependence on nature, but secondly, nature's vulnerability to human depredations—the *fragility*, that is, of both man and nature, for all their notable powers of recuperation. And this means that neither man nor nature is sacred or quasi-divine.*

There is more than a little paradox in the view, when it comes from ecologically-minded preservationists, that we need to revert to older, mystical attitudes to nature. For ecology, however much some of those who praise ecology would like to persuade us otherwise, is a serious scientific attempt, dependent on the aid of such technological innovations as the computer, to understand what scientists still find mysterious—the ways in which populations respond to environmental fluctuations. This manner of looking at ecology is unpopular with those, like Theodore Roszak, who hoped that ecology would replace scientific analysis by 'a new science in which the object of knowledge will be rather like the poet's beloved: something to be contemplated but not analysed, something that is permitted to retain its mysteries'.[8] But if Roszak and his counter-cultural followers are disappointed to discover that ecology is after all another branch of science, that it

* It may be true that in hunting societies—the example most often cited—the belief that nature is sacred and animals are capable of understanding served in some measure as a protection against the destruction of species. (Although man the hunter, it would now seem, was largely responsible for the disappearance of a great many of the large mammals—the giant kangaroo in Australia, the moa in New Zealand, the woolly mammoth in North America.) But as matters stand, such beliefs are not merely so out of harmony with our traditions that to attempt to revive them would be to attempt the impossible; they simply would not serve.

dispels mysteries, many of us see in that fact, rather, a demonstration that Western science is still fecund, still capable of contributing to the solution of the problems which beset human beings, even when they are problems of the scientist's own making.

That science is still so fecund is just as well, seeing that, as I have often had occasion to remark, ignorance is one of the most potent obstacles to our solving our ecological problems, an ignorance which only science can dispel. No doubt, the modern West has more knowledge at its disposal than has had any previous society. But it has neither the kind nor the degree of knowledge which it now needs. Our knowledge of the ways in which societies work is not at all comparable in extent with our knowledge of the workings, let us say, of the planetary system; we know little about the atmosphere, the seas, the life cycles of the scarcely numerable varieties of plant and animal life. While absolutely speaking we know a great deal, we are proportionally ignorant, proportionally in relation to what we need to know. The farmer tilling his fields by conventional methods and living in a traditional society did not need to know a great deal. But the task we have now to undertake, in attempting to estimate the long-term effects of our actions both on the biosphere and on human societies, is so immense that in relation to it our ignorance is almost total.

To correct this situation may well require, I am fully prepared to admit, a minor revolution within science. The scientist will be forced, in the unenthusiastic words of one of my scientific colleagues, 'to slosh about in that primordial ooze known as interdisciplinary studies'. He will need to pay more respect to such scientists as work outside laboratories. There is a pecking-order in science; almost everybody pecks the 'natural historian'. The field naturalist is unlikely to find himself awarded a Nobel Prize or even a Fellowship of the Royal Society. But there are already signs that such a revolution is under way, if still very tentatively.* Field studies are beginning to regain something of their previous status—Darwin did not, after all, work in a laboratory—and more and more distinguished scientists are at least dipping their fingers into the 'primordial ooze'. To say that science has need of new directions, however, is one thing, to say that the West ought to abandon its hard-won tradition of critical investigation is quite another; that tradition it needs more than ever before.

What about the view, so often associated with science and

* One of the most significant examples that has come my way is A. B. Pippard's Inaugural Lecture as Cavendish Professor of Physics in the University of Cambridge. It is time, he there suggests, for scientists to turn their attention 'towards the difficult and less elegant phenomena of the real physical world' in contrast with their past concentration on simpler and more elegant natural laws. Coming from a Cavendish Professor, that is really something. See A. B. Pippard: *Reconciling Physics with Reality* (Cambridge, 1972).

technology, that man is master of the world? Must not that at least, if not science itself, be abandoned? Man's dominion can be understood, I have suggested, in a number of different ways, varying in their degree of 'arrogance'. On the minimal interpretation, it 'licenses' men to sustain themselves by making use, in the manner of any other animal, of what they find around them. Or, to drop the confusing quasi-legal talk of 'licences', 'dominion', 'rights', talk of which we have had more than enough, it says that there is nothing morally wrong in men's behaving in this way. Even thus interpreted it is rejected by the sterner ascetics, by, for example, the third-century neo-Platonist Porphyry, who would restrict the diet of such men as hope to perfect themselves to those fruits which plants do not need for reproduction.[9] (This is at least an improvement on the sole bill of fare permitted, on similar grounds, by Samuel Butler's *Erewhon* prophets—rotting fruit and decaying cabbage leaves.) But wherever the boundaries are drawn, I have argued, we can certainly say this much: man can live at all only as a predator, whether on plants or animals. And in order to establish a civilisation he has to go beyond this point; he has to domesticate herds or plant crops and must so far act as lord and master over at least a segment of nature. In so far as he necessarily acts in this way, it is pointless to suggest that man should do *nothing* to disturb existing ecological systems, should *in no sense* attempt to master them.

At the opposite extreme, 'lordship over nature' is interpreted as entailing that nature is wax in man's hands. Interpreted thus, I have agreed, it must certainly be rejected. Indeed, it was never plausible. Cicero's Balbus, boasting that as a result of their navigational inventions men had now mastered the wind and the waves, had never experienced, so much is clear, the force of a tropical cyclone. Even now, in claiming mastery over nature, men are whistling to keep their courage up. If their science, once converted into technology, enables them to control their immediate natural environment more effectively than can any other animal, it also constantly reminds them, as Karl Popper has particularly emphasised, of what they cannot do. As ecology has now sufficiently demonstrated, the doctrine that nature is infinitely malleable is not merely an illusion—comforting, perhaps, to human beings in their helplessness and encouraging to them in their aspirations—but a dangerous delusion.

An intermediate interpretation, however, can be framed thus: men, uniquely, are capable of transforming the world into a civilised state; that is their major responsibility to their fellow-men. The virtues of civilisation, no doubt, are now sometimes questioned. Once more the 'noble savage' hunts his ecological way through intellectual drawing-rooms. Hsün Tzu's advice to his Chinese contemporaries:

> You glorify nature and meditate on her
> Why not domesticate her and regulate her?
> You depend on things and marvel at them:
> Why not unfold your own ability and transform them?

finds itself reversed, as advice to the West:

> You have domesticated nature and regulated her
> Why not glorify her and meditate on her?
> You have unfolded your own ability and transformed things:
> Why not depend on them and marvel at them?

This would, indeed, be the 'great refusal', the rejection of all that man has discovered he can achieve. No doubt, the West needs more fully to realise that it 'depends on things' and so far to 'meditate on' and even to 'glorify' nature. But it cannot now turn back, my argument has constantly suggested, even if it were desirable that it should do so; only by transforming nature can it continue to survive. There is no good ground, either, for objecting to transformation as such; it can make the world more fruitful, more diversified, and more beautiful.

If we ask, indeed, what human beings add to the world by their presence in it, there is, I should say, only one possible reply: civilisation. Were it not for his ability to civilise, man would be no more than a predator amongst the rest, more powerful, more aggressive, more violent, more skilful in capturing his prey but in no other respects superior, and in many respects inferior, to the prey he hunts. And man's great memorials—his science, his philosophy, his technology, his architecture, his countryside—are all of them founded upon his attempt to understand and subdue nature. Through their struggles with nature men have discovered their potentialities and developed those forms of enterprise which constitute their civilisation. I have included the countryside in the list of man's memorials, because even the landscapes we now so greatly admire—the landscapes of Tuscany or of England or of Kyushu—are largely the creation of human enterprise, of human struggles. When Cowper wrote 'God made the country; man made the town', he was simply mistaken. The eighteenth-century English countryside Cowper knew and loved was largely of human creation. (What god, for the matter of that, would not be proud of having created eighteenth-century Bath?) That is what, however obscurely, Hegel and his followers saw, and passed on to the

Marxists. It is not merely out of arrogance that men think of themselves as having a 'duty to subdue nature'; it is only they who can create. So far, and only so far, they can rightfully claim 'dominion over nature'.

Nor, however implausible the doctrine that nature exists only to serve man, is there any objection to the weaker view, to which Descartes subscribes, that whatever exists in nature is of some use to us. This is not, as it might at first seem to be, an empirical hypothesis, for there is no way of falsifying it. It always remains possible that something will turn out to be useful which we have cast aside as useless. But it can act as a guiding principle, encouraging men to look for uses in unexpected places, discouraging the destruction of what might eventually turn out to be of vital importance to them. In that form, it should certainly not be cast aside as 'rubbish'.

The danger in destroying is, of course, a point on which the ecological critics have particularly insisted. And quite clearly one has to concede, as Ehrlich puts it, that 'any tinkering with an ecosystem may result in unforeseen and deleterious consequences'.[10] But, as we have repeatedly had occasion to note, man has had no option but to live dangerously. If he had let himself be too alarmed by the fact that, in a certain sense, he does not know what he is doing, he would never have ventured beyond his immediate environment. Nor would he, certainly, ever have embarked on the domestication of animals, let alone agriculture or industry. Indeed, if we follow to its logical conclusion Ehrlich's description of man as a dangerous tinkerer, we can scarcely stop short of that picture of man's relationships with nature composed at the very end of the nineteenth century by W. S. Blunt, the ecologist's poet-laureate.*

Here is 'unspoiled Nature' as Blunt sees it:

> Thou dost remember, Lord, the glorious
>   World it was,
> The beauty, the abundance, the unbroken face
> Of undulent forest spread without or rent or seam
> Thy lakes, Thy floods, Thy marshes, tameless,
>   unbetrayed,
> All virgin of the spoiler, all inviolate,
> In beauty undeflowered, where fear was not nor hate.

And here is man, that 'lewd bare-buttocked ape':

---

* This poem, Blunt tells us, was 'written to some extent in collaboration with the late Herbert Spencer'. It sounds like it.

Man the senseless knave
Who struck fire from his flint to burn
Thy gorses brave,
Thy heaths for his lean kine, who, being
the one unclean,
Defiled Thy flower-sweet Earth with ordure
heaps obscene,
To plant his rice, his rye.[11]

But the virtues of civilisation, many of us would wish to argue, are not to be so lightly set aside. It is one thing to recognise that human action has unintended consequences; quite another to suggest that man is nothing but the defiler of nature. Lewd he often is, no doubt, but the bareness of his buttocks is not the only thing which distinguishes him from the ape; if the 'glorious world' of Blunt's imagination was a world without hate—although scarcely, as he suggests, without fear—it was also a world without love, without art, without science, without philosophy, with no Venice, no Nara, no Salzburg.* These are as much consequences of man's 'tinkering' as are 'ordure heaps obscene'. That we ought to attempt to try to preserve the spirit that creates them, I shall not even bother to argue.

It is a much more particular assumption, however, that the democratic institutions, the spirit of enterprise, the liberal attitude, characteristic of the modern West are worth preserving and maintaining. That requires separate argument. No one with any knowledge of history could have any illusions about Western civilisation, modern or ancient, with its record of violence, cruelty, fanaticism, puritanism and avarice. What is particularly tragic is the way in which the best and the worst have so often gone together, as the history of Florence from the thirteenth to the fifteenth century vividly exemplifies. Everything was there, genius in literature, painting, sculpture, science; cruelty and violence of the lowest, least forgivable, kind; even the egalitarian terrorism of Giano della Bella. But it remains true, I believe, that

---

* Ian McHarg, in a much-reprinted paper rhetorically entitled 'Is man a planetary disease?', is prepared to lay it down that 'Algae know about creativity but man does not'. There is no depth of masochistic nonsense to which in their moods of self-denigration men will not descend. In Roeg's 1970 film *Walkabout* not man in general but only civilised man is diagnosed as a disease. The gentle self-reliant aborigine is contrasted with civilised men and women who are cruel, cold, mean-spirited, sexually repressed, devoted only to their possessions, utterly ruthless. Western art is depicted as childish play, its science as trivialities in a desert, its literature as a rambling story at once pointless and cruel, its education system as a training in futile snobberies, its industry as rusted *débris*, its technology as an instrument of slaughter, its mathematics as empty formulae. If this indictment—or the picture of civilisation in Godard's *Weekend*—is at all points justified then, certainly, I should have no policy to advocate except mass suicide. The alternative—the hunting savage—arouses in my heart no enthusiasm whatsoever.

nowhere outside Western civilisation have men so often risen to such great heights. This by no means implies that cultures which are not Western in type are valueless. No one who has even the slightest acquaintance whether with their cultural achievements or their social structures could possibly take that view. In its dealings with other cultures, I should freely grant, the West has often shown itself at its arrogant, bigoted, greedy worst. But neither the simple sensualities of Tahiti nor the complex ritual of ancient Japan enabled the human spirit to expand to its fullest extent. A craftsman, a certain type of artist, might have found in such a society all that he needed, but a philosopher, a scientist, a dramatist, would not. The West has not conquered the world solely by the force of its arms or the flashier attractions of its consumer goods. The richness and diversity of Western culture even a country like Japan has found profoundly stimulating, for all the importance of its own achievements.

One of the more fashionable forms of contemporary cant condemns as 'racialist' —now an all-encomposing form of abuse— the description of any form of society as 'higher' or 'more advanced' or 'better' than any other. No doubt, as I have granted, a less 'advanced' society can possess virtues which a more 'advanced' society lacks. The fact remains that there are familiar and quite proper ways of grading societies: in terms of the diversity of their culture, their humanitarianism, the degree of liberty they offer their citizens. By any of these criteria the liberal democratic West stands high. (Nor will it do to reply that this is not surprising, since the West invented these criteria. What other criteria are we offered?) Its range of cultural achievements in science, in philosophy, in art, is unequalled; few of its citizens starve in the streets or live by exhibiting their deformities; never before has personal liberty been so widely diffused. If we judge modern Western democracies imperfect this is only by applying to them those absolute standards which the West has taught us. We take it for granted that they contain no Untouchables, no Etas; we condemn them, quite rightly, because they still discriminate against certain of their members, still confine personal liberty by absurd and pointless laws, still do not adequately educate their citizens, still do not do all that they might to help those—inside or outside their territories—whose life is nasty, brutish and short. If the liberal democracies collapse, this will be because they have aroused in their citizens aspirations which no society will ever completely satisfy, not because those aspirations are worthless.* To *seek* their

* It is very misleading, of course, to speak of the 'West' in a monolithic way. I have often been told, if I wrote in modified praise of Western civilisation, that I have forgotten Newark and New York. The tragedy of New York no one could forget; that city and its inhabitants

destruction, with whatever noble aims in mind, is to attempt to destroy the only sort of society which has ever come near to fulfilling those aspirations.

The view that ecological problems are more likely to be solved in an authoritarian than in any such a liberal democratic society rests on the implausible assumption that the authoritarian state would be ruled by ecologist-kings. In practice, there is more hope of action in democratic societies. In the United States, particularly, the habit of local action, the capacity of individuals to initiate legal procedings, the tradition of public disclosure, are powerful weapons in the fight against ecological destruction. The democratic states should rather be condemned, I have suggested, when they are tempted into exactly the same vices as the totalitarian states: spying, soothing utterances from central authorities, face-saving, bureaucratic inertia, censorship, concealment.*

What about the metaphysical outlook characteristic of the West? That, I have tried to show, is exceptionally complex and diversified, by no means to be summed up as the view that nature is wax in man's hands. Nor is the West, I should add, irrevocably committed to that Aristotelian-type metaphysics for which nature consists of substances with distinct properties, each of which can be separately modified without altering anything else. One of the most important alternative suggestions, dating back in essence to Heraclitus, is that the world consists of complex systems of interacting processes varying in their stability. Each such system—of which a human being is one—can survive, like a flame, only so long as it can interact with surrounding systems in certain particular ways, drawing upon and giving out to the systems around it. It can die by choking on its own wastes or because it has exhausted its resources. That way of looking at the world, which ecological investigations help to substantiate, makes it perfectly plain why 'You can't do one thing at a time'; it destroys, too, the belief that human beings are somehow different, outside the eco-system, whether as villainous intruders or heroic manipulators. But it

---

should be preserved for eternity in plasticised aspic as a memorial to the grandeur and the misery of the human condition. Newark, I confess, but seldom crosses my mind, less often than, let us say, Aarhus. Why should it? But Newark is no more typical of the West than is Calcutta of India or Osaka of Japan. I see no reason for believing, either, that it shows the West, as in a science-fiction mirror, what it is certain to become. Indeed, it is reminiscent of the eighteenth century rather than prophetic of the twenty-first. In many fundamental respects, America is a very old-fashioned country.

* In so far as the ecological movement necessarily involves a critique of the creeping bureaucratisation so characteristic of our society, it has a social and political importance extending well beyond its immediate ecological ends; in so far as its practical policies would tend to encourage that bureaucratisation, it represents a social danger. For not only are man and nature fragile, so too is liberal civilisation, as the tragic history of inter-war Germany so vividly reminds us.

does so in a manner not in the least mystical, not in the least anti-scientific in spirit, not in the least implying that there is something intrinsically wrong with any attempt to make the world a better place.

On such a view man's uniqueness is not metaphysical; it lies, like the peculiarities of a flame, in the special character of his relations with other systems, his ability deliberately to transform them. Christians have thought otherwise. Ecological critics of the West are justified in arguing that Christianity has encouraged man to think of himself as metaphysically unique, as supernaturally above, rather than naturally immersed in, the ebb and flow of processes. What is ecologically dangerous in Christianity, indeed, is not that it denies the sacredness of nature but that it encourages men to believe that they are 'sons of God' and therefore secure, their continued existence on earth guaranteed by God. So far it encourages *hubris*; it makes of nature something which can be ravaged with impunity. Man, it must certainly be recognised, has no tenure in the biosphere.

Christian theology, however, has in the past proved itself to be remarkably flexible. Theologians are now busily attempting to work out new attitudes to nature, still consonant in a general way with traditional Christianity but reverting in important respects to a prelapsarian conception of man and man's role and denying that men have a 'sacredness' which animals do not possess.[12] For my part I more than doubt whether Christian theology can thus reshape itself without ceasing to be distinctively Christian, whether it can bring itself to deny, in the light of its central theology, either that man is *metaphysically* unique—as a soul to be saved—or that in the end his survival is *metaphysically* guaranteed.* Only if men see themselves, I should rather argue, for what they are, quite alone, with no one to help them except their fellow-men, products of natural processes which are wholly indifferent to their survival, will they face their ecological problems in their full implications. Not by the extension, but by the total rejection, of the concept of the sacred will they move towards that sombre realisation.

The rejection of Christianity by no means immediately entails, however, the acceptance of a doctrine more conscious of human limitations, as is sufficiently obvious both in the Soviet Union and

---

* Much stress is now laid, however, on Paul's 'the whole creation groaneth and travaileth in pain together until now' (Rom. VII: 22). This is taken to imply that not only man but the whole creation anticipates salvation. There have for long been those, indeed, who expect immortality for animals, although no one in the West, perhaps, has gone so far as those Eastern teachers for whom even a blade of grass can aspire to Buddhahood. Christianity would be wholly transformed, however, were it to be supposed that cats and dogs were as much 'sons of God' as are human beings and are called upon in the same way to seek after salvation.

contemporary China. Nothing could be more ecologically damaging than the Hegelian-Marxist doctrine that nature, before man operates upon it, is mere potentiality. Two traditional attitudes are, I suggested, more promising—the first, that man should think of himself as a steward; the second, that in his attempts to transform nature he should cooperate with it. The 'stewardship' attitude is often said to be peculiarly Christian; this I have denied. It is linked rather with the idea that man forms part of a chain of improvement, that he has responsibilities to those who come after him, responsibilities arising out of his attempt to preserve and develop what he loves. In its fullest implications this is a peculiarly Western and modern concept, dating back to Kant. Its ecological importance is manifest.

As for the view that man should co-operate with nature, this cannot, of course, be taken literally. Nature is not a semi-divine entity with aims which human beings can share. Against any such an interpretation, Robert Boyle rightly protested. Interpreted less literally, however, it suggests, as we have already seen, a policy of ecological wisdom: to try to control pests by diversifying crops rather than by insecticides, to construct tourist hotels so that they make use of, rather than cut across, existing drainage contours, to grow what can be grown with least damage to the countryside. And so on, modestly but effectively. Read thus, it is by no means rubbish.

To accept it does not commit us, however, to Barry Commoner's 'third law of ecology'—'nature knows best'.[13] It is true enough— as, like Ehrlich, Commoner argues—that every human intervention in an ecosystem is likely to disturb the workings of that system in a way that is detrimental to some member of it. So much is true of every change, man-induced or nature-induced. But it by no means follows, as his 'law' might seem to suggest, that every such change, or even most such changes, will be detrimental to *human beings*. Unlike the watches to which he compares them, ecological systems were not designed for man's use. When men picked seeds off plants and sowed them on cleared ground, they acted in a way that was detrimental to the organic life which was accustomed to feed on the fallen seeds. But only the most unreconstructed primitivist would suggest that the actions of our agricultural forefathers were destructive of human interests. A nature left entirely alone as 'knowing best' would support only the dreariest and most monotonous of lives. Even the primitive hunter found it necessary to burn; the fires he lit have transformed the face of the earth.[14]

It is, indeed, absurd to suggest that man can find in nature, at hand for his taking, all that he needs to live a good life. So much, in principle, the authors of Genesis saw: nature has its 'thorns and thistles' which man has no option but to root out. In his essay on 'Nature', J. S. Mill mounts a general attack on the injunction that men ought to 'cooperate with nature'. 'Her powers,' as Mill puts it, 'are often towards man in the position of enemies, from whom he must wrest, by force and ingenuity, what little he can for his own use'.[15] One may well warm to the enthusiasm with which Mill attacks the more sentimental nature-lovers. Anyone who lives on the inhospitable shores of Australia will certainly appreciate his feelings. To think of nature as an 'enemy', however, is not the alternative to thinking of it as a 'friend'. Natural processes, as I have constantly emphasised, go on in their own way, indifferent to human interests. But we shall do best to learn how they operate, not supposing that they will immediately respond to our whims or miraculously suspend their modes of operation so as to permit us harmlessly to convert rainforests into agricultural lands or rivers into sewers.

What of the view that the West now needs not only a new concept of nature but a new set of moral principles to act as a guide in its relationships with nature? That, I have argued, is not entirely wrong-headed. During most of the West's history, as we have observed, its moral philosophers, Stoic or Christian, denied that man's relationship with nature is governed by any moral considerations whatsoever. From Montaigne onwards, however, to say nothing of his neo-Platonic predecessors, sceptics and humanists took a different view. And by the end of the eighteenth century, as I have pointed out, even Christians began to argue, although often against fierce opposition from their co-religionists, that callousness towards animal suffering was morally wrong. Nor is cruelty to animals a unique instance of such a change of heart. Well over a hundred years ago an editorial writer in the Melbourne *Age*—and newspaper editorials are not given to moral innovations—could assert that 'he who cuts down a tree unnecessarily is a criminal'. One has only to look at some regions of England, or France, or Italy, to see that, as much as in Japan, the land, for all the hardship involved in working it, has been loved. As Leopold recognised, there are 'seeds' in the West of the morality he advocates in which the active cherishing of nature is accounted good and its wanton destruction evil, even if it would be unsafe to assume, with Victor Hugo, that such a new morality will *inevitably* come to dominate the West.

The traditional moral teaching of the West, Christian or utilitarian, has always taught men, however, that they ought not so to act as to injure their neighbours. And we have now discovered that the disposal of wastes into sea or air, the destruction of ecosystems, the procreation of large families, the depletion of resources, constitute injury to our fellow-men, present and future. To that extent, conventional morality, without any supplementation whatsoever, suffices to justify our ecological concern, our demand for action against the polluter, the depleter of natural resources, the destroyer of species and wildernesses.

One of my colleagues, an ardent preservationist, condemns me as a 'human chauvinist'. What he means is that in my ethical arguments, I treat human interests as paramount. I do not apologise for that fact; an 'ethic dealing with man's relation to land and to the plants and animals growing on it' would not only be about the behaviour of human beings, as is sufficiently obvious, but would have to be justified by reference to human interests. The land which a bad farmer allows to slip into a river did not have a 'right' to stay where it was. The supposition that anything but a human being has 'rights' is, or so I have suggested, quite untenable.

This insistence on the primacy of human interest does not imply, however, that the only question at issue is whether someone's *income* will decline as a result of the silting of the river. The silting of a sparkling river, the replacement of a forested slope by an eroded hillside, is a loss to mankind even if it does not lessen anyone's income. To cause it to happen constitutes an act of vandalism, the destruction of something worth enjoying for its own sake. Only in so far as Western moralists have suggested otherwise, have suggested that no form of human activity has any value unless it involves a direct relationship with God or, for moralists of a more secular cast of mind, a relationship to a narrowly conceived economic prosperity, can the West plausibly be said to need a 'new ethic'. What it needs, for the most part, is not so much a 'new ethic' as a more general adherence to a perfectly familiar ethic.

For the major sources of our ecological disasters—apart from ignorance—are greed and short-sightedness, which amount to much the same thing. (The greedy man pursues the object of his greed in a manner which is indifferent to the means employed and to the wider consequences of his pursuit. The short-sighted man, more commonly described as 'practical', displays that special form of indifference to consequences which refuses to look beyond the present or the immediate future.) There is no novelty in the view that greed is evil; no need of a new ethic to tell us as much.

Our society, however, has officially denounced greed while in practice subscribing to Horace's maxim: 'By right means if you can, but by any means make money.' (Just as it officially denounces violence while in fact admiring it, glorying in it—as its favourite forms of literature make perfectly clear—except when it is employed by those it condemns on other grounds.) To tell men that they must now moderate their zeal for possessions, must give up what have been highly profitable pursuits, must surrender established economic rights, is to risk condemnation as a fanatic. No doubt it is formally recognised that there are ways of making money that are not entirely virtuous. But even the successful thief often excites admiration rather than contumely; the most devastating of land-developers may hope to be rewarded, in British countries, with such signs of public esteem as a knighthood. As the young Marx once wrote, 'money is the jealous God of Israel before whom no other god may exist'—and the worship of it, as he also argued, has given birth to an 'actual contempt for and practical degradation of nature'.[16] It is not 'rubbish' to suggest that our society actually, although not in its explicitly-enunciated moral principles, does honour to violence, short-sightedness and greed. What this brings out, once more, is that new modes of behaviour are much more important than new moral principles.

I am not, when I condemn greed, condemning the making of money—that would be like a eunuch condemning sexual intercourse. All I am condemning is the view that every pursuit is valuable just in so far as it is a way of making money or that money-making is the rational norm in comparison with which all other pursuits are irrational and abnormal. Every free society has been a commercial society, and the connection is not a merely accidental one. But certainly there is little hope for us unless we can moderate our desire to possess.* We shall do so, however, only if we can learn to be more sensuous in our attitude to the world, more ready to enjoy the present moment for itself, as an object of immediate pleasure, instead of frenetically seeking the power and security that possessions offer.

It is at this point that the moral outlook of the West is not merely inadequate but dangerous—in virtue of the puritanism it inherited from Augustine and, beyond Augustine, from Plato. We have already seen how, for example, this puritanism adversely affects the prospects for population control, by restricting the publicising of birth control methods and by condemning all sexual relationships which do not have procreation as their aim. But the more general puritan attack on sensuousness, its denial that the enjoyment of sensual pleasures for their own sake can ever be right and proper, has also had, as we have also suggested, more widespread, less obvious, ecological consequences. Admittedly, one

---

* The 'we' in this sentence is not that patronising 'we' which means 'everybody except me and the enlightened few I am addressing'. It means all of us: 'You! hypocrite lecteur!—mon semblable,—mon frère'.

has only to look back on the art, the architecture, the literature, the man-made landscapes, the townscapes, of our Western past to observe that the puritanic tradition has never wholly destroyed, even in the West, man's sensuous delight in the surfaces of things, in sights and smells, in sounds and tastes and touches. But it is as if the smoke of the industrial revolution had destroyed men's eyes, ears, noses and sense of touch, or as if only by seizing upon and making their own the familiar tenets of what had been a minority puritanism could men justify the ugliness which they were creating around them. A more sensuous society could never have endured the desolate towns, the dreary and dirty houses, the uniquely ugly chapels, the slag heaps, the filthy rivers, the junk yards which constitute the 'scenery' of the post-industrial West and which it has exported to the East. Only if men can first learn to look sensuously at the world will they learn to care for it. Not only to look at it, but to touch it, smell it, taste it. As we said, Plato—like every other authoritarian, like Stalin and Skinner in our own century, like the Protestant Church (legate in its own eyes of an authoritarian deity)—severely condemns the sensuous man, the lover of sights and sounds. And one must grant to him that a purely sensuous life, in which sensuousness is never kindled into love, love with the responsibility and care it brings in its train, is impoverished, sub-human and incapable by itself of solving ecological, or any other, problems. But, on the other side, the attempt to be 'super-human' by rising totally above sensuousness issues, as I have elsewhere argued in more detail, in a way of life no less impoverished, no less sub-human, and is utterly destructive, into the bargain, of man-nature relationships.*

The traditions I have so far explored, whether with sympathy or antipathy, have a long history. I have said almost nothing as yet about a factor which many would regard as far more ecologically significant than metaphysical principles and moral ideas—industrial growth. I cannot conclude without considering, however inadequately, the problems it raises. Industrial growth is a new phenomenon and the attitudes of mind it has generated, however powerfully, are still so new that it is somewhat odd to call them traditions. It is only very recently that nations have boasted of their Gross National Product, that a society has condemned itself, or been condemned, because its per capita growth rate is low, that

* Only a Canute who took his courtiers seriously and pretended to sweep back the tide by sweeping with the ebb would think it necessary to defend sensuality, I shall no doubt be told, in so 'permissive' an age. But permissiveness is not necessarily sensuous. More often than not, it takes the form of obscenity—a sub-variety of violence (who has ever seen a sensuous American film?)—or of grossness as in the Berlin of the 'Thirties, with those female mud-wrestlers and transvestite sexual grotesqueries so vividly depicted in Fosse's film version of *Cabaret*. In spirit, both obscenity and grossness are Augustinian. Remember, too, that 'sensuous' does not mean 'sexual'. For more on the importance and the limits of sensuality see *The Perfectibility of Man*.

consumers have come to expect an endless flow of new types of product, that industry has been geared to meet the needs of an affluent society. Here, many would say, lies the real crux of our problem. The changes of heart to which I have drawn attention—the intimations of a new, more considerate attitude to nature—are, on this view, of no fundamental importance. It is the crudest sort of sentimentalism—rubbish, my critics would say—to see in the spectacle of Boy Scouts collecting bottles or 'conservation' groups preventing the construction of this or that freeway anything more than a middle-class game. At best the participants in such enterprises are like children constructing a sand barrier to protect their castle from the tide-turned sea. At worst they distract attention from the fundamental issues. For what is at fault, so it is said, is the total system, the scientific-technological-industrial complex on which the middle-class reformers depend for their livelihood and their social position.

This is one of the points where I find myself least certain of my ground. The issues involved are so large, so complex, so difficult that I can do little more than raise them. To what degree is the further emancipation of the human spirit, in the East as well as in the West, inevitably tied up with the advance of industry? Can resources safely be diverted from industrial development to less-despoiling tertiary activities? Can industries be cabined and confined without undermining the spirit of enterprise which has brought them to birth? On the face of it, one can no doubt reply that the historical connections between industry and freedom are not inevitable. There can be heavy industry, as in Russia, where there is little or no freedom; neither Greek democracy nor the Enlightenment came into being within a highly industrialised society. There are good reasons for believing, furthermore, that the emergence of large industrial complexes represents a threat to, rather than a necessary condition of, the further emancipation of mankind. Yet one is still left uneasy about our capacity, without destroying liberty, effectively to redeploy our forces.

Not uncommonly, we are told that what has to be abandoned is the ideal, much loved by politicians, of economic growth. This concept, however, is far from being a perspicuous one, and its ambiguities are of first importance. If economic growth is defined as the more effective utilisation of scarce resources, better economising, then what is commonly described as economic growth may in fact be economic recession. Let us take a simple case. A park is built over to provide new office areas. The park had made available such scarce commodities in an urban context as space, light, quiet, air, the sight and smell of flowers and trees and shrubs. Should not the construction of such buildings count as economic recession and the reverse process, the destruction of buildings to construct parks, as economic growth?

Not, no doubt, if growth is measured in terms of the Gross National Product, as this is conventionally defined. And this means that the supposition that the Gross National Product is a satisfactory measure of the quality of a society's life must certainly be abandoned; there is something wrong with any measure which suggests that it constitutes 'economic growth' when parks, shops, hotels, theatres, neighbourhoods, are destroyed in order to substitute banks and insurance offices. But throughout the developed world, in Japan as well as the United States, attempts are being made to find a better index of economic growth than the Gross National Product—'an amenities index', or a 'stock index', which would take into account the destruction of amenities and natural resources as well as the flow-through of goods. The problems of constructing such an index are manifold; we have already touched on some of them. It is so much easier to quantify and compare the value of marketable goods than it is to compare the loss in amenity arising out of the destruction of a park with the economic gains from the offices which have taken its place.

Even presuming, however, that a solution can be found to this technical problem, we have still to ask whether our society can *afford* to substitute parks for office buildings, or more generally to reduce its Gross National Product. (It must be remembered that population is bound for some time to increase.) This is a point in respect to which some conservationists are remarkably insouciant. 'By the use of such specious arguments as the loss of jobs, the lowering of living standards, and the raising of prices,' one of them has written of the anti-ecologists, 'they are endeavouring to turn the citizen away from those who are striving to save a viable environment for future generations'.[17] But the spectacle of an unemployed man or an old-age pensioner faced by rising prices is at least as pitiable as the spectacle of an oil-soaked mutton bird. Arguments which direct attention to economic costs are not necessarily 'specious'.

On the other side, the question now is whether the liberal-democratic West can afford *not* to cut down its industrial activity or, at the very least, to alter its direction. We can perhaps speak of an 'ecological transition', a point at which a country's industrial activity reduces rather than enhances the quality of life of its citizens, at which increased industrial activity, at least in its conventional forms, is profitable only when its costs are estimated by grossly inadequate methods of accounting, accounting which entirely ignores the public squalor it creates. Its citizens have a

per capita income more than enough to permit them to live enjoyable lives, so far as that capacity depends on income; they have
a national product sufficient to support adequate social services.
Sweden, Japan, the United States, to take only three examples,
have all passed that point; they can afford to devote part of their
income to the solution of their ecological problems and to
compensate, by way of better social services, for the resulting
increases in prices. Whether they will do so is, of course, quite a
different matter. But in fact their rate of population growth is
already moving towards zero; to varying degrees, Japan more
slowly, they are introducing sharp-toothed legislation against
pollution; they are at least more aware than they were of the need
to preserve wildernesses and wild species. Their middle-class
ecological reformers reflect rather than disguise deep social forces.
It is not absurd to hope that they may be able to find the resources
to solve their major ecological problems.

One difficulty is to avoid the costs of industrial slow-downs,
or re-deployment, from falling very unevenly. It is not the
reformers who would lose their jobs if, to take a very minor
proposal, regulations were introduced which made it illegal for
automobile companies to change their models except in so far as
by so doing they saved resources or diminished pollution. No
doubt, every citizen might have to meet increased taxation. But
that is nothing compared with seeing one's entire mode of life
vanish overnight. It is cruel foolishness to suggest that people
would be perfectly content to turn their lathes into pitchforks.

So far we have looked at changes in the rate of industrial growth
only from the point of view of developed countries. But it could
also greatly affect the developing countries, whose conviction that
they would bear the brunt of any attempt on the part of Western
nations to solve the world's ecological problems is clearly reflected
in a number of the consensus resolutions put forward by the 1972
Stockholm Conference. Consider, for example, the eleventh
'principle': 'The environmental policies of all States *should enhance
and not adversely affect the present or future development potential of
developing countries.*' Or even more strikingly, the twenty-third
principle, not in the original proposals but introduced in the
course of discussion: 'Without prejudice to such criteria as may be
agreed upon by the international community . . . it will be essential
in all cases to consider the system of values prevailing in each
country, and the extent of the applicability of standards which are
valid for the most advanced countries but which may be *inappropriate and of unwarranted social cost for the developing countries.*' In other
words, do not expect the developing countries to proceed as if
they had reached the point of 'ecological transition'!

It is sometimes suggested that the West cannot afford to lower its rate of industrial development precisely because it has the responsibility on its shoulders for the developing countries. This, as it stands, is hypocrisy. Aid to developing countries represents a miniscule fraction of the national income of most of the developed countries; the proportion is unlikely to increase. Much of the aid, furthermore, is useless, its nature determined by the interests of the donor rather than by the needs of the recipient. If—with the caveats we have already entered—the West were to give up its pollution-creating synthetic products and lower its tariffs, it might substantially improve the position of the developing countries while at the same time alleviating its own ecological problems. But that would involve real sacrifices.

One must not, however, exaggerate. Some forms of aid have been genuinely helpful. And the effectiveness of other forms of aid has been nullified by greed and corruption at the point of reception rather than at the point of donation. The developing countries are not unnaturally fearful lest, should the developed countries begin to concentrate on their ecological problems, even this degree of aid will cease. They fear, too, that if they attempt to limit industrial growth, the industrial countries will reduce their imports from the developing countries. If, in the course of writing this book, I have ever felt cheerfulness breaking in, a moment's reflection on the plight of the developing countries has been sufficient to dispel it.

So long as one keeps one's eyes solely on the liberal democratic West, the prospect is a little more encouraging, if only because the solutions for a number of problems converge. It is not only in order to solve their ecological problems that the Western countries need to transfer resources from industry to tertiary services; new transport systems, decentralisation, population control, are as essential for urban as for ecological renewal. In order to solve that set of problems which Galbraith has collectively designated as 'public squalor', the West, to a striking degree, would have to embark on precisely the courses of action which are essential for the solution of its ecological problems. (The opposite situation holds in the developing countries; there lies the tragedy.)

What troubles me, however, is that it is hard to see any way in which the West can change its economic habits which does not entail the shifting of decisions about choices from the market to governments. This has already happened, of course, to a large degree; those income-earners—most of us—who have not learned the art of tax-evasion will have a large part, perhaps the greater part, of their income spent for them by the government. Whether this process can be carried further in a manner which does not entail the gradual emergence of a bureaucratic police state and the stifling of enterprise is, for me, the question of questions. Is Sweden, as has recently been argued, the prime example of creeping totalitarianism?

To sum up, I find it impossible to sum up, to arrive at any neat, tidy, quotable conclusions. As I have written, I have become more and more conscious of the complexity of every problem I have touched upon. I have tried to clear some intellectual ground, so that the alternatives before us are a little less obscured by undergrowth, but the problems remain. Yet nothing could be worse than to allow ourselves to slip into the doomsday mood of paranoic melancholia. The elderly, especially, are only too liable to this mood, whether taking pleasure in the reflection that by dying they will miss nothing but calamities or seeking an illusory grandeur as prophets of death and destruction. But in the young, too, apocalyptic prophecy can serve as a substitute for the overwhelming responsibility of action.

There is certainly a risk that we shall be utterly discouraged by the implications of Barry Commoner's 'first ecological law'— 'everything is connected to everything else'—for this makes it appear that to act at all is the height of imprudence. But fortunately I do not, before I swat a mosquito, have to calculate the consequences of my act on the sun's output of cosmic rays or the eutrophication of Lake Erie. It is just not true that everything I do has effects on *everything* else. What we do need always to remember, however—and this is sufficiently alarming—is that the unintended consequences of our actions are often surprisingly remote in time and place from those actions. (Skin cancer forty years after exposure to the sun; the excess fertiliser from my garden feeding algae in a remote stream.) Commoner's 'law' somewhat resembles the old Heraclitean dictum 'expect the unexpected'. Valuable as a warning, it is useless as a guide to action.

What in general I have emphasised is that, if the world's ecological problems are to be solved at all, it can only be by that old-fashioned procedure, thoughtful action. We may, of course, think to no purpose; by acting thoughtfully we may make matters worse. As we know quite well in our personal lives, we are sometimes saved by rashness, destroyed by prudence. Looking before we leap may make cowards of us. But there is no alternative policy. Mystical contemplation will not clean our streams or feed our peoples; no invisible guiding hand, whether Providence or History, guarantees our salvation. In the biosphere, as I said, man has no tenure; his own folly may, at any time, lose him his precarious occupancy.

How and what we think, however, is determined not only by

our brain structure but by the nature of the possibilities our society leaves open to us, the forms of thinking its traditions permit and encourage. The modern West, I have argued, leaves more options open than most other societies; its traditions, intellectual, political, moral, are complex, diversified and fruitfully discordant. That gives it the capacity to grow, to change: it nurtures within itself the seeds of innumerable revolutions. It is inventive—not only technologically, but politically, administratively, intellectually. Its flexibility gives it a better, not a lesser, chance of solving its problems. Admittedly, its central Stoic-Christian traditions are not favourable to the solution of its ecological problems—those traditions which deny that man's relationships with nature are governed by any moral principles and assign to nature the very minimum of independent life. But they, I have sought to show, are not the only Western traditions and their influence is steadily declining.

If, a century hence, men live worse lives than they do today, that will not be because the traditions of the West have bemused them; greed, ignorance, shortsightedness, fanaticism, are not Western inventions. How in fact they will live I have not dared to guess. My sole concern is that we should do nothing which will reduce their freedom of thought and action, whether by destroying the natural world which makes that freedom possible or the social traditions which permit and encourage it.

REFERENCES

CHAPTER ONE *Man as Despot*

1 Aldo Leopold: *A Sand County Almanac with Other Essays on Conservation* (New York, 1966), p. 238.
2 ibid., p. 245.
3 Editorial, 'Towards an ecological ethic', *New Scientist*, 48: 732 (31 December 1970), p. 575.
4 Lynn White: 'The historical roots of our ecologic crisis', *Science*, 155: 3767 (March 1967), p. 1204.
5 'Brahma, Shiva and Vishnu: three faces of science', *Australian Annals of Medicine*, 4 (1969), p. 354.
6 For a fuller account of these distinctions see K. Nielsen: 'Ethics, problems of' in Paul Edwards (ed.): *Encyclopedia of Philosophy* (New York, 1967), vol. 3, pp. 117–34.
7 Compare Genesis 9: 2–3 and 1: 29.
8 James Thomson: *The Seasons* (London, 1744), 'Spring', ll. 239–40.
9 Genesis 3: 17–19.
10 *Summa Theologiae*, 1a, 102, 3.
11 Quoted in A. O. Lovejoy and George Boas: *Primitivism and Related Ideas in Antiquity* (Baltimore, 1935), p. 27.
12 W. K. C. Guthrie: *A History of Greek Philosophy* (Cambridge, 1965), vol. 2, p. 249. Compare Plato: *Laws*, 782.
13 Chuang Tsu, 19: 22 in James Legge: *Sacred Books of the East* (Oxford, 1891), vol. 39, pp. 277–9.
14 Hans Kelsen: *Society and Nature* (London, 1946), p. 80.
15 Jubilees 3: 8, in R. H. Charles: *The Apocrypha and Pseudepigrapha of the Old Testament* (Oxford, 1913), vol. 2, p. 17.
16 Genesis 8: 17 and 9: 10.
17 Job 38: 26–7.
18 Job 39: 5–6. The Revised Standard translation is clearer at this point than the Authorised Version.
19 Psalm 104: 10–11.
20 *Republic*, bk. 1, 343*b*, based on the translation by A. D. Lindsay.
21 Ezekiel 34: 3–4.
22 Henri Frankfort: *Kingship and the Gods* (Chicago, 1948), pp. 342, 344.
23 Alfred Biese: *The Development of the Feeling for Nature in the Middle Ages and Modern Times* (London, 1905), p. 25.
24 L. C. Birch: *Nature and God* (London, 1965), p. 90.
25 Psalm 11: 4. On this general theme see R. de Vaux: *Ancient Israel: its Life and Institutions*, trans. J. McHugh (London, 1961), bk. 4, ch. 1.
26 Psalm 50: 10.
27 Robert Boyle: 'A free inquiry into the vulgarly received notion of nature', in *The Works of the Honourable Robert Boyle*, vol. 4 (London, 1744), p. 363.
28 Charles Davis: *God's Grace in History* (London, 1966), p. 25.
29 Saadia Gaon: *The Book of Beliefs and Opinions* (Yale Judaica Series, New Haven 1948), vol. 1, as quoted in Norman Lamm: *Faith and Doubt* (New York, 1971), p. 86.
30 A. Cohen: *The Teachings of Maimonides* (New York, 1968), p. 49.
31 Moses Maimonides: *The Guide for the Perplexed* (1: 72), quoted in Norman Lamm: *Faith and Doubt*, p. 95.
32 John Calvin: *Institutes of Religion*, trans. F. C. Battles (London, 1961), bk. 1, ch. 14, 22; vol. 1, p. 182, and in many other places.
33 G. P. Marsh: *Man and Nature* (New York, 1864), p. 35.
34 Aristotle: *Politics*, trans. W. Ellis (London, 1912), bk. 1, ch. 8, 1256*b*.
35 *Institutes*, 1, 5, 5; vol. 1, p. 58.
36 Lucretius: *De Rerum Natura*, bk. 5, l. 199, trans. T. Creech, 1682; revised version in H. Shapiro and E. M. Curley: *Hellenistic Philosophy* (New York, 1965), p. 62.
37 Cicero: *De Natura Deorum*, bk. 2, in H. Shapiro and E. M. Curley, *Hellenistic Philosophy*, p. 433 (my italics).
38 E. V. Arnold: *Roman Stoicism* (London, 1911), p. 205, footnote 39.
39 Act II, Scene 1, ll. 16–17.
40 George Berkeley: *Alciphron* (London, 1732), Dialogue 4, §14, ad fin.

41 Immanuel Kant: *Critique of Teleological Judgement*, pt. 2, 22, 431, as trans. J. C. Meredith (Oxford, 1928), pp. 93–4. On the Stoics see M. Pohlenz: *Die Stoa* (Göttingen, 1948), p. 85.
42 Luke 12: 6–7.
43 I Corinthians 9: 10–11.
44 Educated Christians could not but be struck by the resemblances between Pauline and Stoic teachings—especially Seneca's. That explains, if it does not excuse, the author of the forged letters which were for so long believed to prove that Seneca got his ideas from Paul. See J. N. Sevenster: *Paul and Seneca* (Leiden, 1961), which tends to exaggerate, however, the differences between Paul and Seneca.
45 Origen: *Contra Celsum*, IV, 75; trans. H. Chadwick (Cambridge, 1953), p. 243.
46 Psalm 104: 14.
47 Psalm 104: 17–21.
48 *Contra Celsum*, pp. 243–4.
49 Cicero: *De Natura Deorum*, II, 60, 153, adapted from the translation by H. Rackham, Loeb Classical Library (London, 1951), p. 271.
50 Robert Jungk: *Tomorrow is Already Here*, trans. M. Waldman (London, 1954), p. 17.
51 Cicero: *De Natura Deorum*, II, 60, 151, p. 17.
52 Francis Bacon: *Religious Meditations*; 'Of Heresies' in *The Works of Francis Bacon*, ed. Spedding, Ellis and Heath, vol. 7, p. 253.
53 *Of the Advancement of Learning*, bk. 2, Dedication, §6; *Works*, vol. 4, p. 286.
54 *Novum Organum*, Aphorism CXXIX; *Works*, vol. 4, p. 114.
55 'On the Interpretation of Nature', *Works*, vol. 3, p. 222.
56 ibid.
57 *Novum Organum*, Aphorism CXXIX; *Works*, vol. 4, p. 115.
58 *New Atlantis*; *Works*, vol. 3, p. 156 (my italics).
59 René Descartes: *Discourse on Method*, bk. 6, in *The Philosophical Works of Descartes*, trans. E. S. Haldane and G. R. T. Ross (Cambridge, 1931), vol. 1, p. 119 (my italics).
60 Descartes: *The Principles of Philosophy*, trans. E. S. Haldane and G. R. T. Ross, in *Works*, vol. 1, p. 271.
61 H. C. Carey: *The Past, the Present and the Future* (Philadelphia, 1848), p. 95.
62 Henry More: *Antidote against Atheism*, bk. 2, ch. 9, 3 in *Opera Omnia* (London, 1679), vol. 2, pt. 2, p. 82.
63 John Ray: *The Wisdom of God Manifested in the Works of the Creation*, 3rd ed. (London, 1701), pt. 1, p. 197.
64 ibid., pt. 1, p. 202.
65 See the account of Linnaeus in Immanuel Kant: *Critique of Teleological Judgement*, pt. 2, 21, 427, p. 89.
66 Sigmund Freud: *Civilisation and its Discontents* (Vienna, 1930), §11.
67 *Man and Nature*, p. 43.
68 David McLellan (ed.): *Marx's Grundrisse* (London, 1971), p. 94.
69 Friedrich Engels: 'The part played by labour in the transition from ape to man' (written in 1876 but not published until 1896, in the *Neue Zeit*), in Karl Marx and Friedrich Engels: *Selected Works* (London, 1950), vol. 2, pp. 82–3.
70 ibid., p. 85.
71 ibid., p. 90.
72 M. N. Pokrovskiy: *Brief History of Russia* (10th ed. 1931), translated and quoted in I. M. Matley: 'The Marxist approach to the geographical environment', *Association of American Geographers' Annals*, 56 (1966), p. 101.
73 See especially I. P. Gerasimov: 'A Soviet plan for nature', in A. Meyer (ed.): *Encountering the Environment* (New York, 1971), pp. 197–208.
74 See Wing-Tsit Chan: *A Source-book of Chinese Philosophy* (Princeton, 1963), for samples of their work.
75 Rhoads Murphy: 'Man and nature in China', *Modern Asian Studies*, 1: 4 (1967), p. 315.
76 For quotations illustrating the man-nature relationship in China see Derk Bodde: 'Harmony and conflict in Chinese philosophy', in A. F. Wright (ed.): *Studies in Chinese Thought* (Chicago, 1953), pp. 56–7.
77 Translation by Hu Shih, in his *The Development of the Logical Method in Ancient China* (Shanghai, 1928), as quoted in Wing-Tsit Chan: 'Chinese theory and practice with special reference to humanism', in C. A. Moore (ed.): *The Chinese Mind* (Honolulu, 1967), p. 37.
78 Rhoads Murphy: 'Man and nature in China', p. 319.

CHAPTER TWO *Stewardship and Cooperation with Nature*

1 *Phaedrus* 246b. See on this theme the discussion in R. P. Festugière: *La Révélation d'Hermès Trismégiste* (Paris, 1953), vol. 3, ch. 2, p. 74, and the further references in E. R. Dodds: *Pagan and Christian in an Age of Anxiety* (Cambridge, 1965), p. 22n.

2 Hugh Montefiore: *Can Man Survive?* (Fontana ed., London, 1970), p. 55.
3 Genesis 2: 15.
4 John Black: *The Dominion of Man* (Edinburgh, 1970), pp. 48–9. Black is Professor of Natural Resources in the University of Edinburgh.
5 1 Corinthians 4: 1; 1 Peter 4: 10. Compare on this theme Wilfred Tooley: 'Stewards of God', *The Scottish Journal of Theology*, 19: 1 (March 1966).
6 Quoted from Rev. Edward Payson: *Memoir, Select Thoughts and Sermons* (3 vols., Portland, 1846), vol. 3, pp. 444–5, in C. S. Griffin: *Their Brothers' Keepers: Moral Stewardship in the United States* (New Brunswick, 1960), p. 7.
7 Matthew Hale: *The Primitive Origination of Mankind* (London, 1677), sect. 4, ch. 8, p. 370.
8 ibid., the previous paragraph. Compare Genesis 3: 17, 29.
9 George Herbert: 'Man', first published in *The Temple* (1633), quoted from C. C. Clarke (ed.): *The Poetical Works of George Herbert* (London, 1863), ll. 25–7, 49–55. The phrase 'the laureate of the Church of England' is from the introduction by John Nichol, p. vi.
10 James Schall S.J.: 'Ecology—an American heresy?', *America*, 124 (27 March 1971), p. 308.
11 Following the translation in A. D. Nock: 'Posidonius', *Journal of Roman Studies*, 49, p. 12. The reference is to Clement of Alexandria's *Stromateis*, 11, 21, 129. But the reading is doubtful.
12 *Hermetica Asclepius*, 1, 8, as quoted in C. J. Glacken, *Traces on the Rhodian Shore* (Berkeley, 1967), p. 146. Compare Festugière: *Révélation*, p. 74.
13 Karl Marx: *Economic and Philosophical Manuscripts* (1844), here cited from *Writings of the Young Marx on Philosophy and Society*, trans. and ed. L. D. Easton and K. H. Guddat (New York, 1967).
14 *The Vocation of Man*, in *Johann Gottlieb Fichte's Popular Works*, compiled by W. Smith (London, 1873), p. 331.
15 P. Teilhard de Chardin: *The Future of Man*, trans. Norman Denny (London, 1964), p. 12.
16 Romans 8: 22. For a fuller account of Teilhard see John Passmore: *The Perfectibility of Man*, pp. 251–9 and the references there cited.
17 Herbert Marcuse: *One Dimensional Man* (London, 1964), ch. 9, p. 236.
18 ibid., p. 240.
19 W. A. Gauld: *Man, Nature and Time* (London, 1946), p. 124.
20 *Spectator*, 414 (25 June 1712).
21 Compare Joseph Warton: *An Essay on the Genius and Writings of Pope* (London, 1782), vol. 2, p. 183, describing the illustrations to Giovanni Andreini's play *L'Adamo* (1617).
22 Edward Malins: *English Landscaping and Literature 1660–1840* (London, 1966), p. 99. See also on this theme Russell Noyes: *Wordsworth and the Art of Landscape* (Indiana, 1968), ch. 1.
23 G. A. Jellicoe: *Studies in Landscape Design* (London, 1960), p. 27.
24 Quoted in F. B. Artz: *From the Renaissance to Romanticism* (Chicago, 1962), p. 164. Source not cited.
25 John Bradford: *Ancient Landscapes* (London, 1957), p. 149.
26 Ian L. McHarg: *Design with Nature* (Philadelphia, 1969), p. 1.
27 ibid., Introduction, p. viii.
28 J. S. Mill: 'Nature' in *Three Essays on Religion* (London, 1904), p. 14.
29 Luke 3: 5 quoting Isaiah 40: 4. Isaiah has 'exalted' where Luke has 'filled'.
30 J. S. Mill: 'Nature', p. 15.
31 The language of 'seeds', although not the concept, I derived from conversation with Kenneth Boulding.

CHAPTER THREE   *Pollution*

1 E. J. Mishan: *The Costs of Economic Growth* (Harmondsworth, 1969), p. 37, n. 3.
2 The literature on pollution from a scientific point of view is now overwhelming. For a good non-sensational account see A. S. Boughey: *Man and the Environment* (New York, 1971), chs. 10–12. Perhaps the best general book on the topic is Barry Commoner: *The Closing Circle* (New York, 1971). See also the periodical *Environmental Pollution* (since 1969).
3 See his discussion-contribution in N. Polunin (ed.): *The Environmental Future* (London, 1972), p. 320.
4 For the importance of this distinction, see L. B. Slobodkin: 'Aspects of the future of ecology', *Bio-Science* 13: 1, reprinted in R. Disch (ed.): *The Ecological Conscience* (New Jersey, 1970), pp. 71–90.
5 See, for example, W. R. D. Sewell et al.: 'A guide to benefit-cost analysis', in Ian Burton and Robert W. Kates (eds.): *Readings in Resource Management and Conservation* (Chicago, 1965), pp. 544–57. Some of the problems are briefly brought out in Albert Lepawsky: 'The quest for quality in the administration of resources', in S. V. Ciriacy-Wantrup and J. J. Parsons (eds.): *Natural Resources: Quality and Quantity* (Berkeley, 1967), pp. 167–9.

6 R. D. Cadle: 'Is clean air possible in an industrialised society?' in W. H. Helfrich (ed.): *Agenda for Survival: The Environmental Crisis* (New Haven, 1970), pp. 135–48.

7 Commoner: *The Closing Circle*, p. 57. See also John Maddox's chapter on 'The pollution panic' in his *The Doomsday Syndrome* (London, 1972).

8 'A blueprint for survival', *The Ecologist*, 2: 1 (January 1972), pp. 1–43.

9 Glenn C. Stone: *A New Ethic for a New Earth* (New York, 1971).

10 Oscar Wilde: 'The decay of lying', *Nineteenth Century* (January 1889), reprinted in *Collected Works* (London, 1948), p. 909.

11 J. K. Huysmans: *A Rebours* (Paris, 1884), ch. 2.

12 Bernard Berenson: *Sketch for a Self-Portrait* (London, 1949), p. 133.

13 On the relationship between pollution and order see Mary Douglas: *Purity and Danger: An Analysis of Concepts of Pollution and Taboo* (London, 1966), ch. 2.

14 'A blueprint for survival', p. 5, sec. 162 (italics mine).

15 Mishan: *The Costs of Economic Growth*, Preface, p. 15.

16 Herbert Marcuse: *An Essay on Liberation* (Boston, 1969), Preface, p. ix.

17 E. A. Starbird: 'A river restored: Oregon's Willamette', *National Geographic* (June, 1972), pp. 816–35.

18 S. Keen and J. Raser: 'A conversation with Herbert Marcuse', *Psychology Today*, 4: 9 (February 1971), pp. 35 ff.

19 Compare *New Scientist*, 49: 737 (4 February 1971), p. 236.

20 Compare S. E. Finer: 'The political power of private capital', *The Sociological Review*, new series, 3 (December 1955). The successful campaign against anti-pollution measures in California in 1972 illustrates the power of the unemployment issue.

21 See J. M. Edelman: *The Symbolic Uses of Politics* (Urbana, Ill., 1964).

22 New York, 1970. See also W. O. Douglas (reprint): 'The corps of engineers: the public be damned', in W. Anderson (ed.): *Politics and Environment* (California, 1970); F. M. Potter (reprint): 'Everyone wants to save the environment', in R. Disch (ed.): *The Ecological Conscience*, pp. 130–40.

23 See R. U. Ayres: 'Air pollution in cities', and N. Wollman: 'The new economics of resources', in W. Anderson (ed.): *Politics and Environment*.

24 Garrett Hardin: 'The tragedy of the commons', *Science*, 162: 1243 (13 December 1968), pp. 1243–8. Compare Beryl L. Crowe: 'The tragedy of the commons revisited', *Science*, 166: 3909 (28 November 1969), pp. 1103–7.

25 A. C. Pigou: *The Economics of Welfare* (4th ed., London, 1932), p. 184.

26 See E. J. Mishan: 'The postwar literature on externalities: an interpretative essay', *Journal of Economic Literature*, 9: 1 (March 1971), pp. 1–28.

27 See David Spurgeon: 'Replacement for phosphates' (reprint) in R. M. Irving and G. B. Priddle (eds.): *Crisis* (Toronto, 1971), pp. 53–7.

28 For American instances see M. I. Goldman: 'The mess around us', in M. I. Goldman (ed.): *Controlling Pollution: The Economics of a Cleaner America* (New Jersey, 1967).

29 Compare Dennis Livingston: 'Pollution control: an international perspective', in W. Anderson (ed.): *Politics and Environment*, pp. 319–35. Much has happened, however, and very rapidly, since Livingston wrote.

30 Compare R. U. Ayres: 'Air pollution in cities', in W. Anderson (ed.): *Politics and Environment*, esp. pp. 97–8.

31 James M. Buchanan and Gordon Tullock: *The Calculus of Consent* (Ann Arbor, 1962), p. 91.

32 Brian Barry: *Political Argument* (London, 1965), p. 257.

33 For a discussion of this method and its limitations, see J. H. Dales: *Pollution, Property and Prices* (Toronto, 1968). There is a briefer account in his 'Land, water and ownership', *Canadian Journal of Economics*, 1: 4 (1968), pp. 791–804, reprinted in R. M. Irving and G. B. Priddle (eds.): *Crisis*.

CHAPTER FOUR *Conservation*

1 Compare O. C. Herfindahl: 'What is conservation?', in *Three Studies in Minerals Economics* (Washington, 1961), pp. 1–12.

2 *The Declaration of Governors for Conservation of Natural Resources* is reprinted in I. Burton and R. W. Kates (eds.): *Readings in Resource Management and Conservation* (Chicago, 1965), pp. 186–8. For the history of the conservationist movement see S. P. Hays: *Conservation and the Gospel of Efficiency* (Cambridge, Mass., 1959). The arguments put forward by the leading conservationist Gifford Pinchot in his *The Fight for Conservation*, first published in New York in 1909, are remarkably like more recent arguments.

3 See the documents included in F. E. Smith (ed.): *Conservation in the United States: a Documentary History* (New York, 1971), esp. vol. 2 on *Minerals*, ed. W. T. Doherty.

4 See the tables in D. H. Meadows et al.: *The Limits to Growth* (London, 1972), Table 4, p. 56.
5 Norman McRae: 'The future of international business', *Economist*, 242: 6700 (22 January 1972), p. xvi.
6 'Prophet of nuclear power', Alvin Weinberg talks to Dr Gerald Wick, *New Scientist*, 53: 779 (20 January 1972), p. 140.
7 Eugene Rabinowitch: 'Copping out', *Encounter*, 37: 3, p. 95.
8 See 'The energy crisis', pts. 1 and 2, in *Science and Public Affairs: Bulletin of the Atomic Scientists*, 27: 8–9 (September–October), 1971.
9 See M. K. Hubbert: 'Energy resources', in M. K. Hubbert: *Resources and Man* (San Francisco, 1969).
10 Immanuel Kant: 'Idea for a universal history with a cosmopolitan purpose', Proposition 8, in *Kant's Political Writings*, ed. H. Reiss, trans. H. B. Nisbet (Cambridge, 1970), p. 50.
11 William James: *Pragmatism* (London, 1907), ch. 3.
12 J. S. Mill: *Autobiography* (London, 1873), ch. 5.
13 For more detail see John Passmore: *The Perfectibility of Man*, pp. 195–7.
14 Francis Bacon: *The Advancement of Learning* (Oxford, 1926), bk. II, XXI, 11.
15 Immanuel Kant: *Religion within the Bounds of Pure Reason* (bk. III, div. 1, 1) and *Idea for a Universal History*, Eighth Proposition. In his *The Contest of Faculties* (sect. 10) he ascribes even less importance to human goodwill as distinct from Providence. These last two works can now be conveniently read in *Kant's Political Writings*, ed. H. Reiss, trans. H. B. Nisbet.
16 Jay Forrester: *World Dynamics* (Cambridge, Mass., 1971). He gives a brief account of his work in two articles in *Ecologist*, 'Alternatives to catastrophe', 1: 14–15 (August–September, 1971), and in 'Counterintuitive behavior of social systems', *Theory and Decision*, 2: 2 (December 1971). Large scale simulation studies are also being conducted at the University of British Columbia, Vancouver.
17 First Report of the *Royal Commission on Environmental Pollution*, Chairman: Sir Eric Ashby (London, 1971), pp. 38, 41. For a brief account of the argument on the other side see David Gates: 'Weather modification in the service of mankind: promise or peril?' in H. W. Helfrich (ed.): *The Environmental Crisis* (New Haven, 1970).
18 Hugh Montefiore: *Can Man Survive?*, p. 55.
19 *The Contest of Faculties*, 6, trans. H. B. Nisbet, p. 182.
20 For Fichte, and for detailed references, see John Passmore: *The Perfectibility of Man*, pp. 231–2.
21 Henry Sidgwick: *The Methods of Ethics* (7th ed., London, 1907, reissued 1962), bk. 3, ch. 13, p. 381.
22 ibid., bk. 4, ch. 1, p. 414 (my italics).
23 T. L. S. Sprigge: 'A utilitarian reply to Dr McCloskey', in M. D. Bayles (ed.): *Contemporary Utilitarianism* (New York, 1968), p. 263.
24 See the graph in 'Blueprint for survival', p. 7.
25 See ch. 8, 'The unit cost of extractive products', in H. J. Barnett and Chandler Morse: *Scarcity and Growth: The Economics of Natural Resource Availability* (Baltimore, 1963). This book is an excellent example of the more optimistic economic writings on conservation.
26 Joan Robinson: *Economic Philosophy* (Harmondsworth, 1964), p. 115.
27 John Rawls: *A Theory of Justice* (Cambridge, Mass., 1971), p. 285.
28 On this general theme see John Passmore: *The Perfectibility of Man*, pp. 299–302 and 323–5.
29 Macfarlane Burnet: *Dominant Mammal* (Melbourne, 1970), ch. 9; Pelican ed. (Harmondsworth, 1971), p. 182.
30 Quoted in Russell Lord: *The Care of the Earth* (New York, 1962), p. 235; Mentor ed., p. 190.
31 Harrison Brown: *The Challenge of Man's Future* (London, 1954), p. 219.
32 M. P. Golding: 'Obligations to future generations', *The Monist*, 56: 1 (January 1972), p. 86.
33 ibid., p. 99.
34 ibid., p. 98.
35 'Blueprint for survival', p. 21.
36 ibid., p. 16, citing Stephen Boyden: 'Environmental change: perspectives and responsibilities', *Journal of the Soil Association* (October 1971).
37 P. R. Ehrlich and R. L. Harriman: *How to be a Survivor* (London, 1971), p. 73.
38 Quoted in H. W. Arndt: 'Socialism in changing societies', *Quadrant* (March–April 1972), p. 34.
39 Pigou: *Economics of Welfare*, p. 29.
40 C. P. Snow: *The State of Siege* (New York, 1969), p. 43.
41 As quoted in *The Australian*, 26 May 1971.
42 *Royal Commission on Environmental Pollution*, p. 9.

CHAPTER FIVE   *Preservation*

1 Plutarch: 'Whether land or sea animals are cleverer', in *Moralia*, 12, 964–5, trans. W. Helmbold, Loeb Classical Library, p. 353.
2 *Sand County Almanac*, p. 269.
3 See F. Fraser Darling and N. D. Eichhorn: 'Man and nature in the national parks', in W. Anderson (ed.): *Politics and Environment*, p. 221.
4 This is the title under which G. P. Marsh published the second edition of his *Man and Nature* (New York, 1874). The quotation is from p. 327.
5 David Lowenthal: 'Daniel Boone is dead', in A. Meyer (ed.): *Encountering the Environment* (New York, 1971), p. 52.
6 R. L. Means: 'The new conservation', in ibid., p. 2.
7 Garrett Hardin: 'The economics of wilderness', reprinted from *Natural History* (1969) in C. E. Johnson (ed.): *Eco-Crisis* (New York, 1970), p. 176.
8 *Principles of Political Economy* (London, 1848), bk. 4, ch. 6, 2.
9 J. K. Galbraith: 'How much should a country consume?', in H. Jarrett (ed.): *Perspectives on Conservation* (Baltimore, 1958), p. 92.
10 R. L. Means: 'The new conservation', in A. Meyer (ed.): *Encountering the Environment*, p. 2.
11 Lake Pedder Action Committee: *Lake Pedder* (Adelaide, 1972), p. 35 (my italics).
12 C. E. Norton: *Letters*, II, 95 n., as cited in Hans Huth: *Nature and the American* (Berkeley, 1957), p. 173.
13 Bertolt Brecht: *Tales from the Calendar*, trans. Y. E. Kapp (London, 1961), p. 110.
14 T. K. Whipple, 'Aucassin in the Sierras', *Yale Review*, New Series, 16 (July 1927), p. 714, quoted in P. J. Schmitt: *Back to Nature* (New York, 1969), p. 176.
15 In C. E. Johnson (ed.): *Eco-Crisis*, p. 175.
16 J. G. von Herder: *Reflections on the Philosophy of the History of Mankind* (trans. T. O. Churchill, London, 1800), bk. 8, ch. 2, sect. 3.
17 Cotton is quoted in Edward Malins: *English Landscaping and Literature* (London, 1966), p. 8. On this theme in general see Marjorie Nicolson: *Mountain Gloom and Mountain Glory* (Cornell, 1959).
18 See D. S. Wallace-Hadrill: *The Greek Patristic View of Nature* (Manchester, 1968), pp. 87–91.
19 The quotation is from John Cassian: *Colloquia* (III), xviii, 6, and xix, 5. On this complex question see especially G. H. Williams: *Wilderness and Paradise in Christian Thought* (New York, 1962), esp. p. 41.
20 See 'Luther on the Creation', in J. N. Lenker (ed.): *Martin Luther: Precious and Sacred Writings* (Minneapolis, 1903), vol. 1, pp. 64–5.
21 Thomas Burnet: *The Sacred Theory of the Earth*, bk. 1, ch. 9.
22 The quotation from Hopkins is in 'Inversnaid', *Poems of Gerard Manley Hopkins*, ed. R. Bridges (London, 1918).
23 The views of the New England settlers are as summed up by Nathaniel Morton, keeper of the records for the Plymouth Colony; quoted in S. L. Udall: *The Quiet Crisis* (New York, 1963), p. 13.
24 Tertullian: *De Anima*, in A. Roberts and J. Donaldson (eds.): *The Writings of Tertullian*, vol. 2, p. 481; Ante-Nicene Christian Library, vol. 15.
25 F. Fraser Darling: 'Man's responsibility for the environment', in F. J. Ebling (ed.): *Biology and Ethics*, Symposia of the Institute of Biology, no. 18 (London, 1969), p. 119.
26 *Babylonian Talmud*, Seder Mo'ed, vol. 1, trans. I. Epstein (London, 1938), 128b, ch. 18, p. 640.
27 Compare on this theme Edward Westermarck: *Christianity and Morals* (London, 1939), ch. 19.
28 Augustine: *The Catholic and Manichaean Ways of Life*, trans. D. A. Gallagher and I. J. Gallagher (Boston, 1966), ch. 17, p. 102.
29 The argument is cited in Plutarch: 'The cleverness of animals', *Moralia*, 964, p. 347.
30 See Arthur Schopenhauer: *On the Basis of Morality*, trans. E. F. J. Payne (Indianopolis, 1965), pt. 2, sect. 8, p. 96, and pt. 3, sects. 19, 7, pp. 175–82; J. S. Mill: *Principles of Political Economy*, bk. 5, ch. 11, §9; John Laird: *A Study in Moral Theory* (London, 1926), pp. 296, 302; Hastings Rashdall: *The Theory of Good and Evil* (London, 1907), vol. 1, pp. 213–15; Leonard Nelson: *System of Ethics*, trans. N. Guterman (New Haven, 1956), p. 136.
31 Montaigne: *Oeuvres Complètes* (Paris, 1925), vol. 3, p. 246 (my italics).
32 Hume: *Enquiry concerning the Principles of Morals*, ed. L. A. Selby-Bigge, sect. 3, pt. 1, §152, §145.
33 Jeremy Bentham: *Introduction to the Principles of Morals and Legislation*, written 1780, published 1789, ed. J. H. Burns and H. L. A. Hart (London, 1970), ch. 17, §4, note b. In some other editions the chapter number is 19.
34 First published in London in 1892. The revised edition (1922) attempts to reply to Ritchie's criticisms—referred to below—but not, in my judgment, successfully.
35 H. L. A. Hart: *The Concept of Law* (Oxford, 1961), p. 7.

36 D. G. Ritchie: *Natural Rights* (London, 1894), p. 107.
37 Foreword to *Sand County Almanac*, p. xviii.
38 Compare Roslind Godlovitch: 'Animals and morals', *Philosophy*, 46: 175 (January 1971), pp. 23–33, revised in S. and R. Godlovitch and John Harris (eds.): *Animals, Men and Morals* (London, 1971). But Godlovitch is mainly concerned with the much stronger principle that we ought to *prevent* animal suffering.
39 John Ray: *Three Physico-Theological Discourses* (London, 1903). Quoted from the third edition (1713), p. 149, in A. O. Lovejoy: *The Great Chain of Being* (Harvard, 1948), pp. 243, 365.
40 See especially P. S. Martin and H. E. Wright (eds.): *Pleistocene Extinctions: The Search for a Cause*, Proceedings of the 7th Congress of the International Association for Quaternary Research (New Haven, 1967), vol. 6; in *Nature* (1967), 215: 5097, pp. 212–13, and in *Natural History* (January 1968), pp. 73–5 the controversy is continued by L. S. B. Leakey and P. S. Martin.
41 Quoted in A. O. Lovejoy, *The Great Chain of Being*, p. 77.
42 *Le Milieu Mystique* (1917) quoted in Henri de Lubac: *The Religion of Teilhard de Chardin*, trans. R. Hague (London, 1967), p. 13. Compare John Passmore: *The Perfectibility of Man*, pp. 253 ff.
43 J. S. Mill: *Principles of Political Economy*, bk. 4, ch. 6, par. 2.
44 Compare C. S. Elton: *The Ecology of Invasions* (London, 1958), pp. 145–53.
45 From *Dīgha Nikāya*, 1.4 ff., in W. T. de Bary (ed.): *The Buddhist Tradition* (New York, 1969), p. 34.
46 Cowper: *The Task* (1785), bk. 6, ll. 562–3.
47 The quotations are from the basic texts of the Jain scriptures in William Gerber: *The Mind of India* (New York, 1967), pp. 73, 80.
48 Albert Schweitzer: *My Life and Thought*, trans. C. T. Campion (London, 1933), p. 271.
49 Albert Schweitzer: *Civilisation and Ethics* (1923), trans. C. T. Campion, 3rd ed. (London, 1946), p. 244.
50 Karl Barth: *Church Dogmatics*, vol. 3: *The Doctrine of Creation*, ed. G. W. Bromiley and T. F. Torrance (Edinburgh, 1961), pt. 4, p. 350.
51 ibid., p. 355.
52 See the *Babylonian Talmud*, vol. 1, Shabbath 129a, ch. xviii, p. 644.
53 A. G. Baumgarten: *Ethica Philosophica* (Halle, 1763), §398.
54 For a case-study description of five such conflicts see Roy Gregory: *The Price of Amenity* (London, 1971).
55 See also on this theme R. D. Guthrie: 'Ethics and non-human organisms', *Perspectives in Biology and Medicine* (Autumn, 1967), pp. 52–62.

CHAPTER SIX *Multiplication*

1 P. R. Ehrlich: *The Population Bomb* (New York, 1968), p. 166.
2 Compare N. Lee and P. J. W. Saunders: 'Pollution as a function of affluence and population increase', in P. R. Cox and J. Peel (eds.): *Population and Pollution* (London, 1972).
3 See Barry Commoner: *The Closing Circle*; P. R. Ehrlich and J. P. Holdren: 'One-dimensional ecology', *Ecologist*, 2: 8 (August 1972), pp. 11–21.
4 U.N. Population Commission (9 April 1963).
5 Quoted in Barbara Ward and René Dubos: *Only One Earth* (Harmondsworth, 1972), pp. 217–18.
6 Alfred Sauvy: *General Theory of Population*, trans. C. Campos (London, 1969), p. 266.
7 Simon Kuznets: 'Economic aspects of fertility trends in the less developed countries', in S. J. Behrman, L. Corsa and R. Freedman (eds.): *Fertility and Family Planning: A World View* (Ann Arbor, 1969), pp. 175–6. See also R. A. Easterlin: 'Effects of population growth on the economic development of developing countries', *Annals of the American Academy of Political and Social Science*, 371 (January 1967), pp. 98–108, reprinted in T. R. Ford and G. F. de Jong [eds.]: *Social Demography* (New Jersey, 1970), pp. 264–75.
8 Sir Matthew Hale: *The Primitive Origination of Mankind* (London, 1677), sect. 2, ch. 9, p. 211.
9 Archibald Alison: *The Principles of Population and their Connection with Human Happiness* (Edinburgh, 1840), vol. 2, pp. 529–31.
10 Tertullian: *De Anima*, ch. 30.
11 Colin Clark: *Population Growth and Land Use* (London, 1967), p. 157.
12 P. R. Ehrlich: *The Population Bomb*, p. 45.

13 Jean Mayer: 'Food and population: the wrong problem?' *Daedalus*, 93: 3 (Summer 1964), pp. 830–44, reprinted in K. C. W. Kammeyer (ed.): *Population Studies* (Chicago, 1969), pp. 459–71.

14 Colin Clark: *Population Growth and Land Use*, p. 155.

15 For further observations on this theme, see Garrett Hardin: 'Interstellar migration and the population problem', *Journal of Heredity*, 50 (1959), pp. 68–70.

16 The 'theory' dates back to 1929. See D. O. Cowgill: 'Transition theory as general population theory', *Social Forces*, 41 (March 1963), pp. 270–4, reprinted in T. R. Ford and G. F. de Jong (eds.): *Social Demography*, pp. 627–33.

17 See John Maddox: *The Doomsday Syndrome*, p. 55.

18 See W. D. Borrie: *The Growth and Control of World Population*, pp. 228–9. Several of the contributions in D. V. Glass and R. Revelle (eds.): *Population and Social Change* (London, 1972) are devoted to this same theme.

19 Simon Kuznets: 'Economic aspects of fertility trends in the less developed countries', p. 162.

20 Compare A. J. Coale: 'The decline of fertility in Europe from the French Revolution to World War II' in *Fertility and Family Planning*, pp. 13–19.

21 W. D. Borrie: *The Growth and Control of World Population*, p. 229.

22 K. Davis: 'The theory of change and response in modern demographic history', *Population Index* (October 1963).

23 For a good brief account see J. J. Spengler, 'Optimum population', in the *Encyclopedia of the Social Sciences* (New York, 1968).

24 See E. P. Hutchinson: *The Population Debate* (Boston, 1967), ch. 8.

25 Sir Charles Davenant: *An Essay upon Ways and Means of Supplying the War* (London, 1695), p. 144, as quoted in E. P. Hutchinson, *The Population Debate*, p. 63.

26 Alfred Sauvy: *General Theory of Population*, pt. 1, ch. 6.

27 See Jack Parsons: *Population versus Liberty* (London, 1971).

28 L. R. Taylor (ed.): *The Optimum Population for Britain* (London, 1970), p. xxi.

29 See, for example, P. R. Ehrlich and R. C. Harriman: *How to be a Survivor* (London, 1971), pp. 36–8.

30 See the articles in S. F. Singer (ed.): *Is There an Optimum Level of Population?* (New York, 1971).

31 See, for example, P. R. Ehrlich and R. L. Harriman: *How to be a Survivor*, pp. 34–5.

32 Quoted in L. H. Day: 'Concerning the optimum level of population', in S. F. Singer (ed.): *Is There an Optimum Level of Population?*, p. 285. See also Alfred Sauvy: *General Theory of Population*, pt. 2, ch. 4; and K. E. Boulding: 'The menace of Methuselah', *Journal of Washington Academy of Sciences* (October 1965), pp. 171–9.

33 Alfred Sauvy: *General Theory of Population*, pp. 401–2. The quotations about the only child are cited by Sauvy from Robert Debré: 'La famille heureuse ou l'optimum familial', *Population* (October–December 1950).

34 For the pressures on education generated by population growth see N. R. Glass, K. E. F. Watt and T. C. Foin: 'Human ecology and educational crises', in S. F. Singer: *Is There an Optimum Level of Population?* pp. 205–22.

35 R. Pressat: *Population*, trans. R. & D. Atkinson (Baltimore, 1971), p. 99.

36 Colin Clark: *Population Growth*, p. 258.

37 Colin Clark: 'Do population and freedom grow together?', *Fortune* (December 1960).

38 J. J. Spengler: 'Demographic factors and early modern economic development' in D. V. Glass and R. Revelle (eds.): *Population and Social Change*, pp. 87–98.

39 Robert Allen: 'Limits of demographic growth' in E. Goldsmith (ed.): *Can Britain Survive?* (London, 1971), p. 37.

40 D. J. Bogue: 'The end of the population explosion', *The Public Interest*, 7 (1967), pp. 11–20, quoted in W. D. Borrie: *The Growth and Control of World Population*, p. 273. See also his comments.

41 See Stanley Johnson: *Life Without Birth* (London, 1970), pp. 216–17, on the IUD campaign in India.

42 See B. D. Kale: *Family Planning Enquiry in Rural Shimoga (Mysore)* (Vidyagari, 1966), pp. 57–9.

43 See J. T. Noonan: *Contraception, A History of its Treatment by the Catholic Theologians and Canonists* (Cambridge, Mass. 1965), pp. 34–6.

44 See N. E. Himes: *Medical History of Contraception* (N.Y., 1963 reprint), ch. III, which is mostly derived from a Talmudic scholar, Solomon Gandz. See also J. T. Noonan, *Contraception*, pp. 51–2.

45 See Lucien Legrand: *The Biblical Doctrine of Virginity* (London, 1963).

46 See J. T. Noonan: *Contraception*, p. 129, quoting Augustine: *The Good of Marriage*, 3.3, 8.9, 17.19.

47 Tertullian: *De Anima*, ch. 30. See also A. O. Lovejoy: ' "Nature" as norm in Tertullian', in *Essays in the History of Ideas* (Baltimore, 1948), esp. pp. 332–5.

48 Tertullian: *To his Wife*, ch. 5 in *Writings*, vol. 1, p. 285.
49 *Summa Theologiae*, 2.2, 152, art. 2.
50 *Summa Contra Gentiles*, III, ch. 136.
51 See the article on 'Continence', *Dictionary of Moral Theology*, ed. Pietro Palazzini, trans. H. J. Yannone (Baltimore, 1962).
52 Quoted in J. T. Noonan: *Contraception*, p. 518.
53 Anne Fremantle: *The Papal Encyclicals in their Historical Context* (New York, 1956), p. 290.
54 A. F. Zimmerman: *Overpopulation* (Washington, D.C., 1957), p. 103, cited in R. M. Fagley: *The Population Explosion and Christian Responsibility* (New York, 1960), p. 185.
55 Martin Luther: *Letters of Spiritual Counsel*, trans. T. G. Tappert (London, 1955), *Library of Christian Classics*, vol. 18, p. 273.
56 Paul Althaus: *Grundriss der Ethik* (1931), p. 91, trans. in Karl Barth: *Church Dogmatics*, vol. 3, pt. 4, p. 141.
57 J. T. Noonan: *Contraception*, p. 197.
58 Cited in Daniel Sullivan: 'A history of Catholic thinking on contraception', in W. Birmingham (ed.): *What Modern Catholics Think about Birth Control* (New York, 1964), p. 57.
59 Letter to C. G. Schütz, 10 July 1797, trans. in A. Zweig: *Kant: Philosophical Correspondence* (Chicago, 1967), pp. 235–6.
60 Quoted in H. S. Harris: *Hegel's Development: Towards the Sunlight 1770–1801* (Oxford, 1972), p. 309.
61 See *The Lambeth Conferences 1867–1930* (London, 1948), pp. 94, 103.
62 *The Lambeth Conference* (London, 1958): 'The family in contemporary society', 2, 147–8.
63 *Babylonian Talmud*, Niddah 13B.
64 Karl Barth: *Church Dogmatics*, vol. 3, pt. 4, p. 144.
65 *Humanae Vitae*, 11.
66 ibid., 16.
67 See for example, A. Valsecchi: *Controversy: the Birth Control Debate 1958–68*, trans. Dorothy White, with introduction by Gregory Baum (London, 1968). This also includes the encyclical, in an English translation, cited above.
68 See, for example, T. D. Roberts (introduction): *Contraception and Holiness* (London, 1965), or the three volumes on *The Problem of Population* issued by Notre Dame University in 1964–5. Although these were published before the *Humanae Vitae*, the argument still continues on the same lines, as in the letter of dissent, signed by some five hundred distinguished American scholars, published in *Commonweal* (23 August 1968).
69 *Summa Theologiae*, 3 (supp.), 41, 1.
70 Lincoln Day: 'Natality and ethnocentrism', *Population Studies* (March 1968). Compare R. Pressat, *Population*, pp. 76–7.
71 I take the quotations from A. H. Khan: *Islamic Opinions on Contraception*, a pamphlet published from the East Pakistan Government Press (Dacca, 1963), p. 4. The source is there given as the Cairo Edition of Al-Ghazzali, 1939, vol. 2, pp. 52–4.
72 W. D. Borrie: *The Growth and Control of World Population*, p. 172.
73 Compare N. H. Fisek: 'Prospects for fertility planning in Turkey', in S. J. Behrman, L. Corsa and R. Freedman (eds.): *Fertility and Family Planning*, pp. 467–76.
74 See Stanley Johnson: *Life Without Birth*, ch. 8.
75 ibid., p. 178.
76 *The Song of Savitri*, from the *Mahabatra*, bk. 3, trans. in Edwin Arnold: *Indian Lyrics* (London, 1883).
77 Mencius, trans. D. C. Law (Harmondsworth, 1970), bk. 4, pt. A, 26, p. 127.
78 See, on this theme, J. M. Stycos: *Human Fertility in Latin America* (Ithaca, 1968).
79 Compare on this whole question Kingsley Davis: 'The demographic foundations of national power', in M. Berger (ed.): *Freedom and Control in Modern Society* (New York, 1954).
80 Catholic Woman Doctor: *A Talk to Catholic Wives* (London, Catholic Truth Society, 1959), p. 26. Quoted, with other similar examples, in Phillip Appleman: *The Silent Explosion* (Boston, 1965), p. 83.
81 These passages are quoted in D. Schulder and F. Kennedy: *Abortion Rap* (New York, 1971), pp. 155–6.
82 Karl Marx: *Theories of Surplus Value* (written 1861–3), excerpted in R. L. Meek (ed.): *Marx and Engels on Malthus* (London, 1953), reprinted as *Marx and Engels on the Population Bomb* (Berkeley, 1971), p. 137.
83 Friedrich Engels: *Outlines of a Critique of Political Economy* (1844), excerpted in R. L. Meek, pp. 57, 59, 63.
84 R. Pressat: *Population*, p. 122.
85 Compare D. M. Heer: 'Abortion, contraception and population policy in the Soviet Union', *Demography*, 2 (1965), pp. 531–9, reprinted in D. M. Heer: *Readings on Population* (New Jersey, 1968), pp. 208–17.
86 Quoted in W. D. Borrie: *The Growth and Control of World Population*, p. 259.

87 On this theme see also Alfred Sauvy: *Malthus et les deux Marx* (Paris, 1963) and W. Petersen: *The Politics of Population* (New York, 1965).
88 *Letter to Kautsky* (1 February 1881), in R. L. Meek (ed.): *Marx and Engels on Malthus*, p. 120.
89 *Capital*, vol. 1 (1867), in ibid., p. 94.
90 Compare Stanley Johnson: *Life Without Birth*, pp. 208–9, 20–8.
91 Alfred Sauvy: *General Theory of Population*, p. 354.
92 W. D. Borrie: *The Growth and Control of World Population*, p. 141.
93 Compare J. J. Spengler: 'Demographic factors and early modern economic development', in D. V. Glass and R. Revelle (eds.): *Population and Social Change*.
94 On Indian marriage age in its relation to the Hindu tradition see K. M. Kapadia: *Marriage and Family in India* (London, 1958), ch. 7.
95 The facts about India cited above are all from W. D. Borrie, *The Growth and Control of World Population*, pp. 166–8. The final calculation he takes over from the Indian demographer, Agarwala.
96 P. K. Whelpton, A. A. Campbell and J. Paterson: *Fertility and Family Planning in the United States* (Princeton, 1966).
97 See J. Parsons: *Population Versus Liberty*, pp. 311–12.
98 See studies reported in E. Pohlman: *The Psychology of Birth Planning* (Cambridge, Mass., 1969), chs. 3 and 10; and for the historical trends, Judith Blake: 'Ideal family size among white Americans', *Demography* 3 (1966), pp. 154–73.
99 Pohlman: *The Psychology of Birth Planning*, p. 56.
100 See L. Rainwater: *Family Design* (Chicago, 1965), p. 150.
101 See J. J. Spengler, 'Values and fertility analysis', in *Demography* 3: 1 (1966), pp. 109–30, and the discussion in D. M. Heer: 'Economic development and the fertility transition', in D. V. Glass and R. Revelle (eds.): *Population and Social Change*.
102 Visid Prachuabmoh: 'Factors affecting desire or lack of desire for additional progeny in Thailand', in D. J. Bogue (ed.): *Sociological Contributions to Family Planning Research* (Chicago, 1967), pp. 364–409.
103 Galatians 3: 28.
104 Compare E. Westermarck: *Christianity and Morals* (London, 1939), pp. 338–40.
105 Tertullian, 'On female dress', bk. 1, ch. 1, in *The Writings of Tertullian*, vol. 1, pp. 304–5, Ante-Nicene Christian Library, vol. 11.
106 1 Timothy 2: 11–15.
107 Aquinas: *Super Epistolas S. Pauli Lectura*, ed. P. Cai (Turin, 1953), vol. 2, p. 229.
108 *Summa Theologiae*, 1, 92, 2, reply to obj. 3.
109 Martin Luther: *Vom ehelichen Leben* (1522), in *Werke* (1907), 10, 11, 301, 13.
110 For a woman's protest on this point see Sally Sullivan: 'Woman, mother, or person', in W. Birmingham (ed.): *What Modern Catholics Think about Birth Control*, pp. 204–14.
111 J. S. Schapiro: *Condorcet and the Rise of Liberalism* (New York, 1934), ch. 10.
112 *Laws of Manu*, trans. G. Bühler, in F. M. Müller (ed.): *The Sacred Books of the East* (Oxford, 1886), vol. 15, v, 154, p. 196.
113 ibid., IX, 13–19, pp. 329–30.
114 Philo: *Special Laws* (3.20.113), quoted in J. T. Noonan: *Contraception*, p. 87.
115 T. Malthus: *An Essay on the Principle of Population* (6th ed., London, 1826), p. 172.
116 Étienne Dumont: *Bentham's Theory of Legislation*, trans. C. M. Atkinson (London, 1914), vol. 2, ch. 12, p. 39. First published in 1802, based on manuscripts by Bentham.
117 Robert Wallace: *Various Prospects of Mankind* (London, 1761), p. 119. Published anonymously, Wallace, like Malthus, is criticising perfectibility.
118 Tertullian: *Apologeticus*, in *Writings*, vol. 1, pp. 71–2.
119 Figures cited in L. A. Westoff and C. F. Westoff: *From Now to Zero* (Boston, 1971), pp. 148–9 from Gallup Polls. See also the articles in R. E. Hall (ed.): *Abortion in a Changing World* (Columbia, 1970). The best general theoretical discussion is in Daniel Callahan: *Abortion: Law, Choice and Morality* (London, 1970).
120 Paul Ramsay: 'The morality of abortion', in *Life or Death* (Seattle, 1968), pp. 61–2.
121 Garrett Hardin: 'Abortion—or compulsory pregnancy?', *Journal of Marriage and the Family*, 30 (1968), pp. 246–51, excerpted in Garrett Hardin: *Population, Evolution and Birth Control* (2nd ed., San Francisco, 1969), p. 301.
122 Sripati Chandrasekhar: 'Abortion in India', in R. E. Hall (ed.): *Abortion in a Changing World* (New York, 1970), vol. 1, p. 250.
123 Akhter Hameed Khan: *Islamic Opinions on Contraception* (Dacca, 1963), p. 5, and J. T. Noonan: *Contraception, passim*.
124 J. T. Noonan: *Contraception*, p. 91.
125 For a brief exposition of the conventional view see V. J. Bourke: 'An ethical consideration of artificial contraception', in W. Birmingham (ed.): *What Modern Catholics Think about Birth-Control*.
126 J. L. Thomas: 'Marriage and sexuality: the Catholic position', in D. N. Barrett (ed.): *The Problem of Population* (Notre Dame, 1964).

127 F. E. Flynn: 'Natural law', in *Catholic Messenger*, 78 (1960), as excerpted in Garrett Hardin: *Population, Evolution and Birth Control*, p. 253.
128 V. J. Bourke: 'An ethical consideration of artificial contraception', p. 21.
129 For an illuminating account of the difficulties in which moral theologians have found themselves in the attempt to distinguish such operations from sterilisation, see J. T. Noonan: *Contraception*, pp. 451–60.
130 Rosemary Ruether: 'Birth control and the ideals of marital sexuality', in *Contraception and Holiness* (London, 1965), p. 78. See also on the rhythm method generally, the same author's: 'A question of dignity, a question of freedom', in W. Birmingham (ed.): *What Modern Catholics Think about Birth Control* (pp. 233–40). For a defence of the method against these criticisms see the Jesuit A. Nevett: *Population: Explosion or Control?* (London, 1964).
131 J. T. Noonan: *Contraception*, p. 440; and on Augustine, p. 120.
132 See, for example, the *Laws of Manu* III, 46–50 (Sacred Books), pp. 85–6.
133 See R. A. McCormick: 'Family size, rhythm and the pill', in D. Barrett (ed.): *The Problem of Population: Moral and Theological Considerations*, p. 71.
134 M. K. Gandhi: *Birth Control* (Bombay, 1962).
135 *Encyclopedia Judaica*, article on Celibacy.
136 Vidya Prakash: *Khajuraho* (Bombay, 1967), p. 156, n. 1.
137 For a summary account of the possibilities see Bernard Berelson: 'Beyond family planning', *Science*, 163 (1969), pp. 533–43. Berelson's analysis follows the same pattern as my analysis of ecological problems (ch. 3 above); I am concentrating, for the moment, on the moral issues. See also Kingsley Davis: 'Population policy; will current programs succeed?' in *Science*, 158 (1967), pp. 730–9.
138 P. R. and A. H. Ehrlich: *Population Resources Environment* (San Francisco, 1970), p. 273, n. 14.
139 K. E. Boulding: *Economics as a Science* (New York, 1970), p. 149.
140 Compare on this general theme M. P. and N. H. Golding: 'Ethical and value issues in population limitation and distribution in the United States', *Vanderbilt Law Review*, 24 (1971), pp. 495–523. The Goldings, however, are only concerned with the United States.

CHAPTER SEVEN *Removing the Rubbish*

1 F. Fraser Darling: 'Man's responsibility for the environment', in F. J. Ebling (ed.): *Biology and Ethics*, Symposium of the Institute of Biology, no. 18 (London, 1969), p. 119. On this general theme see also George Seddon: 'The rhetoric and ethics of the environmental protest movement', *Meanjin*, 31: 4 (December 1972), pp. 427–37.
2 Aldo Leopold: *A Sand County Almanac*, p. 253.
3 C. E. Rolt (ed.): *Dionysius the Areopagite on the Divine Names and the Mystical Theology* (London, 1920), p. 107. Compare the diagram from the fourteenth-century mystic Henry Suso in A. Nygren: *Agape and Eros*, trans. P. S. Watson (London, 1953), facing p. 616, with the diagram in 'Ecology: the new great chain of being', *Natural History*, 77: 10 (December 1968), p. 9.
4 On this theme, see Henri Frankfort: *Kingship and the Gods*, as quoted on p. 10 above.
5 Plato: *Critias*, trans. B. Jowett (Oxford, 1892), 111*b, c*.
6 R. W. Emerson: *Nature: Addresses and Lectures* (Boston, 1876), p. 10.
7 Compare S. L. Udall: *The Quiet Crisis* (New York, 1963), pp. 48–55.
8 Theodore Roszak: 'Ecology and mysticism', *Humanist* 86: 5 (May 1971), p. 136. See also Norman Brown: *Life Against Death* (London, 1959), pt. 5, ch. 15, p. 236, and my summary in *The Perfectibility of Man*, pp. 306. See also Passmore: 'The revolt against science', *Search* 3, 11–12 (November–December 1972), pp. 415–22.
9 Porphyry: *De Abstinentia* IV, 20.
10 P. R. and A. H. Ehrlich: *Population Resources Environment*, p. 182.
11 Wilfrid Scawen Blunt: 'Satan absolved: a Victorian mystery' (1899), in *The Poetical Works of W. S. Blunt* (London, 1914), vol. 2, pp. 266, 275.
12 See, for example, J. B. Cobb: *Is it too Late? A Theology of Ecology* (Beverly Hills, 1972), and what was said above about Barth and Schweitzer.
13 *The Closing Circle*, p. 41.
14 O. C. Stewart: 'Fire as the first great force employed by man', in W. L. Thomas, Jr. (ed.): *Man's Role in Changing the Face of the Earth* (Chicago, 1956), pp. 115–33.
15 J. S. Mill: *Three Essays on Religion*, p. 15.
16 Karl Marx: 'On the Jewish question', in L. D. Easton and K. H. Guddat: *Writings of the Young Marx on Philosophy and Society* (New York, 1967), pp. 245–6.
17 Denis Puleston: 'Protecting the environment', *New Scientist* (28 September 1972), p. 558.

SUBJECT INDEX

NAME INDEX

Abel, 12
Adam, 6, 7, 8, 13n., 19, 29, 31, 33, 36, 108, 156
Addison, Joseph, 36
Al-Ghazzali, 146, 204
Alison, Archibald, 131, 143, 202
Allen, Robert, 203
Althaus, Paul, 204
Anaxagoras, 11
Anderson, John, vii
Andreini, Giovanni, 198
Anger, Kenneth, 93n.
Appleman, Phillip, 204
Aquinas, Thomas, 6n., 7, 15, 31, 32, 113, 117n., 119, 142–3, 146, 156, 205
Aristotle, 13–14, 33, 56, 134, 156, 158, 160, 196
Arndt, H. W., 200
Arnold, E. V., 196
Artz, F. B., 198
Augustine, 15, 19, 32, 79, 111–12, 142, 166, 188, 201, 203
Ayres, R. U., 199

Bacon, Francis, 18–20, 24, 27, 33, 80, 197, 200
Balbus, 14, 15, 16, 17–18, 178
Barnett, H. J., 200
Barry, Brian, 69, 199
Barth, Karl, 122–3, 145, 152, 202, 204
Basil the Great, 108
Baumgarten, A. G., 124, 202
Bede, the Venerable, 6n.
Bella, Giano della, 181
Bentham, Jeremy, 84, 85, 91, 114–15, 159, 201, 205
Berelson, Bernard, 206
Berenson, Bernard, 56, 199
Berkeley, Bishop, 15, 196
Biese, Alfred, 196
Birch, L. C., 10, 196
Black, John, 29–31, 198
Blake, Judith, 205
Blueprint for Survival, 52–3, 58, 68n., 93, 95, 199, 200
Blunt, Wilfrid S., 180–1, 206
Boas, George, 196
Bodde, Derk, 197
Bogue, D. J., 140, 203
Borrie, W. D., 131n., 203, 204, 205
Boughey, A. S., 198
Boulding, Kenneth, 168, 198, 203, 206
Bourke, V. J., 164–5, 205, 206
Boyden, Stephen, 93, 200
Boyle, Robert, 11, 185, 196
Bradford, John, 198
Bradley, F. H., 53
Brecht, Bertolt, 106, 201
Brown, Harrison, 89–90, 200

Brown, Lancelot, 36–7
Brown, Norman, 206
Buchanan, J. M., 69, 199
Büchner, Georg, 118
Burnet, Sir Frank Macfarlane, 88, 96–7, 200
Burnet, Thomas, 109, 119 201,
Butler, Samuel, 178

Cadle, R. D., 199
Cain, 12
Callahan, Daniel, 205
Calvin, John, 13, 14, 29, 196
Campbell, A. A., 205
Carey, H. C., 21, 197
Carr-Saunders, A. M., 134
Cassian, John, 108, 201
Celsus, 16
Chadwick, Sir Edwin, 64
Chamberlain, N. W., 154n.
Chandrasekhar, Sripati, 163, 205
Charles, R. H., 196
Cherokee Indians, 8
Chrysippus, 15
Chuang Tsu, 7–8, 196
Churchill, Winston, 96n.
Cicero, 14, 15, 17, 18, 178, 196, 197
Clark, Colin, 131–2, 138, 149, 202, 203
Clement of Alexandria, 198
Coale, A. J., 203
Cobb, J. B., 206
Cohen, Abraham, 196
Commoner, Barry, 128, 185, 194, 198, 199, 202
Comte, Auguste, 3
Condorcet, Marquis de, 156
Coombs, H. C., 98n.
Corinthians, 197, 198
Cotton, Charles, 107, 201
Cowgill, D. O., 203
Cowper, William, 121–2, 136, 179, 202
Crosland, Anthony, 94
Crowe, B. L., 199

Dales, J. H., 199
Darwin, Charles, 14, 23, 177
Davenant, Sir Charles, 134, 203
Davis, Charles, 11, 196
Davis, Kingsley, 203, 204, 206
Day, L. H., 203, 204
Debré, Robert, 203
Declaration of Governors, 73–4, 199
Descartes, René, 18, 20–2, 24, 27, 114, 180, 197
Deuteronomy, 16, 124
Diderot, Denis, 156
Dodds, E. R., 197
Douglas, Mary, 199

210